F
C12   Calisher, Hortense.
          Tattoo for a slave.

TATTOO
FOR A
SLAVE

ALSO BY HORTENSE CALISHER

TATTOO
FOR A
SLAVE

HORTENSE CALISHER

HARCOURT, INC.

Orlando   Austin   New York   San Diego   Toronto   London

Requests for permission to make copies of any part of the work should be
mailed to the following address: Permissions Department, Harcourt, Inc.,
6277 Sea Harbor Drive, Orlando, Florida 32887-6777.

www.HarcourtBooks.com

Library of Congress Cataloging-in-Publication Data
Calisher, Hortense.
Tattoo for a slave / Hortense Calisher.
p. cm.
ISBN 0-15-101096-X
1. Jewish families. 2. Conflict of generations.
3. Women immigrants. 4. Southern States. I. Title.
PS3553.A4T38 2004   2004001620

Text set in Dante MT
Display set in Charlemagne
Designed by Cathy Riggs

Printed in the United States of America

First edition
A C E G I K J H F D B

TATTOO
FOR A
SLAVE

"Your grandmother never kept slaves," my father says to me suddenly, staring straight ahead as we walk. He should know. Born to her in 1861, in Richmond, Virginia, then the capital of the Confederacy, during what they preferred to call not the Civil War but "the War Between the States," he had been her seventh child, of eight. I, born to him in his sixth decade, by a mother over two decades younger than he, am always eager for these tales that have lain in wait for me, of a childhood that has begun to run alongside my Northern one like its shadow-mate. But he has never said this before.

"What about Aunt Nell?" I say, hushed. Saying "Awnt" as he always does, of the "Mammy" he had adored. Who had adored him back. I found myself wanting one.

"Aunt Nell was a freed woman. My mother insisted on that."

How did you get freed? He didn't say.

He had just come from my grandmother's deathbed. I had been brought in just before. "Say good-bye to your grandmother," he had said. The circle gathered around the great Victorian bed, my two aunts and two uncles, her other remaining children, clearly had not approved, but my father was the head of the family, their support and her favorite.

She lay there much as I had known her, except for the closed eyes. Visiting her by custom every day after school, in her two rooms at the far end of our apartment, I would find her in her sitting room, in her wicker rocker, with its side pocket that held the newspapers she still tried to read on her own. Or I would find her in her bedroom, standing by the two huge wardrobe trunks almost higher than she was, one of them open perhaps, though I was never invited to delve. Though she no longer went outside, the wrappers she wore were always of an outside color, dark gray, and with a thing at the neck that my mother said was a fichu. I was learning a lot that had nothing to do with my century.

As she lay there, the feather mattress she would never discard floated her high, as if it meant to keep her at center still, not just a tiny person who had had a fall. Nowadays we know that the hip breaks before the fall, but this was before. A word that would always have a special sound to me. This is 1924. Born just before the end of 1911, I am twelve.

"Ninety-seven," my one aunt had said, the other one adding softer, "Though out of vanity she only admitted to ninety-four."

Even now a flutter of smiles, though my father, head bent, had not joined in.

"They were married in 1852," an uncle said. "Pa came over from England in '27, we were always told. That book he and his crowd are in lists him as an elder—in 1832. But neither one ever spoke age."

"We could look it up," the second uncle had said. "Maybe time we should."

My father had raised his head, silencing them with a look I already knew the meaning of. *Pay respect.*

Our family doctor, who usually ran in at the slightest, had come and gone, respecting us. As for hospitals, those were for bloody events, like my tonsils. "Will she have to go?" My father's proud smile had reassured me days ago. "We were all born at home. Including you. We die there."

But that, too, had been before. His fists are at his forehead now. She is floating on her pillow. I have never seen her in disarray. Death—please don't do that to her. He must feel the same.

But that was the moment when my mother had glided toward me—so much younger than they, she was never quite of their circle. Whispering, "Wait in Granma's sitting room."

So I had waited. Along with a wicker chair, in its pocket her eyeglasses and on the table across from it the big Chinese vase with never a plant in it, that plainly had come from another household. And high above, centered on a wall at her left and facing the door, the likeness of my grandfather, who must be so long gone that I have never heard any personal anecdote of him. Nor as I wait there does that seem odd to me, even though Southern as my father's dominant side of the family is, I am used to being whelmed in anecdote. Deferential as we are to our background, this comes with an oddity that can put the milder family ones way out of joint. Or else will in time find itself rather "in"—even fashionably aligned?—with the new century, the twenty-first. Where newsworthy men in their seventies and eighties, some of them known to me, would be having babies with young wives.

For we are odder than most, generationally. With a Pa married late and his Pa wed maybe even later in life—well, my own sense of where I am will be elastically stretched. The man in the likeness on the wall may well have been, probably was, born in the eighteenth century. It's a steel engraving, mind you—or a photo made to resemble one? The answer would be in the dates, which we rather run to at times, but I have never heard the date of his death. Sensing only that when "we" came to New York, where "we" were ensconced by the eighteen-eighties, he may have long since become dry-as-dust fact. There couldn't have been anything disgraceful in his history. Not with that stiff distance between nose and lip, plus a collar suitable to the business address and religion as attested to in that book—and, above all, the whiskers. They are the mid-nineteenth century's for sure—those muttonchops.

Meanwhile, back there in the sitting room, all I know is that I am in-waiting, and learning one thing more. When you await the imminent death of somebody, no matter how loved in her elusive distance, no matter how dreaded that event, you will feel yourself death's accomplice. I crouch there, in that guilt. Until there is my father, at the sitting-room door. He is weeping, in a way I've never seen anybody do. Grunts, deep in the chest. I suppose they are sobs. Behind him is my mother. She says, "Take your father for a walk." As if, for the moment, I am of an age with him.

So now we are walking, along pavement where he had held my hand as I tottered on my first four-wheeler skates. Then past the hill where he had shot me off on my Flexible Flyer sled. In his sixties, he has done what he could. But the greatest gift to me, if at times a burden, is something else. As a storyteller in any gathering, as a famed anecdotalist in business life, he has a particular hoard of tales that have lain in wait for me. He has been giving me his youth.

But like any boy-man, emigrating in his teens from the defeated to the conquerors, from army uniforms of one color to another, and even to a different flag, he has doled it out to me in two parts. I'm pretty savvy about that period called the "belle epoque," though as he gilds his New York portion of it, from

Diamond Jim and Lillian Russell seen at Mouquin's and Delmonico, to brass-knuckled John L. Sullivan pounding his opponent while the blood ran, to Mark Twain listened to: *He spoke to you like from next door, but you remember it*—it does begin to sound, as when challenged my father will admit: "Straight down-the-pike American." And later on, I'll be pleased that he never edited for a girl.

I have heard some also about that intermediate New Orleans, where he learned French, as well as certain words like "Creole" and "quadroon," that when I asked did that mean "Colored," he did not reply.

But of Richmond? Only a boyhood, surprisingly rural—melons poached from neighbor gardens, cockfights crept into in hidden barns. Rather Tom Sawyerish really—and as with Tom's Aunt Polly, the women guarded the household, and did what they could to assert its moral tone. Quite a lot, if my grandmother's role here was any token.

For though Confederate Richmond seldom merged in these reminiscences, when it had, so had she. Or vice versa. In one incident, when my father, rapped over the knuckles with a ruler by a teacher, jumped out the school window, never to return, she stood up for him. "Your grandmother ruled us with an iron rod, so to speak. But never used it." No grandfather appeared there. As a merchant's daughter, my own father either downtown in his offices, or away, I never thought to question. My grandfather would have been busy in the dry-goods store, its address listed in that book: "e.s. 17th be Main and Franklin." Perhaps he did help get his miscreant son the son's two lackluster apprenticeships, first at a grocer's: "Couldn't stand reaching in that pickle barrel"; then in an office: "Hated licking those stamps."

When my father sped north, I have no doubt somehow that she had pushed. She appears a second time, unheralded at his

bachelor pad in New York, finding him and his roommate, a
Frenchman named Louis Housselle, sobering up, after a night
out with their "flames"—those frizzed girls whose anonymous
pics still resided in our breakfront's bottom drawer. "Phew. Did
she lick into us"—his roommate too. She had heard of their
rake's progress. How? Perhaps through the Southern underground of émigrés ever visiting us from Richmond, whom I
would come to know: The Pyle family, almost kissing cousins to
us, or others whose grandchildren were at an age to be my play-
mates; the Haases, Evelyn, my age, and her older brother, Man-
fred, whose grandfather would in summer wear the same pale
silk pongee suit and Panama hat that my father sometimes did.
Also the Edels (accent on the last syllable), Lieutenant Commander Albert Edel and his wife, Lee, parents of my friend
Leonore, whose grandparents, the senior Edels, were New York
residents, and when she came from Richmond at Christmas-
time, would regale us, the two of us just edging into our teens,
with whiskey eggnog—he advising us that the amount of liquor
in it would not hurt us, a counsel familiar to me from my own
father's allowing me "a taste" of wine. Mrs. Edel, following my
gaze to the portraits and other mementos on the walls, was
likely to remind us that her father (or was it her grandfather?)
had been mayor of Savannah.

"Memento" still seems to me a fully Southern word. All
those households, like my own and my aunts' and uncles', kept
a similar faith in objects, and in stories. With the émigrés' hope
of passing on what they have come from, and of keeping us as
Southern as they could. "Keep," I hear them saying from their
scattered graves. "Keep."

They all had as well the loose, ramshackle vocabularies that
their birthright seems to breed, hot in the mouth as if they were
spitting peppercorns: "Gee whittakers! Shoot! Crazy chile!" Or

languid with pure love of the syllable: "Hon, you sure look tat-terdemalion." Or they could hold "Ri-ich-mond" in the mouth like a melting fondant—those white sugar bits the aunts always picked first from a box of candy. Yet there was one monosyllable they never had trouble with. I hear it yet. Their recurrent "the waw." A phrase never heard from my father. As his elder sib-lings, they would have been schoolchildren when Grant sacked Richmond, about when my father had been born. But while he gave me his birthplace in the sharply limned details of one who in his late teens had left it forever, their mouths spilled often with the cloudy allusion "Dayun home." Down home.

Also, as women of a generation that had either sewn its own clothes or had this done, they referred to the shades of ma-terials used in terms I thought of as "seamstress colors," and maybe now peculiar to us? *Puce, reseda green, Prussian blue.* Where did I ever hear that litany except at home? Yet though the aunts wore black constantly, often with fancy jet dangles added, they never spoke the word (pronounced as a "blay-uck" nearly "blake") in that connection.

This only came to me when I heard the two talking of their housecleaners.

"Blay-uck as the ace of spades," one says. "Catch her in a dark corner, gives me the grizzles. But lak ole times to have around the house." The last word pronounced with that slight yelp which can almost make it "hoose." This aunt's apartment is so indulgently messy that my once-German mother strives never to sit down in it.

"My new one's a terror," the other aunt says. "Up yere too long. Give her what-for, and she'd bounce. And right sassy. But relishes a tease. Lak they do. 'Never'd think your home folks come from Roanoke,' I tell her. 'When am I going to hear you talk lady-come-to-see?'...Gives me such a glare, I'm most afraid to turn my back on her...But, sister, I wish you'd try her. She sure knows how to clean for *what* people." When they go down the hall to see their mother, as done daily, I say to mine from my corner, "How to clean for *what* people?" I am at school now and another accent has taken over. "She mean that Aunt Mamie's too messy to clean for at all?"

My mother spoke American with a cool, median competence, hard learned. "No, silly." Her sigh implies that we are not as they. "She said 'waht' people. Double-u, aitch, eye, tee, ee, as they say it. *White.*"

So it seeps to me. By osmosis? That fell word, taught ever earlier in biology, which for me will come to signify the cell-creep between the generations, when, somewhere in the dumb show between one's history to date and one's future to be, we latch onto a bit of what we are all everywhere burdened with.

"They're mean." Once said aloud I believe it fully. A habit that will grow. "Real hunkered-down mean. Never say black or white, huh. Unless it's skin."

My mother gave no one her confidence. This including me. I was used to that, expecting no more, even cannily turning to my father, he at sixty-odd ready to heap on his firstborn all the chrysanthemums of love. Yet my mother, arrived at sixteen from a small German town, had had her own legend. A beauty, with a long rope of chestnut hair, her own mother had died giving birth to her. She, fugitive from a stepmother who had packed her off along with the lesser family jewelry, had come from here to my great-aunt, her own mother's sister, and the aunt's husband, a pair who still lived in Yorkville, New York's thriving German section.

My mother's father, the conventional *Haustyrann*, was by then parent of a son by the stepmother. Had my maternal grandfather connived in or accepted my mother's departure, or, in the pattern of the times, scarcely noticed?

I never heard her mention him. She, like any *Backfisch* (the German word for flapper, which, escaped from her once, had enchanted me), had been taught to embroider like a recording angel and had brought a full dowry to the New World, this including the dozen long, ruffled knickers that my great-aunt's maid, taunted by the other maids serving the backyards of that house block on East Seventy-ninth Street, had refused to hang on Aunt Adler's distinguished laundry line. A humiliation, never forgotten, that will hang like a dirty pantaloon swinging in the chancy breeze of my mother's first brush with *Amerika*. "Greenhorns, those maids," she would say. "Just like me." The going rate for them having been fourteen dollars a month.

For if I interpolate her here, in what is intended as a Southern story to the hilt, and will be, this is because, during all her life with us, she herself would be an interpolation. (As you may note from that pronoun, ever shrinking into itself in its alum dip: us.) While it further seems that much of the reportage on any family must always be qualified, as in parenthesis?

Hedwig Lichtstern (who changed her name, no doubt on the double, to Hattie?) and my father (who in a book I have of his, dating from his early manhood in New Orleans, had in turn signed himself *J. Henri*, for Joseph Henry Calisher) had met in Saratoga at the races, she under the chaperonage of her aunt and uncle-in-law. The first decade of the twentieth century was a happy playground for the spectator sporting rich, and the merely comfortable Yorkvilleians joyfully followed suit. This coming from both the group habit of the Turnverein clubhouse and an awareness that in the new republic a frequent appearance at the fashionable event, in the proper clothes and with an air of well-filled pockets, is how a new society, the coveted "social" one, is ever made.

Though the Adlers, my great-aunt Nettie, and my great-uncle by marriage, Sigmund, inhabited only a floor of a brownstone (if the coveted second floor that had the big bay window), this nevertheless quite separated them from those who, disdaining even the single brownstone, lived in the mansions off Fifth Avenue and were constantly photographed in the glossy brown weekly rotogravure section.

Yet the Adlers knew how to comport themselves in their own style. At the races, Sigmund, owner of a flourishing bakery business, would have split for box seats on sale, located well behind those frontline ones, which were no bigger, but family inherited. Both aunt and niece would have been dressed with an elegance, just under showy, that the seamstresses would have executed well. In *Tante's* picture by the fashionable Sarony, her brocade evening bodice was one to be envied now. *Onkel,* in reassuring burgher vestment, was at her side. Both the elders were fluent in English, if with a plummy accent not quite *Hochdeutsch,* but near, and well above that ridiculed comic dialect known as *Plattdeutsch.*

How would my father have met them, he offsided in his own enclave of drawlers who by then had been almost a hundred years in America? With a sister, Mamie, whose husband (either dead or long lost but in any case never mentioned) had come of ancestry that had served in the American Revolution. J. Henri himself had by then been a member of the Hundred Years Club, founded by businesses of that ilk. His firm, Oakley & Co., being touted as the second oldest (after Colgate) and dealing chastely in soap and scents.

How did she and he meet? Two hints. The first is a dashing picture we have of him, seated but wearing a yachting cap, though he was not notably fond of the sea. Though wont to hum at me at bedtime: *"O, I've been to Eu-rop, Ey-rop—and Stirrup,"* a saying not traceable to the South, perhaps derived from Britain by his own father—he had never been abroad, or never had the chance. To which in those days one went by sea.

Secondly: How did he acquire Oakley & Co? The kind of small "refined" occupation that its former owner, a scion of the Rhinelanders, they once heavy in New York real estate, might choose? "Old Austin Oakley, he took a shine to me." As a young bachelor, one could say that in those days, without implying sex. "Had no heirs, or none that wanted the business, and first job I had up here, I worked like a drover for him. Sold it off to me like the gentleman he was. At a price I could pay."

How long a time that had taken, or whether there was interest paid, he never said. He himself, maybe taking his cue from Austin, was never to be a sharp businessman. Took both his elder brothers, Aaron and Nat, and his elder sister Flora's husband, Clarence, in with him. Took in a brother of one of his brother's wives as his bookkeeper, who cheated him but, after a plea, was forgiven and hired back. After both the brothers' deaths leaving both home office and factory half unattended and him away selling, the profits meanwhile seeping away—he was still a soft touch for their wives.

Peep at the pair, she and he, Hattie and Joseph, that day— from perhaps an adjacent box? Or from two separate small portrait photos in the thick lasting cardboard of the times. She and her girlfriend are each wearing one of the great platter hats, tea-tray ovals—but it is my mother who looks the queen. Imagine her then, sitting in the box, face tilted toward the horses, or else standing up, slim and curved, in perhaps the same or a similar long white Gibson girl linen skirt I still have, binoculars ready at her side, her face looking as calm as it always will be, under all the wifely rages to come. As the lone younger consort, breasting that seasoned elder clan, whose strict mustardy judgments lie so hidden under their easy caroling. One day, postpartum my brother, born six years after me, she will go suicidal, but recover. Through all, her face will remain serene. In the box, should she part her lips, perhaps to answer the stranger in the next box, or else lifting his hat to her from the aisle as if he knew her, her accent, twelve years after her arrival in this country, will be perfection. Even if, with its slightly broadened "a," as in "cahn't," for the squawked and unspellable New York "cain't," her speech is a trifle beyond her station in life.

In my father's photo, close to that same time, he's wearing a black bowler, whereas in race time he'd have been wearing the straw hat with the black band, as in all the summers to come. Or no: if in a box, more likely bare headed. At fifty (who would think it?) with a full head of black hair that may have an enduring tendency to curl but has been barbered by the best, and underneath, the flourishing handlebar mustache to match, he's handsome but not vulgarly so. In the photo, which would be in winter, he is high collared, a white one, of course, and in the topcoat with velvet revers, all correct. In August, he would have been suited in the cream-colored pongee, as in all the summers I knew him. If standing, he is merely of medium height, or slightly more, though by the time I knew him, he may have shrunk from youth's taller bone.

Not that this ever worried a man cocksure of his centrality in life and time. Who yet would have deemed it utter crudity to say so. As well as foolish beyond monkey land to say it with a gun, as the region where he was born would have entitled him. See him then, a mongrel mix of German-Polish (border city of Kalisch) fathered by an emigrant from Britain (London, or Manchester?), cousined in that connection by Sephardim named De Sola and Seixas, mothered by a Dresdener (surname Bendan, most likely originally ben-Dan, as in the rabbinate), and all of him convinced, by mere nativity, that he is Virginian to the core.

Who introduced them? Though I pestered, she could never come up with a name. *Tante*, applied to, said, "We could see Joe was a gentleman." *Onkel*, grunting from his armchair, "She was too good for any German we introduced her to." And time to get her off their hands?

See my father, honorable merchant, filial son, but maybe to my grandmother too much in his groove as a man-about-town. Shouldn't a favorite son have family? By then it was almost past time. My mother, on the other hand, like many a female then and now, has been cultured to believe, and perhaps carries even in her soma, her ordinary flesh, that her provenance in this New World, if not in eternity, will depend on a man. Besides, though dressed for the rotogravure, with a profile to compete with most of the beauties there and rather more dulcet speech, she is convinced that as an immigrant, though some of those soar, because of her "clodhoppers" she will remain forever a peasant. Coiled at the heart of her psyche and all too present in her conversation are her size-ten feet.

Yet half a ploy? To conceal from her family-to-be the profession she had actually worked at, apparently almost since she had got off the boat. A *dummkopf,* who could read and write only German script? What were they to do with her? Work in a factory? The Adlers and their neighbors were already too genteel. Far as the latter were to know, she went to work "at *Onkel's.*" On the nearly all-German block where they lived, north side of Seventy-ninth, near Lexington Avenue, any young person, even those born here, might have done the same. If there was a family business, or contacts, you jumped to it. Whether or not you got on with your relatives, as she luckily would have, had nothing to do with it. Or whether you had harbored another choice.

Individualists struck out, of course; that was what some there had come for. Or found out that they had, once here. (But not likely a girl.) Yet, when I learned, though not until I was a sophomore in college, what she had instead gone and done for more than a decade until her marriage, I saw that she had struck out, in the limited way that snobbish distaste (Bakery! Bread!) plus a face to sell, had made possible.

I would learn her secret because it was by then 1929, when "luxury" manufacturers like my father's—he dealing in perfumes like the one called *Toujours Moi,* which name he had patented, and satined-up rouges and powders—had been among the first to suffer. Oakley's no longer sold soap. Might have been better if they had.

"Go to work" was her solution for me.

"Leave college?" I see her nod. Not straight up. Faintly cocked to the side with a slight jealous smile. "Hattie," my father would say gently, when so informed. "Tuition would be only a drop in the bucket, m'dear." He storming, when she persisted with that stubbornness which perhaps did come from the peasantry, "You have no business experience...and I won't have this poor girl—" Not finishing his sentence, he left the room.

"No," she'd said low, in his wake. "I only see the bills."

But he had to leave on his trips; she could pressure from home. I went to the Occupation Bureau at school. Saturday salesclerk, nine-to-five, four bucks per. Coming home after a few times to inform her proudly, "I sold three hundred dollars' worth. At fifteen dollars per. They sent the buyer around to ask me how I did it." And how had I? "Dunno." Only saying to each customer, my eyes alight as I held up a dress, "Isn't it lovely?" Because to me they were—and I'd gone through the whole year wearing last year's one new dress as often as I could. And they had seen the yearning, perhaps...One customer, who bought three dresses, even said, "Look, honey, you've been so helpful, could I buy you one?" As my family forever warns, my face tells everything. Though, of course, I had had to decline.

Then one day the Occupation had come up with something extra: "To model," I told her. "Only for dresses. Not bathing suits. But I have to have your permission, since I'm only seventeen. But it's aboveboard." By then I was coming to know that some things were not. "And we, ten of us froshies are all to go together." "Models" then, though not notorious, verging toward professional, even when nude and properly posing for a known artist or a life class, were as yet far from the demicelebrities they would become, as half-actresses, stars in their corner of the lens, candidates even for the films.

Her hand hid her mouth. Was she laughing? My irregular features, as blended with another's, had never satisfied her Teutonic need for the strict confirmation, recognizable at a glance as beauty, which had been her lot. "But it seems I must have the figure for it," I quavered. "They sent the head of their showroom to our dance class. She chose." I had danced my way through the term (as one could in the college that had a Martha Graham assistant in the Phys Ed Department) and I was good at it. Originally sent off for training at age six, because my mother had feared that I was already destined to be *ein Lump*, I had labored. The sound of *Lump* is a dread one, in a language that for all its treble beauties has diphthongs no bass drum can equal.

"Seventh Avenue?" she says from behind the hand. "Well, it's not as sleazy as once. But any trade you take your clothes on and off for, people assume that after five o'clock, you do the same." Then she clammed up.

Why then did she cede me the permission after all? Only grumbling, to my father, "We're paying all that money so she can dance the clock around, with scarves? Like that Isadora who strangled herself." My father replying proudly, "Don't worry about our girl, Hattie." (By which he of course meant "my girl.") "She's got bookmarks all over her. Hanging even from the nose." He was always one to elaborate. And wanting me to read all the books for which his youth had never had time. Though once in a while, during my progress toward senior class, we were to share the one or the other on our shelves that a traveling drummer had had time for.

"Don't you worry, Hattie," he'd repeated, patting my cheek fondly. "One day, she blows that nose, only words will come out."

Our family life progressed by such verdict, rolling along like the player-piano music at which anybody could take a punch. The victim usually being present to receive his or her due.

Standing there I felt what it was to have parents who so differed in their expectations of me.

"Well," she said, "I wash my hands of her."

For him, I could do no wrong. I was his heir.

For her, college was the armor she hadn't had.

While for me, rescued from *Lump*-hood as seemed to be happening, all I further craved was a nose like anybody's, with boogers in it.

Meanwhile consoling myself that their marriage can't have been that ill a match. After all, it had produced me.

(I should have wondered how she knew about Seventh Avenue. But did not.)

How the match was arranged will take all this child's lifetime to make clear. Along with other matters—like whether there is "class," upper or ignorable, in "America"; (to say "the States" is not the same.)

And along with how slavery is managed. In the Commonwealth. In the household. In the memory.

I give it to you as it comes. In patches. As I know it now. And in parentheses.

On a humid day at the track I would later know so well, the air is a thin mustard; the mountains crowd in from forty miles away. On a rainy day the glad-clothes ooze home, wet rags, the guests of a nonsorting cosmos that has dumped. You have won less than you should, or more…But on this good day, it's as if you have already bet right on the Exacta. All is doubled, yet in place, from the lake-blue sky to a turf already speckled with the gold dust to be made. Women in the stands have cheeks like almond cream and ruby smiles, or else, when they flump, hindquarters no bookie would take a chance on. Hats are dashing beyond belief, awful or amusing, each as if born on the head under it, each wearer by God suitable to this day. Won't be many more days like this to the season. But the seasons will continue to sheen in and of themselves—well past the favorites. And winning every race.

Almost nothing we'll find out about my mother, either her dates or her inner self as she sees it, will come from her. Or more than sift, as one lived with her. My great-aunt must have known on which October sixth, that is of which year, her niece had been born. *Onkel* Sigmund had after all sponsored her to come. But elder women of *Tante's* time were often collectively coy on the age of marriageable girls. It would be from my father's pride, cocky at having wed someone twenty-two years younger, and he never denying his age, that we could count up. In my humbly awestruck way, I had been documenting them both ever since I had been of conscious mind, having no remembrance meanwhile of just when I had learned my letters.

According to my aunts, my father's sisters, they happy to quote a silly cousin from Richmond, thereby excusing them from sneer, it had been "a whirly-wind courtship," their middle-aged brother (and staff of life for their mother and them) gone dotty over a maiden, single for the twelve years she'd been here. Who, for all she was "handsome, in that Rhine-maiden way of hers" (my one aunt taught music in night school and got free tickets to the opera), no stalwart had snapped her up. On their wedding day, August 9, 1910, she was twenty-eight. Her wedding shoes had to be white satin, "which makes the feet look bigger," and would be worn only once. Years after her death, during a period of penury and required dinner parties, I wore them to shreds, with a strangely doubled displacement—she filled them yet.

The wedding exists only in the caterer's bill (saved by my mother) for the home reception at the Adlers'. In certain drawers of our household, or in the piano bench, say, one could come upon engraved menus of dinners with many courses. Or opera librettos—some of these tattered, some perhaps used only once, as well as ticket stubs, some autographed by the composer or the actors. All the record of a life as a man-about-town. This pretty little "Bill rendered" receipt for the lobsters, ices, and champagnes of the decade is her great flourish, ending all that.

I had no lore of weddings. Even those of my first cousins had occurred when I was small. No rabbi was mentioned, though there was no religious difference. "A prominent judge," I recall her volunteering, with satisfaction. "Your father knew a lot of those from that club." Certainly there was nothing underhand about the affair. Rather, just the demure one that you would expect of a bride and groom so far apart in age but tastefully joining. She wore his wedding present, a delicate diamond-and-platinum "lavalier," of the kind that there would be few occasions for afterward.

I was born sixteen months later, should anyone care to know, and she was given either "the bar pin," as those brooches were then called, or "the dinner ring," my brother and I never being sure later which celebrated whom. The events of the body, and of the body politic—never any guarantee that they go in sync. How could metal and chips smooth over our oddity? Yet in a household like ours, where the ages were all awry, and the two halves so unmatched, I all the more wanted the family story to be as unremarkably joined in time as most.

Two differing backgrounds didn't bother me; on the contrary, I had attended an extra lycée of languages, whereby I would never be able to pronounce "five" other than as "fahv" and still repress an urge to say *"Bitte,"* when thanked. (Though this doesn't quite mean "you're welcome." For that, the Germans echo "please.") But an extra treasure of time had been laid on me, by virtue of a father at fifty perhaps only slightly out of kilter, yet also the next-but-last son of that muttonchops, my grandfather. Who had not begun his own string of followers until 1853. While that book he was in, a *History of the Jews of Richmond,* written by Herbert Ezekiel in 1917, had listed him as already an "elder" of a synagogue in 1832.

From the history of our own Revolution, drummed into us at my public school as if there had never been another one, I at least knew that lives had been shorter then. With all the weights of life, in particular of government, arrived at earlier. Yet I couldn't put him only in his twenties then. In his thirties perhaps, with a "dry-goods" business brought with him maybe, and shortly reestablished. All of which might mean that he had been born in the 1790s? The best I could do for him, the latest, was—1798?

In the company of my school buddy Ginny, a year older than me, whose father was thirty-five and climbed poles for the telephone company (and whose mother had had her tubes tied so as not to doom them forever to more babies in their tenement), my out-of-whack progenitors somehow didn't bear talking about. She even had an aunt who was in her twenties. My dowager aunt Flora had had a great muff of rippling white hair as long as I had known her; my own father was iron-gray.

As a city child, I went often to museums, getting what I didn't know was my "cultural" life, without fuss. At Saturday

matinees "we girls" from high school who crowded the cheap
seats (fifty cents) sat awed during the play (maybe *As You Desire
Me* with Judith Anderson or *Hedda Gabler* with Blanche Yurka)
but fell agiggle at intermission; theater was not sacred. It was
what you did, the way movies with popcorn are now. But in the
museum, osmosis already working like a benevolent virus that
had been waiting for me, I walked the aisles silent and alone.
Home again, that assessing transferred. My family's past stretched
behind me, flattened and two-dimensional. A minor tapestry,
faded, but with me the eager dog at the bottom border, muzzle
lifted to all the odors of identity above.

I had never yet seen a racetrack. My father and a crony had
once taken me to the nearby Yankee Stadium, where my comment on the slowness of the game: "It's like potsie" (a kids'
game where one chalked squares on the pavement and hop-
scotched after a thrown skate key), had sent the crony into
stitches. "We must take her to meet the Babe." From his idola-
trous citing of batting scores, I knew who this meant: Babe
Ruth. He hadn't appeared any more than the Christ child would
have. Or my mother, who would have had no taste for this
crowd-pleaser pleb event. But the track would be like a tapestry
too—this time of a hunt. A double one, as the museum had
shown. Which aims rated tops?—the masters' or the animals'—
you would have had to be there to know.

About family history one always wants to know more. Unless one is shamed by it? My mother maybe had a trace of that.
My father's pride in our origins seemed to take care of everything. Sometimes, as I heard early, it could be taken to be too
much self-pride. "Oh, Joe?" my aunts would mutter. "Joe was
born with his medals already on him."

When that occurred, my mother turned red for him; I'll say
that for her. (Though in restaurants where, bolstered by his
New Orleans gourmandise, he was inclined to send back a dish

too poorly cooked, her blush and her stifled "Joe" was for herself.) When she spoke this time, turning her back on the aunts, it was for me. "When you grow up," she said, "remember to always speak kindly of the persons you owe."

I was surprised at her gumption, what with her equivocal position in our house. Yet humility is a prism, all of whose sides a child is not yet equipped to see.

But by then, having been told where they met, I felt myself of an age to know how. For this I could apply only to my father. He, valuing me more than she did, which I'd known ever since I'd known anything, would feel my entitlement, indeed always answering any question. I thought her not capable of that, or else she would get it wrong. Whereas all the time, she, having to make her stand in this nest of the better-educated, must have had an intelligence as primal as her peasant feet. God forgive me for seeing only the feet. But, as in many such triumvirates, buried under my urge to know how those two had got together and made me, was there an acknowledgment that truly together was what they would never be?

Pressed, my father one day answered me, in one of those rare after-dessert intervals when no one of the family had dined with us. Josie, the maid, had gone out with a swain. It was summer and I had no homework. My mother had stepped down the hall in answer to my grandmother, who did not dine with us, but had given up her own domicile at their marriage. Still indomitable, except for some attention by the neighborhood optician, she required little more physical care than the rest of us. Yet her birdcall: "Hattie...Hattie," sounded through the house the livelong day, though more often when her own brood was absent, having either not visited or left.

Not a squawk, nor yet quite a dove's call, the first "Hattie" sounded American enough. In the second, the "a" bent almost to an "e," in what could be thought a European inflection.

Beyond that, my grandmother, though ensconced in that heavily accented household, seemed to have none. Why this should be, I couldn't say, except that each time I was in her rooms, I experienced such a primal response to her small focused presence that her short blunt sentences, mined from the throat and only the greetings and remarks natural to our relationship, came as from a dictionary of the past. As of synonyms of words I had to yet hear, much less to use.

"What could she possibly want?" the aunts would say, if they had happened to linger long enough to hear her. To me, that "Hattie...*Hattie*," hovering in the air like a strong-winged butterfly, then vanishing, was merely one of the songs of the household.

"What did she want?" my father might say to my mother returning. My mother's replies were commonplace: "Her glasses to be picked up," or "Josie forgot to pick up the tray," though clearly my mother had stayed longer than for that. If he didn't see that my mother was drawn there like by magic, I wouldn't tell him, which would be disloyal. He was the adorer. If his wife served her mother-in-law, to him that was how it should be.

Conversationally, he is forthright, an embracer of what you are, not a questioner. Nor can he flatter indiscriminately. Miss Lil, as he called her, manager of the factory and archive of all its formulas, once sighed at me, with a tug at her gypsy hair and at the daubings on her blouse, "What does he have to be so honest for? Your father could sell the Golden Gate Bridge to a congressman." On the bus home from Jersey, where the factory was, I repeated what she'd said. We'd made the bus easy, last of the queue, just as it was about to depart. Bustle was unknown to him. (I grew to think of that style, too, as geographical; that false Southern laze which can be so quick on the draw.) He guffawed when I told him what Lil had said, "Bet she wishes I would." He squinted down at me, "Would you?"

With a man who could multiply "gross" amounts in his head, yet shake it over my mother's disappointment in a bargain, saying, "Guess you got too much for your money," you had to wonder what he was asking. My father's vocabulary, too, was mutant, often studded with words I heard nowhere else—and grabbed at from any era. Moving up from the South, where "democracy" meant solidarity, to the North, where it didn't: "Curdled my politics." So, I knew that although all congressmen were scallywags, one had to negotiate between other uncertainties.

"How much gold is there, in that bridge?"

He'd laughed so hard the driver turned round to look at us, but saw I was serious. Indeed fighting for meaning, as I always was in that house, my questions were often seen as jokes, not inadvertent.

"Lil has too much get-up-and-go for her own well-being," he says. "Or for Oakley & Co.'s comfort." He pats my cheek. "Rest assured, daughter," so often a phrase of his, it's like a sudden camera flash. "Rest assured, we have to be honest. Else our children won't be." For a minute he looks somber. "Not that we have to go over everything with a fine-toothed comb." It's almost a query.

In any case, I have no reply. Even now.

"But I'll tell you how I met your mother," he says. The streets we are reeling past are as cheerless as New York City has to offer, blocks of those five-story houses, ambitioned past the tenements but without their lawless gaiety, and any operas within sealed. Yet he leans forward as to a Golconda.

"I saw her."

He says that as if it's almost enough. Of course it is not. He gives the slight cough that he avers is from "catarrh," but which all of his hearers recognize as the practiced speaker's interval. "Who was she? Couldn't figure out the three of them. The old boy looked German. Those days, so respectable—polished and air-pumped. The older lady following him a step behind, even while she sat. But their charge, she did look as if she might welcome not being so taken charge of. Who she was and where from? Would have been like asking the citizenship of a nymph... You know what those are?...Ah-hah...So instead I walk round to the concessionaire—he knew me—and ask who they are. 'Not regulars, like you, sir,' he says. They'd had their tickets from a family who did reserve regular but didn't often use. 'Never sell, not they. Pass along to friends...You know them, perhaps?' He knows I don't, and why I'm asking." My father laughs. "I don't only slip him a fin. Later on, I sneak back and grease his palm twice." He takes my hands, squeezing them along with his rhythm. "After that, simple. Walk past their seat. Look as if we've met. And finally—tip the hat."

So then, he had been wearing one. A boater, they used to call those straw ones. I saw him tip it as he would have done if out walking with me. I saw the waiter's palm, glistening, heard my mother's always disparaging aside, "Sweet talk, they call it. Butter wouldn't melt in their mouths." Meanwhile not in the least understanding yet what dowry he was giving me, but willing to play patty-cake. "So—you finagled."

"Not on your tintype," he says, though beaming. "That's only for when you and I play cards. No, daughter, I was as honest as the day."

That was a "day" often invoked. For me one that would have had to float up like an oracle for some, but not so for us. We knew what was proper, and spoke for ourselves.

He had sauntered up to the Adlers, saying, "Ah, the Heides are off somewhere, are they, probably on that boat they have at Rye"—for the waiter had told him that too. So my father had saved *Onkel* from admitting that he was no better acquainted with that candy tycoon and Teuton royal than my father, but perhaps had an in with their office manager. Business courtesies—I knew about those, our shelves being full of what the sellers swapped. Including the Roger & Gallet perfume prized by all the family women, but also, when my father's valise was dumped, oddities from corkscrews to Swiss handkerchiefs, to weird games that would die quickly, never again to be met.

There was a word of my father's that my mother knew well, sometimes dropping it to me scornfully, as she watched him with guests, or even with relatives: "Persiflage." Not used on her? Or not that first time. From her lips the word did not fly, airily French. A word more suited to the photos in the breakfront, their coquettish eyes under their fringe. Or to that donor of the set of silver hairbrushes and other articles for the toiletry, on my father's dresser: given him by one Letty Cheatham (pronounced with the "h" silent), the "diseuse" (which "monologuist" or "stand-up comic" or even "performance artist" does not quite define). Irretrievably coy, these footnotes from the old epoque. Yet they summon it. They unfold a level of feeling, or of happy oblivion, that cannot otherwise be described. We are back in the era of vaudeville, of arch pretensions that woo only so far, like a soubrette's décolleté. I see champagne being sipped from glassware so thin that to whisper too near politically would have shattered it.

Safe enough even to take the children to, vaudeville was. Even I, not encouraged toward movies, was allowed it, and maybe that verdict was wiser than appeared. It was sad theater, declining into its own tragedy. Flesh-and-blood, strutting against a shabby backdrop that puffed all too often to the breeze of people behind it, only to be cut off by a curtain that dropped when an act was over like a guillotine. Jugglers were always first, dispensing the disposable, as their faces, clenched behind the soaring balls, seemed to say. Then, deepening the risk, came the acrobats, those sequined eels not meant for the median of air, bravely retrieving their footage each time, your watching little amateur inner self keeping toll with them. Sometimes then, a magician trickster, sometimes not. Always the two dapper spielers, hat brims pulled over the eyes, feet tapping, pinning the marathon jokes on us, one by one...Last act?

Ah, that's the big one. Stage left to stage right, a line of dark men, "Darkies," hacking and twisting, their heads and sweaty faces, joyously not in sync with their *this-away, that-away* hips, their palms crisscrossing their knees mournfully above their slapdash, slapping feet. The feet in those creasy boots that slap so hard they might be empty-toed, but are black and shiny as the faces above them: all blank of eye, teeth grinning go, go, go at the rows upon rows out front, stomping along. A very committed audience, to the minstrel show that was always the last act. In that same theater on upper Broadway—what was its name? Ah, the Audubon—where vaudeville came to its end. As did Malcolm X.

So it will devolve: How, patch over patch, the accents will combine. In *Amerika*.

My father and *Onkel* Adler exchange cards. Eventually the Adlers and he will dine in foursome as his guests at Luchow's, the great gallery of German food and huge replica paintings, with one of whose sirens, one of the more modest, my mother had perhaps been compared. Soon after, he will taste *Tante's Kartoffel Kloss* and capon, which are incomparable. How long the courtship proceeded was never said. But once, when I, off to my senior prom, parading my dress before him, was foolish enough to wonder aloud did I resemble my mother when young?—I got the only cruelty he ever bestowed. Not that he meant it as such. He was only keeping that image. "Never. Not as long as you live will you ever be what your mother was." Treating me then to what he saw that day at the track—and in truth she did have her own style, less fluffy than was sentimentally current but angelically handmade, with maybe that touch of daring suitable to a leftover twenty-eight.

"Pink linen, her dress was. With a line of little black buttons from neck to hem." When it's a man saying that, you see the whole figure within, and the passion, elegiac by then (for he was pushing seventy and she sometimes a shrew)—that had once been behind a man-about-town's eyes.

Consider now the matriarch.

The word is a bulwark, always heavily said. Loose-breasted mamas incarnate is the usual image, they suckling their young with ambition's ichor. Or binding them to the home doorstep with that darning cotton of no visible denier: the apron string. Or heading the breakfast table, neat as archbishops in their morning surplices. Ever weaving behind the family scene, on those ancient looms that wrest something out of nothing—or the reverse. They rule, the matriarchs, often without rod, or hazel switch. What they have is the aura of the birth canal.

Berthe Bendan, or ben-Dan. Born in Dresden. Otherwise, her only other facts are her children: Julius, the eldest and the first to die. (Born October 3, 1853, died December 1, 1885, according to that book.) A young man of parts, the nature of these not precisely known, but one spoken of reverentially by his younger brother, Joseph, and the only one of us to be buried in Richmond; whether he came North with the others is not known. Aaron, later to run the Oakley factory, married my Irish aunt Jo and had one daughter, Ann. Flora, presumably the eldest girl and my senior aunt-to-be. Julia (Cissy). A figure of horror to my mother. "Dirty, unkempt, surrounded by books. Never left her room." Died presumably in the madhouse. Whenever my

father returned from visiting Central Islip, a town that still resounds with childhood dread, he was silent for the rest of the
day. Nathaniel, my gentle uncle Nat, whose sweetness, so often a
mark of the TB sufferers of yore, survives in his photo, though
he did not. Married to my aunt Belle, a lively charmer who took
me, aged nine, to restaurants, often balconied, on which were
women smoking cigarettes. Perhaps a note of that couple's more
frivolous family life. Father of Amy, ambulance driver in World
War I, a talented singer, later married to the Morgan of Sperry
Gyroscope, and of Gertrude, who had worked in Wall Street,
both handsome and had married well. Amy, sent to an Aiken sanitarium with her baby, would die there, presumably of the same
TB, as would the child. "During the waw, we all had rickets,"
Miriam (Mamie), my younger aunt, had said. Last child of my
grandmother's brood, Beppie, formal name unknown. Spoken of
with a tenderness given to the "not quite right," and from the description a Down syndrome.

So that was the end of the line. Six energetic people, cranky
or benevolent, seven if you count Julius in his sainthood—out
of eight. Not a bad score. Though all her influence is now from
the wicker chair.

My father's filial piety pervaded the house like one of Oakley's old-fashioned essences, neither much advertised but drawing in as well his sisters and brothers, whose daily visits,
extended to dinner and late evenings, made them co-inhabitants
of the "main house." Who also hung around to share in the
swag from the valise. While for me, lucky dog at the bottom,
my world was upheld in a balance whose conduct I could observe, whose panorama I might one day join.

My childhood transpired in a globe of comfort whose air—
if I lean in toward the long perspective—I can still nip into, for
a moment's dream. My adults have done something decent,

even fine, but with serious consequence. We have substituted devotion for any wider margin. Being so serenely right in that context, and so exclusively, has maybe saved us from that sectarian righteousness which knows no bounds. But our conversation, as I review it now with these ears, has it a little lost its breadth? Or its impulse? For to all that mixed crowd in our living room, each side of whom once came here for a necessity more than money (our Southerners circa 1830, the older Germans circa 1860), is "freedom" now too raw a word? Too vulgar a policy, for those now settled in an America as spelled with a "c"?

Watching them, I once again travel my heritage. We are past the Silver Jubilee, that apogee of the nineteenth century, and well into mine. How is it that their accents, both the dulcet and the heavy, more and more resemble?

The last émigré—if we move on just short of 1939—will be my mother's half brother. She has long possessed his picture, in German army uniform, circa World War I. After which, unknown to my mother until his son arrived here, he had become a General Motors representative for Bavaria, and according to anecdote, when riding in his white Mercedes and often mistaken for von Hindenburg, would rise and accept the plaudits of the crowd, as if he were indeed their chancellor. But now (that is, back then), it is circa World War II, or just before, and with the same quick impersonation he had solicited my father's sponsorship for him, his son, and his extended family of brothers-in-law and their brothers—as refugees. They are all in our living room back then, including his son, who, arrived months ago, had proudly told us this anecdote. He is my age, and I could understand his shock at what he has found here.

My mother had heard of them only indirectly over these many years—letters in German script from someone in her own dead mother's ignored family, they possibly unaware of her half brother's risen circumstance. In the dread period of the German mark's post–World War I inflation, my mother had taken to sending her German family bundles of used clothing, never acknowledged so far as one knew. Had she done this in return for how they had packed her off? They long ago sending her, in response to *Tante*'s plea for some memento of her sister for her niece, some cheap corals? By then my mother had had her own diamonds—and her own irony?

My cousin has long since told us of his ski hut in the Dolomites, and of other perks of a rich man's son. Having no other skills except the business kind that take capital, and no English, he has had to accept the factory job my father had found for him. After a few months so, he tells us he has warned his father, "In Germany, you are a business genius. Over here, there are dozens like you." Yet when invited to my own first party, all of us newly married and in our mid-twenties, he had complained, "In Germany, when a new person enters the room, everybody turns to greet." Adding later, when he saw my husband carving the ham, "In Germany, no man ever enters the kitchen." When, despite his warning, his father will be forced to come, we are on notice that our relatively modest quarters, nine rooms by then crammed with my grandmother's not-quite-despisable, even grand Victoriana, will utterly disappoint.

In the salon of their Berlin town house, the walls had had a dado of fine paneling, and above that were covered in brocade…And paintings?—I wonder, spending their money for them. For in museums, as I stroll their corridors, meeting corners of Europe somber or bursting with light, some of the walls are so patterned. But he does not respond. I had hoped to be friends with him, as members of the same generation. And, perhaps too sentimentally, to succor him in his terrible severance. But I begin to see that all we may share is in being the same age.

Then comes the weekend on which my two "backgrounds" will collide. The "refugees" (only my mother calls them that) have arrived. *Der Vater,* as his son refers to him (otherwise my mother's half brother and once the man pictured in army uniform), is accompanied by a small retinue of those brothers-in-law or cousins related to him through his mother—my mother's hated stepmother, her father's second wife, and in no blood way connected to us. To my father, whomever he had been pressured to "sponsor" makes no difference. He stands there, firmly being the host, clinking the bottles at the sideboard, determined not to be in any way the rescuer.

When mother and brother meet, she is unable to quaver a welcome. Instead, they double kiss, cheek to cheek. For a long time after, that greeting so common to Europe but then unfamiliar to me, will have an aura of betrayal, past or to come. My mother has, of course, never met any of the retinue. Yet I see that she is entranced with them. They are from the town where all her legends are. But she has her American poise now. Indeed almost *grande dame.* "And your wives?" To a man, they give a domestic shrug, meaning the wives are on the way, or to follow. "We need to establish," the sole one who has some English says like a pleasantry, and we all have a drink on that. Wine and schnapps offered. *Der Vater* himself turns the bottle to peer at the label before he sips. *Joe has quite a cellar,* my mother would normally add, but does not. Geniality takes idiom. She had vowed not to say *Willkommen* at the door, but has found herself the sole translator of any competence and is functioning, but pale. "He looks so like my father," she mutters.

The Germans, as all such are called in this divided house, look uneasy, twirling their drinks, eyes downcast, as if already that is their fate. Yorkville may refer to them that way, sometimes to distinguish such from the Czechs or Hungarians who also live there, but in a German mouth it can mean: Those not here as long as me, as us. *Tante* and *Onkel* Sigmund do not say it, but my mother has picked it up, as useful in a house so divided. On a Sunday afternoon perhaps, to check supplies: "Who's coming?" If the answer is "the Germans," this will mean a *Kaffeeklatsch* with the Adlers, the Lederers, the Engelhardts, the men to have schnapps. Cousins or friends, they have long ago sprouted in each other's ken, like bulbs planted by somebody else in some long-ago town common to them. But among them their origins are not to be bothered with.

If it's the Southern side, they will not be referred to as such, but by name, these numbering not only what aunts and uncles remain, but also a duo of maiden cousins who are regulars, plus any cousins or family friends who are "up from" Norfolk perhaps, or Lynchburg or Richmond—in which case dinner will be in tow.

Although this occasion is for the new arrivals, they are not staying with us; the son, my cousin, has found them hotel accommodations, these not specified. "They'll have money; they made that clear at the outset," my father had said. "Else I could not have done it, for so many...Or even for your two, Hattie, the boy and his father. Not long term." With my father's two brothers, the office and factory managers, long gone, and the Depression dealing its blows, Oakley & Co. is not what it was.

"My two?" my mother had commented. There was of course no reason for her to have his blindly loving sense of family.

Meanwhile at the factory, Lil's oddities were getting worse. "But I can't sack her; she's the only one who really knows the formulas." My mother responding, "Come on, Joe, you never sack." So the house is also divided there. She would have been the businessman. As her half brother clearly is. Or was.

He has the air of a man in company he outclasses. Who is already planning to get far beyond the level he scents here.

...One wouldn't want to exact humility from these men in flight. Or even gratitude. Yet privately I had been prepared to bleed for them. And am finding that hard.

"Their handshake," I whisper to my father, "ick." Like clasping a lump of felt, warmed over. "Like the bones, real sharp ones, are somewhere else." He doesn't always approve of my fantasies, but tolerates them, perhaps as a tendency descended from him. In his "chifforobe," as he calls it, there are poems he once wrote, never seen by me but not cast aside. As for "college," which he funded on my part and found the "dough" for but never had for himself, it is not to be blamed for the education he applauds.

A heap of whispering goes on in our house, but not from him. The sub rosa under-voice is not his style. In that way he still rules, in a voice still prime.

"They not only have lost their country," he says to me. "They know now that it never was theirs...You might go down on your knees, daughter, to your own."

Almost on that note, the Southerners arrive, headed by those survivors, my aunts. Perhaps for once, my mother has wanted to muster a crowd—and in New York, coincidence is easy. It just happens that a pair of our habitués always called "the Abrams sisters," a duo from Richmond, now and then housed by us, are here too.

Since my grandmother's death, there being no reason to move, especially so because of the way we entrench ourselves behind mementos of no value except meaning, her two rooms have been kept exactly as she left them, except for the bedroom's two wardrobe trunks, which after being emptied and their treasure distributed, had been remanded to storage, where they still

are. The Salvation Army having at first refused them, my
mother had found a theatrical supply house where they were
marveled at, but in the end my father had prevailed. This being
an area where he still does.

Sometimes I have an urge to visit those trunks. Telling myself that I will when I am old enough to understand fully why
and not feel strange about it, though I am not yet sure what that
age will be. It is now the autumn of 1938 and, married now, living upstate, I shall soon be twenty-eight. Before the trunks went
away, I was able to study them, regarding them less childishly
than for so many years I had. Finding them wood within and
metal-skinned without, of that suedey tan between light and
dark whose old name I cannot at first remember, then do.
Taupe. They are knuckled at each end with brass, with front fit-
tings that match, and locks that one suspects are simple but appear intricate. They are also not as tall as they once were.

My grandmother, standing with her back to them, is I think
pleased to be encountered again. Some of the dead lose character as time passes but my guess is—not she. She was always exi-
gent, on what at twelve I took to be a demand for good manners
merely. But could it have been for a code of conduct entire?

That night the pair called the Abrams sisters are standing
there with me, regarding the bed, which has been freshly made
and scattered with the small, fancy boudoir pillows over which
women of my mother's era (and not only the Germans) used
to compete. Flowers are on the night table. The sisters, once
schoolmates of my father's and with only a year or so between
them, look like twins, and with their nut-brown hair bobbed
close to their pates, seem eternally middle-aged, with a superior
mien at having remained so, as if this is what the best people do.

"Nanny-hair," a British cousin (visiting us out of the blue,
and although solid enough, like from a bloodline not met since

we left there) had said of them. Longtime denizens of our household, they are my father's era, and as with him, owning a business, harrying as that may be, has kept the two of them spry. Once merely two of the maiden ladies commonly doomed to the porch sociality and honorary committees of his and their birthplace, they have become what he calls "kitchen re-deemed." By cookbooks was the usual way, which might never get beyond the church membership. Or home catering services, which would ignite the whole town, then suddenly pause. But these two have become "Abrams Sisters, Cupcakes," a logo known currently throughout the South, and being wooed by the corporate North. For which dickering they come yearly, as for a stimulant.

"Your mama ask us again, kinely, to stay," one of the duo says. It never matters which.

The other adds gently, "But maybe did she forget we have our hotel reservation? For only a baderoom. But the hotel adds us kind of a extra little office space, no extra charge. Being as they're acquainted with that company comes to dicker."

"Matter of fact, Taylor Trotter, the hotel manager, he put that company on to us," the other one says. Two sets of eyes go shrewd over that contingency. When they next speak, it's in word-over-word chorus, like the too well-married often do. "Taylor's from Norfolk Bays, those Johnny-come-latelies. Thinks we poor nincompoops don't have a prayer he'd be getting a commission on it."

Then they are merry, but singly.

"Used to be that company that wants to buy us out, they dickered us down."

"Nahadays—they bid us up!"

"To a sum you wouldn't believe." Neither can they quite, apparently. "But it's that company makes all the crackers; we

had our lawyer check and since he's pore old Augustus Boet-
tigheimer's boy, we had your dadda's attorney check him."

"Pore old" is no aspersion on Augustus, merely the phrase
for being dead. "Boy," however, when used of a professional, a
doctor, say, or even a banker, may mean that he may not have
come to much.

"Want to know what they're offering?"

When women whisper, putting their hands over their
mouths like that, I used to be shamed for us. Never see the men
at that. Do it under their hats, maybe, those swoopy-brimmed
ones they can then knock back, denying any undercover
exchange. Or hide it in the wallet, where the denominations,
however dealt, are anonymous. But living on, one comes to acknowledge, if not savor, that whether from male or female,
black or white, whether behind borders closed or open, or stew-
ing in those jars of misery that will be the present—or next
war's orphanages—all the secrets will be the same.

"No thanks," I say. "Might talk in my sleep." Kidding is what
I share with these parody Southrons who can still make me, the
Northern-reared, feel reprobate, And meanwhile, let them won-
der who else I might be sleeping with?

"Besides," I say. "You'll never sell."

They stand up straight for those two, their breasts sadly flattened by bras meant to minimize both the flesh and the masculine stare. As girls, they would have had a dully balanced lack of
that sexual pull which we of more gypsy looks tend to draw.
Among the men who were drawn to us, they would have been
dubbed "secretarial." Yet for the moment, twin heads raised,
cheeks flushed, they are a pair out of harness. One of those
matched teams bred to gait one another, and guaranteed not to
break loose. Who somehow have.

"No, we wouldn't." She's Minna, I now recall, the elder one.
The other is Clara. She says, "No, ma'am."

If these two snorted, I'd not be surprised. Nor would I shout, "Whoa."

"Oh? Why not?" Though old enough to ask, I don't feel so.

Clara, with a glance at Minna, gets to be spokesman. "Cain't desert our nigras. You ever seen a roomful working up a batch our receipts, you'd know why. They have the touch for it, always have had—like nobody else. Those cakes rise up under those black hands like filigree, and out the door. And the mammies teach the young ones how."

"Company's out to move the whole operation," her sister grunts. "Won't promise not to. But those nigras rolled us up the hill from a four-burner kitchen. We not rolling them back down."

I'm feeling Southern again. When will this alternation of mine ever stop?

"That bade," a sister says, looking up at its crest, "those high headboards give the most satisfaction. Every good Richmond family had one, our people. Have them yet. Polished walnut, more than double wide, seven and a half foot high. Our folks used to measure us by where our heads reached. Past the pillow bar and we were on our way. Middle of the center panel, right enough for a girl. Top was a bit tall. Grow any farther, we were cautioned, and they might have to stack us in the attic, laid straight out."

People who inherit their humor have a chuckle goes with it. "Those skinny New England four-poster bades? Put the rightful canopy that belongs on them, they too affected for anybody today to live under. Leave it off, and those four pointed colyums, still trying for heaven? How could a body get their proper rest?"

"Saw Granma Calisher on this bade six months before she paysed on," Clara says softly. "She shore did right well there. Beginning to end."

This memorial is what they have come for. To instruct me on a habit I might miss out on up here, they bend their heads.

They are the end of their line, far as I know. Many of our down-home visitors are. Why is it that the end of a tradition so often expresses it, way out of hand?

"She got so tiny," I say. "You knew her younger, Miss Minna, Miss Clara. Was she always so?" Too late I remind myself that they are middling short. When scratching for history, be sure to measure who you're scratching. As for me—I have indeed grown past the pillow bar.

"Uh-uh," they say slowly. "But always slender. Like she was too busy to get fat. Or burned it up." Beyond that they can't really say. "But you'll have photographs," they console, and we nod at each other. We all have those.

My mother sticks her head in through the open door. Our family pace being stately unless it erupts into a hysteria which may or may not clear the air, she is always clocking the tension, and saved daily by imposing the meals. "Su-upper," she lilts, though we are only across a rug from her. Poised there in profile, in the modulated light of an unused room, she is the goddess of supper. "Twenty minutes or so." This is the code for *Time to wash up,* as the ladies will know. "And Josie in the kitchen will want you to tell her how you wish the cupcakes set out." She knits her brow, a message to me for sure, that must wait. Like any Athena, she then vanishes.

"Josie?" one of the sisters says. "She new?'

These days, they often are. My mother has prevailed there; the train of those she had called *Schwarzers,* always my father's assumed help, has been replaced by the Polish ones and the Czechs.

"They marry," I say. In their turn to be absorbed over here, into the great tide. The rhythms between the served and the servers in my nation have always nudged at me to notice, and always will.

My mother's brow had been knit; what is the message? I open the door to Granma's small bathroom for the sisters—it's a sink and toilet only—and leave.

...In her last years, brittle as a bird, she was sponged daily, which can be an act of devotion, perhaps enjoyed by both parties. The annals of home care have even queerer instances, no doubt. (As we minister, in the frail hope of being in our time ministered to?) We here had afterward disposed of that big sponge my father's import agent had procured especially, though its pores, still fresh with a whiff of iodine, tempted toward use. But her silver implements were still on the sink. A buttonhook, a nail buffer, beautifully sharp small brass-hafted scissors that when in need of the delicate we had often borrowed, and the long, double-pronged smug affair that when opened and closed like scissors, expanded and retracted, to do what? My mother had informed me. "To stretch the fingers of a kid glove." Perhaps the sisters, after having taken care of their needs and pawed over the implements on the sink, will pray?

Outside, my mother has waited. In spite of our lack of mutual sympathy, caused, I had to believe, by a mutual discovery that both my features and my mind were always to be too irregular for her, we have moments of flesh-signal, that we recognize at once.

"Your cousin and his father," she murmurs, "they've been in a deadly quarrel about something, ever since the father arrived." She still refuses to "brother" him. It seems that two of the three other men my father had sponsored, though invited today, have walked out on the two of them. With apologies to her, *"Küss die Hand"* and all that of course. But I suspect we won't see them again. The only one left is the one known as the "real brother-in-law." For we have all along suspected (or had my father actually known?) that in the case of the others, no relationship had existed. "But who am I to argue?" my father had said. "Desperate is desperate. We can just hope the authorities let it by." As they had, so far.

The only one now left in our living room besides *Der Vater* and his son, my cousin, is the "real brother-in-law." A man who is either married to the sister of my mother's half brother's wife—or else is her brother. He is the nice one, who knows some English. He has a long-syllabled surname, muttered at entry, which my mother hadn't caught. "Hasenpfeffer?" she jokes. "Wiener Schnitzel?"

Some of the Germans over here comport themselves like honed knives, on the ready in defense of their origin. Others glory stolidly in warrants to their tribal industriousness, from cuisine and homemade beer, to Christmas cards with sparkles on them. Still others avoid *Gemütlichkeit* as they would hip fat, but as if behind those tight lips the tongue flips an aching tooth. My mother may at times briefly resemble one or the other, but cannot be typed.

"What's it all about?" Though she and I are alone in the hall, I now am whispering.

"Come on; what do you think...Money. Plus your uncle's rage at having come down in the world. Worse even than losing his job. Bad as that would be—if that's what happened—to a man in his world, it's a hazard of the trade. Even to be a refugee, if on such a world scale as now. I think your father's wrong. That man can suffer anything if it's on a grand-enough scale to swagger over."

"So what could it be between them? He's always been touting his father to us."

My mother was then a woman of fifty-seven, no longer beautiful in any younger way but with a molding of face, not entirely "sweet," that yet got paid both those adjectives. In repose sad, but with mystery, not glum. She can enjoy, even joke, but will never again be radiant.

I can tell you what caused this, though unrecognized by all then, including herself. Let us look at her as if she is still alive. We are pretending anyway that all here are alive, enough to warrant that kind of scrutiny. And Hattie, born approximately in 1881, since she was about twenty-eight when married in 1910, is like so many women of her time, too untrained to be aware that she belongs to, could be: one of, the intelligent.

When she complained, was ashamed of, those feet that could not poke from beneath a skirt hem with the pretty self-confidence of the ideal of her time—a size four—was she really shivering under the half-unused weight of that other?

"I'm just smelling out what it must be between them, of course," she whispers. "Your uncle—" She sees my face. "All right, half uncle. He'll have given your cousin money beforehand. To be sneaked into the country somehow, in all that pigskin luggage your cousin came over with. Or filtered across the Atlantic somehow. Letters of credit, diamonds, who knows, or maybe transmitted by some third party. And in dollars. Which your cousin, who's no teenager, and witness all his life to *Der Vater's* goings-on. Such a *geschäftsmässig Mann—und mit solchen Ehrenbezeugungen—*" She begins to laugh. "Excuse me, all the umlauts are coming out…Such a businessman, with such honorable references…Not a *von,* but in the back of his white limousine he has the gall to wave to the crowd like one. *Ein König für Industrie und Gewerbe.* Who wants a king of industry for a son. Or expected maybe to be one himself, over here?"

She breaks off, covering her mouth. "Pardon. Forty years almost, it took, to show me *mein Vater, gewiss.* Who maybe didn't send the wrong one to *Amerika.* And do you know, that *Grossvater* of yours, my father, who never wrote me a line in the forty years since I left, didn't die until only last year? And now comes this *Flüchtling,* his son, this refugee, your uncle. Okay, your *halb-Onkel,* who every night this week since he came, we have him to dinner, he sings like a *Heldentenor* at the opera, a hero in the throat. But can sing only of money. And expects the same of his son. Who three times this week did not come here to dinner with." She breaks off. "Your father's very concerned," she says in her normal voice and accent. "He hasn't even offered them a second whiskey."

I have to laugh. So does she. It's such a canny wrap-up of my dad.

"But what has his son done?" For by now I know my young cousin, a young man of sweeping ideas, if all of those pointed one way. Toward him.

At a noise from behind us she moves us down the hall toward the dining room, murmuring as she goes, "I think maybe our young cousin, he must have been trusted with a large sum from over there, maybe his whole estate. With instructions to invest."

"And invested it wrong? Or maybe...maybe not at all?"

We are at the dining room. The table is glowing with fine linen and as much elegant china as a family lacking a butler can handle. I count how many it is set for. Seven. Which means the three of us. And two of them. Including the young master. "*Mutti*," I say. Haven't called her that since I was six. "He hasn't invested it—in Oakley?"

"Good god, no. Your father would never have allowed. Though that would have been better than nothing." For a moment she gleams. "Two new managers brought in, one for the office, one for the factory? Lil paid off—for her formulas? Though once we'd seen your uncle, uh-uh, no, it would never have done. Plus your father would have howled."

I can hear him. "Tit for tat, Hattie? We bring them over out of common humanity—then we get paid for it? Hattie—have you lost your mind?"

Or her morals? But as she smiles into that lost future, I see her capacity, as not seen before.

"So tell me. What my cousin would have done with it. If he has."

"That playboy? With his hangout in the Dolomites? Where he told me the wooden table had been scooped out into bowl shapes, so the soup could be poured right in. Like a fool I said, 'Straight into the wood? Isn't that unsanitary?' To ask that of a German. He smirked at me. I swear I could see my stepmother, his grandmother, in him. She saying, as she used to, 'We have to buy her again. Four times a year. The shoes.'... And he says, 'Of course not, *Tante* Hattie,' looking down his nose at me. 'There was a silver charger shaped to each bowl. *Grossmutter'*— that's her—'had them made for me. *Für mein Geburtstag.* In Switzerland.'

"For his birthday," she translates.

"I know." I say it hard.

"I never know how much you know. German, I mean." Then, not quite under her breath: "Or anything else."

"Why Switzerland? Aren't there enough jewelers, silver-smiths, in Berlin?"

"That's where you park your money, if you can. When the world is tumbling. They sent her old folks there, the *Stiefmut-ters*—to watch over it. In good times, prepare for the bad. The money—that's in the old folks' name. Her father and mother."

"Smart," I say.

"Double smart, the Germans. Always are. Only—then your *halb-Onkel* has to flee out of Berlin, even his army service won't count. But the Swiss are counting. They won't take him in. Nor release the money. Or else the old folks won't. Not for him to come over here. Their son-in-law, your uncle, he fought the war for them. 'The Americans, they beat us,' they tell him. 'And then they sent bundles.'" Smiling, my mother is no longer whispering. "So it is all my fault? 'Go to Australia,' they tell him." Her face changes, in the irony I have come to know. "That is all a *Krawall*, really. They're sitting tight. On his money. The bulk of it."

My German vocabulary is childish, not having been encouraged in a six-year-old during World War I, that last war. *Bitte, das Milch? Danke, vielmals.* But one grown word of my mother's I learned early: *Krawall*. An uproar, a "row," the dictionary says. But in her accounts: "There was such a *Krawall*." Or overheard, to my father, "Again? A *Krawall*? Always the money tinkle."

"But my cousin—he came over. And in style," I say.

"My guess is, he sold the ski hut. The way he regrets when he speaks of it." She always sees what she calls "the ins and outs."

"And with enough left over for his father," I say. "And for the in-laws."

A head shake. "Only the one is a relative. The one who speaks English. And not his. Mine. Through my dead mother. And he paid for himself. The others? Just some rich businessmen your half uncle knew, who had no one over here to sponsor them. Not with the organizations over here having lists already a mile long. Besides, those men, you saw them, not the kind to wait for lists…anyway…swear never to let on to your father."

"Let on what?"

I'm "slow," as she terms it, on the ins and outs. Slow as my father, as she has for years been telling us. Too slow to see the tricks that abound. Among those for whom "honest" is a scornful word for innocence.

"Those men, did you see how quick they lit out?" When she hits her forehead like that, her fist is really aimed at ours. "They paid *Onkel* a fat sum to have your father sponsor them. But thought they were paying your father. That's what they were led to believe."

Both our hands are clapped to our mouths. There we are

mutual, in that underground family suspicion on which she has coached me all too well.

"My half brother didn't mind telling me he had a nest egg," she says. "He means to buy a business with it. 'Better even than *Schatzanweisungen,*' he said. 'What are those?' I said to him. 'You may recall I left too young to know that sort of thing.' He got the point, but he told me. Treasury bonds. But what he had was even better than that. You signal that by rubbing the forefinger with the thumb."

"Cash," I say, awed. "You think—even dollars?"

"All of those men, they were important representatives, they said. Of businesses here. They'll have managed that. 'We had to give him dollars,' one said. 'And dollars he got.' Your uncle had gone to each of them. 'My sister is married to a big one,' he told them. He didn't say *'halb Schwester'*—not that time. 'Her *Mann* is the grand old man of the perfume business,' he told them."

She and I have moved down the hall in the telling. The light from the dining room is on her shamed face.

"A magazine once spoke that about your father. Remember that? When it was still true. And I'd sent it to him. To all those at home."

"Daddy would never. Not in a million years."

"Never. And I told those men that. 'My husband was not involved,' I told them. 'He did it out of the goodness of his heart.' And because he felt out of things. Being from a family so long in this country, no one else over there had solicited him. And what do you know, one of those men said to me, 'We told each other so. The minute we saw him. And that's not *Schwärmerei.*'"

I knew what that meant. Gush. My mother used to say that a lot about the Southerners.

"'*Aber meinen sie,* madame, we know your brother,' the one who speaks English says to me, and then: 'Pardon, *gnädige Frau. Halb.*'"

We are in the dining room now, she absently correcting the knives and forks for angle, shifting the little salt dishes to plumb. "One to a customer," she always says, laughing at herself for being so fond of their mobcap shape. But not now. "'Don't worry, madame,' they say to me. 'He'll get his.' And when they left, shaking hands with us, you know what your father said to me after? 'I felt it. The steel. Inside the hand.'"

There is a noise at the bedroom end of the hall. The polite door creak of those reared to make such a noise.

"Must have been a long prayer," I whisper to her.

When the Abrams sisters reach us, they look, as the old saying went, "refreshed." If you wore no makeup except to powder your nose, other niceties were important, perhaps a pocket hairbrush and a hankie wielded. And the powder would show. To preserve the illusion that this was merely why you had ducked in.

"We took the liberty of a little nap, Miss Hattie," one of them said. I had given up making a distinction. "Laid back the badespread, a'course—all tucked in nice again. Ten minutes does us fine."

As I record that, the fine powder of the years blows toward me, carrying all its variables of domestic etiquette, irritating when you had to observe them singly, yet calming since you then knew what other people were likely to do. It went without saying, although we often said those words—that the Abrams sisters, before lying down, would have taken off their shoes.

"Not at all," my mother says grandly, a phrase that she must have repeated daily, in answer to "thank you's" of one sort or another. "Not at all." Such phrases, repeated in descending treble, did more than make ordinary speech stately. Conduct, the right kind of course, was made all but visible. What this effected was to turn our household into one of the sort the Southerners affectionately called "pokey." Meaning that while we reliably got up enough steam to keep going according to a modest standard of propulsion, our household never spun so full of action that they couldn't pay us a call—even unexpectedly. A social habit that according to my mother could "drive you crazy," and the same for all women recipients similarly at home. Yet any cessation of such visits was dreadfully missed.

What distinguished the routines of the home-women of my mother's time was that in the end many such hazards and dullnesses turned out to be desired comforts—some intermittent, like that one, others much more long term. This was particularly so for the Southern women, who, despite their dulcet speech, were as "opinionated" (a favorite word of their society) as any professional feminist I was ever to meet. Their attitude toward the male being roughly the same.

If, like my uncle Clarence, the husband was never to be more than a pleasantly mannered employee of his wife's family, then she, "turning over" the finances, presumably by investment plus stinginess, came to rule the roost, which my aunt Flora immensely enjoyed. Their daughter Grace was a looker whose easy signals—"I'm a hot property"—were obvious to all. Marrying an upstate Catholic in a hasty home wedding that at age eight I attended bearing a bunch of hydrangeas from the store of dried ones in our living room, she had had a son called Chick and though the husband, Francis, was soon involved in a scandal—a chorus girl drowned from his yacht—she had continued to live with him in their large house, neither speaking to each other for the rest of their lives. This outcome she spoke of as a triumph. Though my junior aunt, a tiny woman with a dry wit, lived alone with her teacher-daughter, their surname being Jacobs, while the daughter went now and then "to Lynchburg," to visit paternal well-to-do aunts and to attend some ceremony

in honor of her paternal ancestor who had fought in the Revolution, my aunt's status, whether separated, divorced, or widowed, was never divulged. Messy as her rooms were, there were
seven of them, on a good block. "Does Daddy support them?" I
once asked my mother, receiving a guarded "Not on your life.
But those aunts down there, they think the world of their niece,
apparently." As for the mythical father, I'm surprised that even
my mother doesn't know the circumstances. "You can bet there
was a marriage, though. My guess is, your aunt was the one to
leave. You know what she's so fond of saying."

That she came North "for the music" was always implied.
"That she shook the dust of the South from her feet."

"Not all of it, unfortunately," my mother said.

Three intelligent women, though. What they have been
able to do—if all they have been able to do, and only according
to custom—was to hang on to their "homes."

In the 1930s, which was where my mother and I were that
evening, colleges were urging women toward the professions.
Teaching was still the safest haven. To be a doctor or a lawyer
was the straightest path, if hard. For the rest, the road was
vague; you had best dig it yourself. For those of us who married,
to keep working was best. For when the children came, the job,
its worth to you and its salary, too often were otherwise ceded
up, while the husband's job was still definitive. Often, as well,
changing communities in the new style. Often leaving that generational center, the old nuclear family, with its fixity and company, far behind.

I knew too many women who, like me, had had to settle for
"homemaker," the new jargon for housewife, with maybe some
scraped-up part-time occupation, or volunteerism—alongside
us the female friendships that could put two or more pared-
down lives in company, for an afternoon.

Just last week one of those, sitting on my porch, where the view was as beautiful as that from hers, had said to me, paraphrasing Thoreau, "Housewives lead lives of desolate separation." I knew what that meant. We were lively, maybe talented, even with some relish for the chores and handcrafts of the home, but immured for the day without company other than that sought artificially, while our husbands, in offices or the professions that involved them with people, likely returned, after a surfeit of that, to a wife whose daily routine, after years of regimented schooling, was now conducted mostly in solitary.

We and the Abramses were just passing my grandmother's sitting room.

"May we peek?" the sisters chorused. We four stood at the door. That wicker chair, why did it so still command?

Up above, high on the opposite wall, my grandfather. Both sisters were staring at him. "Funny thing," one sister said to the other. "Each year up yere, we came and sat with her for a space. Never hardly noticed him up there. 'Cos we never saw him, we keeds, down home. He would have been at the store or somethin'. All the fathers were. Less they had he'p, lak in the ole days. The boun' kind, who you didden have to watch."

"Bound?" The word fell out of my mouth. I could almost hear it hit the base of the cloisonné bowl. "In chains?"

The sisters scowled at me, disgusted. "You No'theners. Never struck you, if you leave people loose, there mought be no place for them to go?" Clara.

"Our paw, our granpaw," Minna said. "Got stuck with four of those who served us. Our two house servants, they went down on their knees to stay, we later heard tell. 'Mars Abrams. Let us stay.' Our granpaw had one principle he taught us all. 'Never split up a family when you buy.' The man worked for him, the wife for us, living in the yard-house he built between.

So he'd made an arrangement. Work out the price he'd paid for them. Then they must go freed; he would help them how. Our mammy was fambly, he said; she would keep with us till she died. But come to find, she'd been married out all along. That left the fella down to our drugstore, whether he was shiftless or too smart for us, the menfolk never could decide. 'Safest to let him gallivant,' Paw told us later. So they did. They let him go. Made a streak for your Harlem. Some of our nigras followed him. Some not. Maybe some of his descendants now working for you all. Like some the others' kin, they still work for us." Minna smiles at us with the superior coolth all our Southrons display when they prate of ancestry. In any form.

"Paw was the instigator," Clara says, crisp. "Staked that boy, I shouldn't wonder. Like years later he staked the two of us. 'Cupcakes?' he said. Nearly fell off his chair, remember, Min? Then he laughs, saying, 'Why not? Whole damn South has a sweet tooth—and maybe the drugstore can fix us up a preservative...' which thank our lucky stars, they didden. We not onto the regulations, back then... Then Paw put a hand on each our heads." She has about choked up. "And we just out of that convent school, St. Joseph's, that all the young ladies had to be sent to, religion regardless, 'Go to it, girls. Gallivant.'"

Southern fathers, ever courtly, even admiring of the spiny-tongued, stiff-backed daughters they sometimes breed—who does that remind me of? Though by then I am nearing thirty, and still denying the "business" of recording that secretly has me by the heart.

But I have figured those two out all right. Clara expands like my father does when once embarked on a story. While my mother glowers in her corner, or maybe brings herself, if in company, to mutter uselessly, "Now, Joe." After the guests leave, he'll apologize. "Now, Hattie, we were brought up to it. We expatiate." As he said the word, it stretched.

Clara does the same. Minna, less patient, goes in for the clinch.

At times my father could warn—himself most—that in business you had to know when to stop "the palaver."

What I was too respectful to note back then will beguile me forever. That all his fancy words for the habits of language were merry ones, and strong. Education, however, signified to him a dreary process, stopped in the eighth grade when that teacher had rapped him over the knuckles. For gazing out the window. Pridefully unused to such treatment, reminding us always, "Your grandmother never had to raise a hand to us," he'd jumped out the window. I saw it as providentially open and not too far from ground level, though he'd never said. And he had never gone back. "At home we had shelves of books: Walter Scott, Shakespeare, that those homespun teacher ignoramuses had never seen, much less cracked."

I knew those editions from our bookcase: print so tiny you had to magnify, Anglo spellings like "labour" and "glamour" and similarly Anglo locutions and punctuations that would clamp my own practice-to-come existentially. Leftover golden sparks cropping up in the cheaper topography to which I had been born. Near them, those thicker tomes that were the bound copies of *Harper's Magazine* for the Civil War years, big as dictionaries, in which stray chapters of a Dickens novel, *Barnaby Rudge, Little Dorrit,* had been inserted, but were never followed up or concluded, my father's scornful forefinger raking the page to tell me why. "Pirated."

In the homes of other families up from Richmond—the Walter Markens, Winstocks, the Pyles, households with whose heads my father played poker, and where I now and then had been the handmaiden bringing cigars—there had been shelves holding much of the same. A half-unacknowledged hoard of English, or Dutch, wrested from milder countries through which these immigrants, fleeing political and religious violences, or merely out to make their way, had passed. I saw them carrying print on their hind legs, you might say, the way bees bring pollen.

To temper as print might, the guns-and-buffalo style of the great new communality?

"*Veni, vidi, vici,*" my father had said, half smiling, when, roaring with a liberal education, I had posed that, about the print. On his own he had pursued education synonyms as he could, acquiring by what he called "self-teaching": a mess of Dante, and "picking up" a little Caesar on the way.

"Paw was the one who *came,*" he said. "Eighteen twenty-seven or thereabouts. We next ones, we were the ones who *saw.* After a war, that's what you mostly do. See the business that has to be done. Some folks from the North did swarm over us, plunder in mind. The South will never stop talking 'bout those carpetbaggers. But quite a few of us came North, carrying exactly the same bags."

"Did you really have one of those?" If so, trusting to our saving habits, or to our inability to discard, I crave to see it.

"Manner of speaking," he'd gruffed. Hadn't I yet learned that a metaphor was as good as a mile? Or that wearing the pince-nez that brought him the world as it was hadn't discharged him from staring at us mostly from over its top. "Matter of fact, we bought me a valise." That, too, seemed to amuse, and I smiled with him. Only much later did I realize that he had left the *vici*—the "I conquered"—to me.

Come back now to the four of us: the sisters, my mother and me, peering into the abandoned sitting room, not quite able to pass it by. Nor to reserve comment. Another habit of the household, and of most who visited it. My mother usually melts some for "the Abrams sisters," even if the very phrase evokes a lifted eyebrow. They have bridged between the domestic, where she is, and "downtown," and the boxes of cupcakes, always heralding their arrival and for which she has constructed a special niche in the walk-in store closet, are more than handy for our daily circle, though she can no longer quite credit the cakes' lack of preservative. "The fact is, I like their tricks."

Also, she believes them both to be still in love with dear Joe, so can feel a certain patronage, in a house where she is not usually on its dispensing side, if no longer quite its recipient.

Catch us then, the four of us, in three variants of age's staircase, the sisters being more or less on the same step. All of us looking in on, and pausing to honor, the woman who had achieved its apex. Although I'm the youngest, I am used to such moments, time with us being so elastic, and the conversation, which I always saw as a meeting of monologues, grayed down even in the sunniest room by the presence of so many elders. I, having already cast my luck with a new generation, perhaps should not dwell so much on what has formed me, but I cannot forgo. Leaning to look is the posture of women. We are a niche, not yet fully singled out. This has its merits. "Perhaps" being its most powerful word?

My mother, chin lifted, is eyeing my paternal grandfather's likeness, up there on the wall. The sisters' presence—or any company?—emboldens her to "open up," though I can never decide whether these larky little outbursts of hers come from the core, making her more what I crave her to be. I realize now I have never been in the sitting room when she was. My time there had been the audiences of a child. I hadn't entered since.

"You know," my mother says slowly, "in all the times I sat with her, I never saw her look at him either. Not once."

The sisters' reply is deliberate, assessing, and a bit greedy. As always when we are pulling at history's strings. "Wayul, the Granpaw, you figure, must have been dade so long? When did he die? Did they come here after he was gone?... Never heard tell. Never thought to... When Joe lit out of school, we were in fifth and sixth grade, he in eighth; he slipping out from the waw destruction wasn't loyal, not to some. Only heard tell about Joe being such a high flyer in New York. 'Til one day, us here for our annual, don't we bump into him in front of the Astor Hotel. He thought we were stayin' there. 'Uh-uh,' we tole him: 'Taylor Trotter, manager the Great Northern? Cheats us blind on the discount but he's home folks.'... And no sooner do we go back there from meeting Joe, we find us two bottles Oakley's perfume at the front desk."

"Toujours Moi," Clara giggles. "That's Joe."

Min is still fixed on my grandfather. "I'll never believe it," she says sly. Like she sure does believe it. "That those two were." She finishes up sharp. "By way of being Unionists. Uh-uh. Not him up there, with those muttonchops."

So that's how the wars end, seventy-odd years thin, after the blood-soaked uniforms, the Blue and the Gray? In a lip-lick of local color? Contravened by how you wore your beard.

"*Nein.*" My mother's voice is cool, instructive merely, as when she had first removed the child's spoon and "pusher" from my small fists and put the knife and fork in them. "*Es war sie.*" It *was she.* And she has said it as if specially to me.

Whether or not they understand German, they get her meaning. She is staring at the wicker chair.

"Oh, you sat with her, Hattie. Always jumped to it, we all knew that. Could hear her nagging at you anytime we came. But our old fuss of a war? No call for you to know about that."

No call? With a stream of emissaries like them? Ever purling in our living room? Where even my father, whose very pores,

after all, drawl naturally, would snort later, "Professional Southerners, save me from them." Until the next time.

"No call for her and me to know?" I say. I feel Northern,
vengeful—and silly, all at once. Yet my mother's confidence has
tendered me more. "With the losers always louder than the win-
ners? Who can help it?"

My mother moves to protest. Guests are sacred. One does
not insult. But a breathed *"Whoo-ee"* comes from both sisters, almost in approval. Their twin stare is now on me. If photographs
can still feel—long exhibited ones being the most likely—then
my grandfather's must be relieved.

"Why—*precious,*" one sister says to me (I've dropped attempting a distinction), the other adds as gently as she, "You've
inherited the family tongue." They haven't to bother identifying
which side of the family.

"When you sat with her," I say to my mother, "what did you
talk about?"

"Ah, you saw that," she says. "That we just sat." She hesi-
tates, soothing the sitting-room door, as to an ally. "Why don't
we sit there for a minute now." She draws in a breath. Even her
sighs are always mute. "For a respite." From the refugees? She
doesn't say that. But the jig is up.

"Those two," Min says, "that father and son in there. You
and Joe deserve an ovation. We paid them our respects. Through
the other one who speaks English. 'So pleased you could come
over,' we said—for what else can you say at such a time? That
young one, he made such a face."

"She always had a reason, your granma. She never called me
without." My mother's still grasping the door. "At that age one
has a lot. Her eyeglasses. Did she let them slide down to the
floor on purpose? Or kick the newspaper out of reach? With
those size-four feet?" My mother's half smiling. "But she soon

caught on. That I'd caught on to her. So, after a while, when I'd come by, she'd say, 'Hattie.' Just that. And we'd just settle down to it." My mother is still smoothing the sitting-room door. "Why don't we just go in and sit a bit."

We four file in. There are enough chairs; Grandmother has always had her audiences. My mother, ceding up authority, sits farthest away.

After we've brooded a minute, Clara says, "The waw knocked out hoopskirts. According to our mother, Granma Calisher never would wear them, not even to hide any of her eight, even when she was carrying. Nor bustles, when they came in." Clara is the dressier sister, if you look close.

"Maybe never one to hide any her sentiments either, those days, sistuh. But who'll ever know? We're talkin' a near centenarian." The word is relished, like they do.

"Oh, come awn, Min. With us, gossip lasts. Passed on, even."

Her sister giggles. "Like what Mumma said that Boo-maw and Boo-paw let fall when they passed on to her and Paw those silver soup spoons."

In her pause, I prepare for an anecdote. It comes.

"So heavy you could scarcely lift them, and those sharp points could near cut your mouth. But the bad debt Paw took them for was notorious. Quarter of a century later, everyone still knew who'd welshed. Member of Boo-paw's congregation. They couldn't sell those spoons for any value, they were told by the jeweler. Monogram takes down the worth. And everybody here knew that crest. And the story. 'Just do me a favor, daughter-in-law,' Granpaw said. 'Just invite us and a former mayor to one of your fancy dinner parties. And serve soup.'"

The trouble with the Southern rhythm is you can get tranced with it, along with its fervors too. I lean forward. The wicker arm has a book pocket, empty now but still firm to the grasp.

"Virginia was fair crawling with Unionists, Daddy always says. Even when it went Confederate and Richmond came to be the capital."

"Joe said that? How would he know? He wasn't yet bawn." And neither were you by a long sight, those four eyes say to me. To leap to defend the legend is a habit ingrained. That's why, in any of our U.S. wars, bar none, recruiters down South do so well.

"I took him see-gars to his poker games." Likely they already knew that; I used to come back wearing as many paper cigar bands the men gave me as I had fingers for. But to state a fact already known like it's a question was a habit we and the Abrams knowingly shared, at least on my father's side. To state a fact so was to further asseverate it, finally clinching it in, as agreed upon by all. On an afternoon-to-evening open house, when our living room had been filled with the soft gabble of our visitors and with us still in collaboration, it was as if one could hear again the whole South questioning itself. While our hard-won, polished oak New York floor and Northern rafters held firm....Sometimes I have trouble with time. In my own life, I mean. Just like him?

"Daddy would be forever maintaining that," I say. "About Unionists." And the poker game had always stopped. Until Walter Markens, the host, would drawl, "Well, emancipation's already been proclaimed, Joe, remember? No need to rub it in." Then, drawing off the band of one of the cigars I brought, he would push it down my left hand's fourth finger, saying, "But we still pledge ourselves to this little hon, here." One of the other players would toss more chips onto his pot, and the game went on. My father, unfazed, dismissed me gently, and I trotted happily back the few blocks between the Markenses' and us, feeling myself an approved participant in what was always referred to, with just the slightest tinge of the infallible, as: *How we do.*

"When Granma died, you sent me for a walk with him, Mother—remember?"

"Your father cried like a baby. Though I wasn't surprised."

"Oh, Joe and she adored one another," the sisters chorused. "And of co'se he was the favorite."

My mother lowers her eyes very slightly. I know her style of disapproval all too well. The sisters aren't quite her preferred company. But she doesn't often get to inform. "No, that would have been the eldest son. I was ten years married before I heard a mention of him. And not from any of them. From somebody up from Savannah who'd known him. Julius. And I just happened to look at Granma when the name was said."

She wouldn't have just happened to. My mother always knew when to look. If only at her own feet. "Joe and his mother, they admired each other. For what each of them had done. For the family."

"That's a funny thing to say, Mother. Like they were in business for the family."

She and the sisters are suddenly a threesome aligned opposite me. Her head cocked, she releases them to speak for her.

They do that together. "Families are."

In the silence after that, the sitting room imposes itself, not quite deserted after all.

"She and you, Hattie," they chatter, "got on extra well, eh? Speakin' German like you both could."

"Ah, no. We spoke only English. From the first we met."

I can imagine how proud she was of that. Nor had I ever heard my grandmother speak German. Until I was grown, I didn't even know she came from there. "Born in Dresden" was about all that was said of her, and not much more of him, my grandfather, except for what was in that book about that group of émigrés early on. As a business, our family hasn't paid that much attention to the files.

"It was kind of a comfort for a child to be with her," I say. "Like she was what people meant when they said 'long ago.'" I glance at the big, ugly cloisonné pot which has some of that, and which has always seemed to be watching me. "And, of course, I never sat when I was in here. She kept me standing. Sitting down was yet to be earned."

The sisters titter. "You were rambunctious, hon. Lak a late chile often is. But Joe and your mother saw to your manners... You and Joe, Hattie, were a first-class match there."

My mother tucks in her chin, not daring to cast me a look. But I can see her swallow. Her neck, though ravaged, is still slender. "Thanks."

"No offense meant."

"And none taken." My mother could be grand. "Matter of fact it was Granma who made our match. Joe's and mine."

"You don't say!"

"Oh, chances are we would have anyway. But she gave us the push." My mother turns to me. "Like to know the first thing she said when Joe brought me to meet her?"

I'm enthralled. By this confidence. From this parent, always the one more remote. Or by contrast so. Via a counterpoise that early on any blubber-mouth could have predicted, and now, after almost thirty years, still in force. Or as my father might quip, in one of his wild quotes ransacked from authors whose identity was lost to him (but when in doubt say Shakespeare), theirs had been a marriage in which, for all its entertainments, they had been "cribbed, cabined, and confined."

"The first thing she said? What?" I croak. I'm accustomed to her irony. I almost see her, the émigré. Empowered by then, and radiant.

"She said, 'Joe says you're twenty-eight. Is that so?' and like it was pulled out of my mouth, I give her the date. She was not near as tiny as when you knew her, though it must have been coming on. I felt she could once have been as tall as me. She thought for a minute, your granma. I felt she was counting up. Then she said, 'You both have my blessing.' And it was done."

But maybe wouldn't have been done without her? I won't ever ask Hattie 'Lightstone' that. But I do ask "And did she ask to live with you two?"

"Not she. Gave Joe what-for, when he suggested that. But your father took that apartment you grew up in, with rooms enough for when that would be. She must already have been eighty-three." My mother's mouth quirks. "And for you, possibly."

"Was she as tiny then?"

"Like I said, not as tiny as when you knew her, though it must have been coming on. In those photographs marked "Calisher Cottage," the one the family had in, I think—Lindenhurst?—she looks thin and spare. But not at all miniature. I always did think, yes, she must once have been as tall as me."

My mother must have been about five foot seven or so, tall for a *Backfisch* of her era, but not dangerously so. In her estimate, I, at five foot nine, am on the edge. Or worse. "The pace was so stately then, Mother." I have all our lives addressed her as that. My grandmother was called Maw. My grandchildren will call their mothers Mom. "Our pace seems so hurried, compared to theirs. Eight children. I shall never manage that."

The Abrams sisters, for the moment forgotten, say nothing. I see them loomed in their nest of those *nigras* still bound to them. Who have "the touch" for cupcakes. Who, perhaps singing those deep-chorded songs of theirs as they set to stir an assembly line of bowls, pour the dough into a railroad snake of tins, and fling their dozens toward the sweet-toothed. As my father said when the Abrams sisters first renewed their acquaintance with him, thanks to our New York residence, "In cookery, it's more often the small operation takes the palm. As in war." Adding softer, "But their mother was a close friend of Maw's."

In our Northern apartment, with the fast-paced city lapping us from below, to puzzle out what controlled or shifted one's days was still amiable, even mandated. Time lingers in every corner, a honey we have brought up from the past. We had once been people who lived in houses. Years later, when I came to live in one, and it our own, I saw how being so fastened to the land could affect the daily. No wonder that the foot could grow large. Or that the once-upon-a-time child of the city reaches down to pull at her root. While the threat of war comes less from the air than from the battalion imagined at the door. Or that my grandmother, by then rarely ambulatory and mulling solitary in the wicker chair years before her death, could rummage back in a war as local as a farmer's market. A war of practice shoots between youths who came in two colors only, the Blue and the Gray, while she once again births. This time the last of her own young.

Or she could at least focus spectacles thick as circlets cut from prisms on the news of 1914–1918, a slangy war, fought by doughboys in trenches, and planes as skinny as mosquitoes whizzing the air, all the dispatches being from an ocean away: "Lo-ong way from Tipperary," and "Hinky-dinky parlez-vous?" singing shoulder to shoulder while the newsboys hallooed it to her from five stories below.

All her sons had either been too young for one war—from Julius born in 1853, or like my father and his remaining brothers, too old—and familied—for the next. She had already had grandchildren, all girls, long before I was born. Who, already women, would serve to keep me longer in my niche as a child? In the final year, 1918, of a war gone from civil to global, her Joe would give her a grandson—my younger brother, Henry—the first male of the muttonchop line in fifty years. And likely to be the last. But I couldn't see her as promoting my father's marriage for dynasty alone. While, as my mother herself has reported, the portrait above had been ignored. Nor had she later on shown much interest in my brother, who had never been made privy to this sitting room.

No secret why she would have been so eager to see her Joe settle. He, at fifty on middle age's cusp, would at last consign those sirens with the too frizzy appeal to the breakfront drawer. There being no evidence, in even the coyest of visitors spinning their topical innuendo, that he had ever since strayed.

I was wishing the Abrams sisters away. My mother and I had never before sat here. Or even been here together. But in a way their duo nullified the personal in them.

"Mother, when you answered Granma's calls, you always sat so long."

"Ah, you noticed that...Well—it was after she started dropping things on the floor on purpose for me to come and pick up. Or hold on to her lunch tray 'til it was midafternoon, that I caught on. 'Just call Hattie,' I told her, 'when you feel like company.' And she said—"

I saw that rictus in my mother's throat again. In the fifty-year-olds, that's where age begins to show. It has a pathos all its own. As it repeats. "'I've lots of company, Hattie,' she said. 'But they are no longer in this life.' So after that—when she called, I came."

A silence. Then: "Everybody paid their respects."

"Everybody."

"And what did she say?" I wanted so to hear. "What did she talk about?"

"We just sat," my mother said. "I grew to know every inch of this room. The carpet pattern. The bumps on the walls. We just sat on and on." She swallowed. "And after a while—it was like we had talked."

"Oh—Hattie," they said. "What an opportunity." Because none of that generation talked personal. You had to pester. Maybe always so, and then maybe, you wormed whatever out of them.

"With Mumma, there were two of us," Min says. "Warn't easy, even so. What she was like when she was a girl like us? She had a hard time saying."

"And so forth." Clara. "We knew how Paw and she were introduced. But after that—she would never say."

They wanted love thoughts. Maybe she saw even then that no man would ever get between the two of them.

"I asked Joe," my mother said. "Where she came from. When. How she and—him up there—met. 'She came from a very educated family,' he said. From over there? None of them listed in that book. So she must have come over alone. There's a wedding announcement—among the family papers Joe has in the vault. Announcing the marriage. At the home of a Mr. and Mrs. Ellis Morris...1852. Of Henry Jacob Calisher and a Miss Betty Benden. Spelled Bee, ee, en, dee, ee, en."

"But that was wrong." Me. "It was Ben-dan."

"So I figured it out. No relatives here. Your granma came alone. Your father knew of the Morrises. People of substance, members of the congregation, your grandfather being an officer at the time, but they were not family...So there it all was—and no wonder she had nobody. The marriage must have been an arranged one...In pioneers you often see how single young women are the most needed. And the minute she arrived—they changed her name."

As with hers. Hedwig. In German sounding softly pretty, with a *hayd* and then the throaty ending *vich*, which Americans can't say. But in English impossible to say—or worse, to read out. As for "Hattie?" My mother had never said whether or not she'd had a choice.

"But Granma was always referred to as Berthe." I had heard my father and the aunts say it. Bairt. Or Bairtuh. Not to her. But to me. Or as in Julius's obit—in the old book. As I say Granma, I think with wonder that she was ever a girl.

"She was always particularly strong-willed, your granma. Mumma always said it." The two tittered. "Though Mumma was pretty willful herself."

"But why would she let herself be sent, then?" I'd cried. "Like a—like a package!"

"Oh—that soon came to me," my mother says. "While we sat. You only have to look at the dates."

"Dates?"

She smiles at our stares. "Hers. I used to figure it out while I'm sitting there. Waiting for her to speak. Ninety-seven when she died. That was 1924. Three years before her centenary. So she was born in 1827. The same year your grandfather came to this country. At least a young man—he born maybe around the century's turn. So—in 1852—same age as Joe, when he married me. And she—whatever had happened in Dresden—or hadn't happened, give or take a few months of the year, she would have been nearly the same as me—twenty-eight first off. As, she'd asked me—made me—confirm. Of course I didn't think any of this at the time—couldn't have. Or that the age difference was—

so alike. So when she gave her blessing right off the dot—and all Joe said was, 'My mother makes lightning judgments—and usually she's right. And she fell for you—how could she not?' I took it as gospel. She was an awesome presence."

"And would remain so," the sisters say, deep. "And maybe thinking it was all destiny. Like when convenient, a fair number of our awesome presences down home tend to do."

I have to laugh. "You Southerners, how you anticipate." Not one of my father's words but might well be. "Small need of psychiatrists. What with the good-old family lore."

"We-ell," Min says slow. "Anyone could see it, Hattie'd be the young wife taking on the load." Geared to hear that—this sitting room—all along.

"And getting fair-enough exchange for it. If an Abrams of Richmond hasn't a right to say that—then who?"

We sink back, in that lull all domestic women recognize, a moment's hooky, gone to gossip even with strangers, perhaps better so, as the prophecy and envy, doubts and warnings harbored to oneself over the washer and dryer, come tumbling out. Or the daily bed-making verdict on one's vanished self. Or even satisfaction in the blowsy routine that will keep the gypsy intellect in health?

I have gone through both. As a quick-married college girl, this night briefly six hundred miles away from husband and child, this is the last time I'll play daughter. What domicile will disappear quicker than the too-solid family house, gerrymandered against all winds? What lasts are always the verdicts delivered to one every morning, as from some seedy columnist the stars seem to find employable. Like me?

"Of course, of course," I cry, looking down at the sitting-room floor where my mother's feet repose, now serviceably black-leathered. I feel a twinge for that lost vanity. From the wall above us my steel engraving of a grandfather—all I will ever have of him—looks down on us. A man whom one might well confuse with one of Queen Victoria's ministers, yet who was denied the privilege of slaves in his own house? Regard, sir, your granddaughter's postmortem glee. At your loss of authority.

Once, when I was in my teens, my father took me to Niagara Falls. Not just to see the Falls, in that oilskin-behind-the-waterfall routine which he thought little of—perhaps because it did not much depend on people like him. Rather, he wanted me to see, indeed stay in, an incredibly louvered, porched, dark-recessed but lighthearted hostel, one of the last—probably to be the very last—of the great wooden hotels. Pure havens of luxury, profligacy, and above all gaiety, of his hallowed youth. "A monstrosity," he said. "But built for joy." He never prated, but as a man of small actions stubbornly pursued, he could put his tenets across. I saw that he wanted to annex me to the ranks of those who were against the tearing down—of eras especially.

As we women brood, there, four so unlike yet linked by the ever-female habit of inserting ourselves willfully into formal history, I dream that my mother's knickers, and my grandmother's trunks, both risen from limbo, whirl like cartoons of old Europe, in the spray of the Falls, and for the nonce upheld there with other flotsam. Small articles of faith dancing in the native light.

"Of course, of course," I say, with that always-limp repetition in which revelation hides best. "A sympathy, that's what it was. Both of you being immigrants."

A word not heard in our house. Perhaps early awkwardness, cynosured as she had mine, takes its revenge. Though when I'd asked her eagerly to tell me about her passage to America, I was still naive. "Not steerage," she'd said sharply. But would not say further in which class. Now she is better armored. I've made her Athena again.

"Josie will be on pins and needles," she sighs. "She rules the roost." My mother's store of middle-of-the-road idiom is admirable—and far easier than mine. Where I was schooled to feel for the common man, but not to his dialect, she, without an ounce of "democracy," is in speech nicely common-denominational. Learning from the tradesman, or from the claque at the knitting shop, is not to be despised. And from avoiding the double-talk (though she certainly hears it) that encircles her.

"Josie," one of the sisters says. Their identity is receding. "Didn't you have one of those, way back, Hattie?"

I look into my hands, waiting for the usual answer.

"I always do. Just rename them. Makes it simpler."

"What do you know," they say. "What do you know. We had Idas." They heave a not quite—whatever it is.

"Mumma was always very tactful. She'd say, 'I'm very forgetful—you don't mind answering to Ida—my first?'"

"And once—," Clara or Minna, Minna or Clara said, "One said, 'No problem, Miz Abrams. I was christened it.'"

Everybody laughs. Doesn't matter—not at all—that we have been through this anecdote before.

"I always wonder," I say. "Like who made the very first recipe?"

"Of what?" one says.

"Of anything," I say, and we all smile the bargaining smile that conversation among our sex teaches. Life is repertoire.

"My half brother and his son—er, new arrivals—will be joining us. The father—I hadn't seen him since he pulled my pigtails—was a, a company chairman in Berlin; he's having trouble with his status here, but looking about. His son—kind of a playboy—knows a little English from the ski crowd at Davos. But manual work was the best Joe could find for him... well. Let's go in. And we're looking forward as always to those cakes." She avoids naming those exactly. My father, whenever advised that the Abramses are hovering, suffers an attack of former roué-ism, "Cupcakes!" he'll snort. "What those two are certainly not. But with their pictures on the wrapper, no less." As he always counsels, the best perfume in the world probably costs less than its bottle.

The next episode in our history I would prefer to avoid, since remembering it always induces a minor sense of shame. Only a minor one—which is the irritation. Nothing like the huge shame that will whelm me when I find out about my grandfather. Rather, I will return to this slight collision between two strains in our households as to the bit of middle-class violence far too median. In the face of the dreadful gap shortly to emerge between "the Germans" and us, the memory of a red weal on a forehead is not enough...Briefly:

"Oh—what a lovely table you do set, Hattie." The Southern drawl does hang in the air so pretty; I'll always see it as the true vehicle for compliment—though in my mouth no longer possible.

"I'm afraid I always overdo the casseroles." The latter are wedding presents from *Tante,* and my mother's disparagement is fake. "She'll have to trot them back into the kitchen to be filled. But that's Josie." Actually, those fat serving dishes, swollen like buttocks at either end and with rosebud-patterned lids, remind both women of Europe—and I don't like noting that my mother is in effect disparaging Josie as well. Also—I cannot prepare our visitors for the two men, father and son, already seated expectantly in the dining room, if to one side. When the father "came over," my young cousin moved elsewhere with him, whether to a hotel or furnished room not disclosed. We can only suspect that they do have funds, at least for the immediate.

In spite of which, invited for the first weeks to daily dinner, they continue to appear for it. As my mother rages, "Out of the blue." And always early enough to greet their host, just home from the office and clinking the sherry from the sideboard. What's more, they are not shy about preferring schnapps.

"Ah, come on, Hattie," my father had counseled, "don't you see why? In a new country. To which they've been relegated. We are their one identity." Adding with a tongue click, "He's no fool."

"Damn right." Swearing is new to her. "Ever reminding us that conditions here are not nearly on the level they're used to. Their maids did not cook—or vice versa. And this time of year—they were always in Paris. At the very same hotel my brother stayed when the army occupied Paris. Where the son— who hadn't stuck long enough at that Berlin gymnasium to learn English—acquired enough from the girls at the Folies Bergère—or from the little dressmaker's assistants, what is it you call them, Joe, the *midinettes?*—so my brother can carp, 'Pity the boy cannot use his French here.'"

"Hattie. The boy works in a factory now."

"Joe. You have too much pity."

For a man, she means.

He flinches. "Learned it at my mother's knee."

We four women now leave the sitting room—a small female cavalcade, trotting down the hall, toward the dining room, where the "refugees," as the newspapers dub those being helped to flee Nazidom, are awaiting us. My mother sometimes varies the term: "Our imports," she'll say, borrowing the phrase from the frail business that supports us all. Oakley & Co. does now and then sell items from abroad. "The trouble being"—quoting what my father is wont to say of such—"you can't always guarantee the quality."

Her joke scares me. Since the arrival of the Germans—both our two and those men who briefly frequented our household—my mother's irony has markedly increased. According to my paternal aunts, a similar increase ("Observations one wouldn't have thought our Hattie capable of," and my father's too-hushed "She kidded a lot; like she wanted to outdo me there") was what, after my brother's birth, had sent her into the hospital. Postpartum psychosis, they call it. As a college-bred girl, recent mother of a small child, and in a new community, I could well understand why, though I hadn't suffered it. The old term for the birth and the period immediately after used to be "confinement." I recall the woman neighbor, fled to my porch, who had so grimly misquoted Thoreau: "desolate" for "desperate." In household women who are capable of more, irony—or depression expressed?—flourishes well.

But tonight my mother, standing at the entry to the dining room, seems unduly satisfied, left hand raised empress style, toward a table set so elaborately that the fumed oak table underneath the long white cloth may indeed be groaning.

"American Beauty roses," she says. "Good God."

"And an orchid," she says. To date my half uncle had never split for flowers. As she had noted. Even citing *der Vater,* their joint parent, who had brought her stepmother a bouquet every Friday night. When, in his world, work had stopped.

"Well. I see some of the family manners have after all survived." She speaks better than she knows, as will shortly appear. *Der Grossvater,* described by my admiring young cousin, his grandson, as at eighty-five still a bull of a man, had not too long ago knocked to the floor a man who had insulted him. "You can take pride in him," my cousin proudly advised. Though my German vocabulary wasn't great, I understood that reflex uppercut in my own long bones. Maybe that sorry tale of money rape wasn't the only reason the *Onkel's* elders have skipped to Switzerland. In Switzerland maybe no one insults?

"But where are the men?" my mother mutters. "Not in the kitchen you can bet. Not them."

But we have passed the living room on our progress down the hall, all the bedrooms being behind us, except for the two tiny maid's rooms, in these apartment houses by custom on the kitchen's other side. Josie's was the larger one. My cousin, while resident, had been quartered in the other, the proximity worrying my mother, but there was nothing else to be done. To have quartered him in the empty suite would have been sacrilege. With this my father—who normally ignored all domestic details other than the food submitted him—had concurred, "If he bothers Josie, I'll read him the riot act." Whether this had been necessary had not been discussed.

"Joe sometimes brings in delicatessen," my mother falters to the sisters. "But surely not today. He's coming home early, in your honor."

The derivation of the stores my father loves now occurs to me—German: *delikat essen.* Dainty eating. And the store for such provender so named: *delikatesse,* I often heard on *Tante's* tongue. In the recurrent waves of immigrants rippling into and out from Ellis Island, our port of entry, the reason for the incoming was always pointed out, the Irish—a midcentury's potato famines, being the best known, and ritually taught. *Tante's* crowd, a couple of decades later, had swarmed in like bourgeoisie, bringing their food and other styles with them. As the Italians had, working class. My father's taste in food has never got over his brush with New Orleans Creole, or the later Mouquin-Delmonico's in New York. Sometimes he details us a dream menu, with lamentations for items on the wane: Oysters from Chesapeake Bay. Or the little Jupiters from the West Coast.

"Peafowl, from not just my own state; they roost in the trees. And from just our neck of the woods: ah-harrr..." All of it, he jests, "from *Hoi-Polloi Cookbook*—which if some smart chef could get it together, he could cash in."

This a dig at *Escoffier*. "There's a strong tie between our nation's food and our politics, daughter. Like anywhere. And you won't catch us entirely with the elite."

But he's not here, maybe to elicit my mother's sub rosa: "There Joe goes again."

Min slips in a boost, consciously polite, "Your chicken fricassee, Hattie. Can't deny we're hopin' for it."

Risky, but to be applauded—and my mother's nod rescues her.

Then the kitchen door swings open, with my father's usual homily, if he's behind it. "Any kitchen of worth has a swing door, eh?" Adding, "So's you can check on your products, eh, sisters?"

Products? Cuisine is the usual term. But not today.

Onkel and nephew are behind him. All three have a glass in hand. Whiskey, by the look of it.

Introductions are flourished—the sisters' more particularly. "*Küss die Hand*. Took a gander at yours. Ladies. These gentlemen have the sweet tooth of their country. You've outdone yourselves, m'dears."

"So you have," I say. "Snagged some." The sisters have known me "since she was so high." As they will say every time. I have to keep in character. But my father's not comfortably so—has he caught nephew goosing Josie again? The hitch being that though she has a steady, she doesn't protest.

He seats us, usually my mother's privilege. With a covert exchange, he puts her at the head, usually his place. I have Clara on my side of the table; he has Min on his, nearest the foot, where

he has placed father and son, side by side. If they have been spatting, as my mother hinted, perhaps a sign they've made up?

He pours the wine. We are not a champagne family; he af-
fects to look down on those. But for our guests he has been
rather displaying his vintages—the Echezeaux, the Puligny-
Montrachet, the Pommard, rolling out the names letter-
perfectly, though only when asked, though the rest of his French
derives from the scentedly risky stuff his friend Housselle put
him on to—Gautier, like *Mademoiselle de Maupin,* the memoirs
of courtesans and the royal bedroom farce of the *Heptaméron* of
Marguerite de Navarre.... plus some Creole.

Earlier on I had seen him set two intended bottles out on
the sideboard. "Château Neuf du Pape. Just right for the ladies,
I think. And they'll likely know the name of it. Though those
two only sip. Not that they'll know the difference." But those
two bottles are no longer visible.

Now the fricassee comes on, a golden triumph of a home
Kocherei, with that winning fillip of irregularity no chef can
supply. The casseroles, trekked back to the kitchen and returned
again, are now warm with vegetables. Normally Josie does
all back-and-forth with the dishes, chin lifted in pride, waiting
silently while my mother ladles out, and the dish being emptied,
is dismissed with a nod—this rhythm going on throughout dinner. At first, as our new "greenhorn," she had to be trained not
to drop casual home-style comments to the diners throughout,
as if she were their equal, but she has learned her manners long
since. Today, however, Josie hasn't appeared. My mother has
brought in the dishes, which, as emptied, have been let lie. I volunteer, but have been refused. Meanwhile the fricassee has
earned its usual compliment, with companion anecdote.

"Remember, Hattie? First dinner you cooked for us up
here, as a bride?" The sisters turn to each other—as they have

done all their lives. "Roasted the chicken with all its giblets inside. Still wrapped."

The laughter bewilders my uncle. My mother explains it to
him.

"Tell him you're now the best cook around," the sisters say.
"Wish we knew German. So many fine receipts." "Receipts" is
the down-home term for recipes. "Hear tell you following in
your mama's footsteps."

"Except for the chicken," I say. "Sure heard plenty about
that."

I see Athena does not welcome my defense. But I am beginning to be sick of my Southrons and their accent—that sugars
my mouth again, the minute I meet up with some. Though my
father's drawl, ever present but with a content more applied to
for meaning, does not affect.

The two Germans weigh heavy on us. My father, too, who
ordinarily is gloomy only in case of illness or death, has fallen
silent. This conversation is not for them. In whatever language.
Nor for my cousin, who though male enough, does not seem to
me yet a man. I think of the pint measuring cup I use, its plastic
incised on one side in grams, the other in pounds, and in liquid
versus solid. There should be such a cup for the weights in family life. Each to be brought to the analyst. Who will recuse himself first, if as involved as me?

"*Onkel,*" I say. Giving him full weight. "*Ihre Frau?*" Your
wife? "*Wo ist sie?*" Where is she?

He stiffens, a bull of a man also. "Also, I need—before they
came... *Ich brauche, vorher—ein* business. *Mann braucht ein Platz.*"
A man needs a place. He asks Hattie the meaning of *vorher.*

We have embarked on that seesaw talk of the elders, still familiar to many American childhoods, where the speech that
comes to them heart-in-throat vies forever with the new slip-

pery clatter that shops you, road-hogs you, outsmarts you at some compromise, but now and then smiles on you. In this land still so full of immigrantsy—if that is a word?

"*Mutti* is not like him, *denkensie*," my cousin says. Half-and-half—as he may do to the end of his life. "*Mein, Vater*—how could he believe this could happen to *Ihm*?" To him.

My father, pushed by my cousin, had finally written the *Onkel*—refusing my mother's tight-lipped offer to transcribe. "No. Let him have it in English. He better come. It's time." And his half-brother-in-law was still—what was he?—General Motors, for—all Germany? Or Bavaria. In the cloud of vaunting he traveled with, confounded by the protective and useless secrecy that can conflict any émigré, we were never really to know. "I'll send him a telegram. Asking Western Union to confirm." That could still be done—summer of 1939. The message read, "Make up your mind. Or I will not further pursue." Two months later, *Onkel* is here. Though not with that smooth excess of luggage, pigskin bright, that did not seem to surprise the custom officers, with which the son had sauntered in.

"*Vielleicht*," my cousin says to me. "*Was ist 'vielleicht'?*"

"'Perhaps,'" I say. *Vielleicht*. Lovely word perhaps, but my mother has never credited it.

My cousin works for a storage company, endlessly shifting the crates. His slender arms, which were not too needed for ski, now have biceps. "*Im* vinter," he has mourned to me, he will "get back" his torso and legs. Their adroitness, he means, for which "the boxes" do nothing—even corrupt. Despite which, the girl he had met on the boat (he had come down the gangplank with her in a duo, like out of a print for something international) had in fact invited him to ski and he had weekended with her twice. "Who pays?" my mother had commented. "Ah, Hattie," my father had replied with a glint. "They say it's always the woman."

Old people flirting; it embarrasses. Twists a forewarning?

I don't much like my cousin but his father partly excuses him—though I've no grounds for why. "Those other men who came when he did, Mother. Ask him did they bring theirs. Their wives. The man who spoke English—a filmist, wasn't he?—I thought he said they had not."

While she asks, I clear the table. No need to hurry, and piling the dirties on the sideboard, at which she usually protests.

My father, blotting his mustache, stares at the two men.

Finally she answers, faltering. "He says there's more and more red tape. Bribery, some. Though that is verboten; you can get shot for it." Her lips are pale. "It's rumored—only one to a family can go. Where there are resources to—to confiscate." I see her swallow. "And, no. None of the other wives"—she puts her head in her hands—"are yet here."

"Hostages?" I whisper to her. "Quick—what's the word for it?"

"*Geisel,*" she whispers back.

My cousin turns red.

"Nah, nah," the uncle says, as soothingly as I've ever heard him sound. *"Du bist verrückt, mein Schwester. Wie immer."*

I know what that means: *You're crazy. Like always.* Said often by her—to me.

"Bring dessert," my father says to me. To thunder such a phrase would be absurd. Nevertheless, it chills. "I'll see to this." He turns to the Abramses. "Sorry to've involved you in this."

My mother follows me.

In the kitchen, no Josie.

"My cousin goose her again?" Or worse?

She prefers not to understand my slang, or protest it, but not this time. Dipping the strawberries into the port, then into sugar, her hand is shaky. "Not him."

"Not—" Her brother. *"Onkel?"*

"I told her to take the rest of the day off. She wouldn't an-swer direct. Gave her some money, and *Tante's* tickets for the dance evening at the Turnverein."

Tante always passes those on. As for the Police Ball, where the crowd is monumentally not yours, nor would you dream of going. But for the solidarity, one subscribes. While these days, at the Turnverein, always the outpost of the "other" Germans. Once graciously extending *zusammenhalt* (togetherness) for a bouncy, beery dream-flight to the homeland, the invasion of that confederation, the *Bund,* and the blackshirts make it dan-gerous now.

The trays, when she has finished them, sparkle like those colored-sugar Christmas cards in which Yorkville used to spe-cialize. Sent by the merchants and professionals, butchers to opticians, which *Tante* and her crowd had willy-nilly patronized, and bought at the stationer's—he head of the *Bund* to which most now belonged. Cards which any child would adore, they are in my psyche still—an accent to which it may still respond?

The berries are in those pressed-glass dishes, thumb-printed on the white sides, red-corolla'ed at the brim, at which my aunts, for whom crystal is par, turn up their noses. "Got them as premiums," my father had said over the top of his newspaper. "Cigar bands of the coffee industry. All over New York, we first came. Only bringing whatever wedding china of your granma's the Blues and Grays between them hadn't smashed. Those cake plates with the cherubs on them mostly." All the aunts had some as well.

As I watch her center the cupcakes in a tray which was *Tante's*, I see how my backgrounds have started to blend. Only trust the inanimate. Though as to the cakes, which come in two sizes: the tinies, poppable into a mouth at one go, or the

graspable supremes, both iced inch-thick in a rainbow of flavors, I see that for these primitives, my mother—from the land
of Dubos tarts, confections of subtle layering and hour-long
beating—has only scorn. Yet pausing at the entry to the dining
room, to sweep a custodial glance at my tray of coffee and
demitasse gear, she looks happy. Speaking to me from the side
of the mouth, she says, "Josie knee'd him"—and we sally in.

From the foot of the table my uncle smiles at her. "*Ach,*
Hedwig…," he says brightly, "for your coffee alone I would
come." He lifts his cup. "Great."

Except for her name, and the guttural *ach,* he has spoken in
English. No—in American.

She puts down her tray, carefully. I sneak down mine, next
to it. Better than throwing it. I feel her heat.

"Stinker. And all the time, you let me translate? What gives
with you?"

"Hattie." My father is staring at his thumbs. "He learned it
in prison camp."

A long breath, expelled. Was it *Schweinhund*: pig-dog? An ex-
pletive escaped from her now and then, its meaning refused.
"*Also.* But the picture you sent us, *Bruder.* Not in prison
uniform."

My cousin, the son, flushes. He is childishly fair for a man;
his cheeks always betray him—that mustn't go down well at the
factory. The father, my dark-haired half uncle, is sallow, like the
women who, buying at *Tante's* Yorkville market, are always in
confab with the butcher on the cuts. Maybe the *Onkel's* wife
is fair?

"*Mutti* sent you that," my cousin sniggers. "Because you
were always sending us the bundles," he says fast, in a German I
didn't know I knew that well.

Bundles of secondhand clothes, yes, to a town house in

Berlin with the brocade-draped walls. My mother, whose hair is now mouse-colored, was once fair, like the woman who died giving birth to her. I had seen the long chestnut-color braid the young Hedwig had come over with. "I could have sold it," she'd said, putting it away again. "But I did not."

I am wishing, wishing, to be out of this entanglement, and upstate again, even at a price. Back in my own solitary daytime household, as the youngest *Frau,* far from her hometown… This handing down—will it never stop?

"I speak the English *also* for business," the uncle is saying. "I learn *besser* at Opels. *Ach,* that was a car. Then comes the GM line. Likewise."

Likewise. That word my mother is forever using. A kind of bowing word, salaaming to the new country? Seldom heard on native lips.

Der Onkel gestures at the cake tray. Inclining first to one sister, then the other. "*Und so,* you do these such for business, *gnädigen Frauen.*" With a nod begging us all to excuse, a signeted hand reaches for one of the tinies. He smacks his lips. "*Schmeckt gut. Ja, und* I see *im Küche* those so many boxes. *Fabelhaft.* You do well." He leans back, suddenly a sharer, nurturing. "*Hause gemacht,* made in house, you tell them?" The head drops for a sec but lifts again. "So did we." He leans back, head going side to side, chuckling at the general world. "You *Amerikanisch.* Sell? Like maestros you do it. Buy? Like kids."

"Ludwig—," my mother says. Warning.

He squints at her. "Loovis. Since now."

Her face is a muse's. "Lewis. And the last name?"

His face. Who knows yet that smile's meaning? As he says it. From their family name, Lichtstern, but as translated, not quite correctly. As suggested by the kindly Adlers, or self-assumed? She has never quite said.

"Lightstone *sehr gut,*" he says. "I get it secondhand. And you did *sehr gut* with it." He tips a salute to my father.

The two sisters—we had almost forgotten them. They are tranced, if only with the gossip they will bring back. What will they say?

"And I soon do more *besser,*" he says. "*Besser wie*—was *ist* this neighborhood? *Besser* even, *wie* Riverside Drive."

"Knock it off. If you get what that means."

"*Ach,* Cho. To speak once more *Amerikanisch.* To—how do you say?—'gas with the boys.' Out of Berlin we would go. Team from Michigan, team from us. To Amsterdam, *ja. Für*: Blowout. *Aber Trieste mehr elegant ist.*"

He slaps his son on the knee, "And we take this *Spitzbube* along." His eyes screw. "It will be for the last time. They know it. *Aber* I do not."

"And when we get to Berlin back—*der* grandvater—mine, Hattie, not yours, is already in Switzerland, family house to us—tickets on the hall table for us. To *Amerika.*"

Clara is leaning forward, her ruffled *jabot* breathing with her. I know its name because I have inherited a box of them, so marked, from the trunks, along with Granma's black thread-lace shawl and white opera cloak embroidered in scarlet. A short cloak, and of a circumference that might indicate its owner had after all once worn a hoopskirt. Also two black fans (carried maybe in her wifehood), one with silver sequins, one with painted-on white butterflies. Did one—could one—conceal babies, the not-yet-born ones, under the hooped tent, that would have swayed as one walked? Driving her middle-aged suitor (for by then my father's father, Henry Jacob, must have been in his fifties) to an energy that eventually in time had produced those eight?... The cloak still hangs in my own closet, its fine-grained stuff still perfect after 150 or more years (1852–2002), only its long, braided neck roll showing wear, both long ends still hung with the silky white tufts of goat hair that when I first saw them made me both laugh and be repelled.

But now, as I write this—I watch my mother queening it over the Abrams sisters, from the marriage nest she herself had made. "Opera" was often my mother's term, lodged in a yearning in part unfulfilled. From her I would inherit a drawerful of elbow-length white kid gloves along with the leftover boas— kept through the Depression years and sported now and then, in the harlequin-checkered entertainments we managed "on a thin dime" now and then.

But the cloak? Part of a dowry from Dresden, which its cloth makes likelier, I am now convinced. For what other reason would it have been saved out of ninety-seven years of garments, unless worn in the parlor of the Morrises? It had been Berthe Bendan's wedding cloak.

So now am I able to see her as a young woman? Though, like my mother in her wedding hour—no longer a young girl.

So—back to Clara. The history of women comes in patches and flashbacks and stuffs, but may be no less durable?

"Hied off to Switzerland—just lak tha-at?" she says. "Minds me of our poppa and his paw. No love lost, between those two. Two men in the jewelry line in a near-dead city, which Richmond was afterward. Arguing whether they should stay with eighteen-carat gold for quality, or go for fourteen. Both of them with their jeweler's eyepieces in." She hoots. "And every customer from roundabouts knowing Paw's was in his blind eye..."

"That's why Clara and I—we never spat about quality," Min says.

I seldom interrupt the elders. You learn more listening. But this I have to make sure of. "Which carat was Paw, your grandfather, for?"

"For the eighteen, of course." She smirks. "Old folks always are."

"Your boxes, the list of ingredients still says 'farm eggs,'" my father says. "And 'flour milled so fine you can powder your face with it.'" He grins. "Any decent flour is. About the same as any decent face powder. As our Lil would agree. But I'm blessed if I can see how you manage new-laid eggs. Not for the area you cover." He looks over at *Onkel.* "From Baton Rouge to Baltimore, sir—if you know the map. And making goo-goo eyes at the East Coast. Or Nabisco is. The company that's dallying to buy these ladies out."

"Na-beesco?" *Onkel* says....I think of my long-gone freshman French teacher, M'sieu Le Grand, confessing that no European can say the short "i."

"Sure, farm eggs, Joe," Clara is saying. "Just not from very small farms. But new-laid—at the time."

My father has two boiled eggs, fresh as he can get them, every morning. As delivered from a Long Island supplier who comes in every second day. The violinist, Yehudi Menuhin, was rumored to require the same, wherever he toured. My father avers that he can tell when the hens are "off." I see them wandering about the barnyard distractedly. (While Menuhin skirts—but surmounts—a false note.)...

"Cold storage—?" he says. "Clara. You can't mean." He winks. "Or do you prevaricate?"

My mother's eyes go up in her head. Your father, she warns, can he never call a spade a spade?

The word means "lie" but the sisters don't bristle. "Our life savings are involved, Joe," Min says. "What's a little beatin' round the bush?"

"Nabeesco," *Onkel* says with reverence. "*Ein Kartell.* And all from—*Was meint Keks,* Hattie—how you say it?"

"Crackers."

"All from those they did it." He drains the shot glass still in his fist. "Buy small." He wipes his mouth. "Thi-ink Big." The "i's" are short. He rests the fist on my cousin's shoulder. "From Berlin I tell him what to buy. The guys from Detroit, they are buying shares in it. A liddle outfit, *Kugellager*." He smacks his lips. "*Die Amerikanisch singt mir immer so.* Ball bearings, *ja*. Midout ball bearings, *Mann* can *nicht* fight a war. And we are going to fight." He is seesawing between English and German—in almost another patois. I see how this lends the speaker a kind of citizenship. A quick study, my *halb-Onkel*. "So then I cable him. By then, to say: I am leaving, is dangerous. To do business with the U.S., still legal—even the Nazis must deal."

So he cables my cousin to go shares with the Detroit guys on the ball bearings. Plus the two-word code that means he himself is on the way. "So I cable *mein* son: 'Buy. *Grüss Gott.*'"

That same greeting-of-old still heard on the streets of Yorkville, as once (according to my mother, half condescending, half wistful) in Bavaria. *Salute God.*

My uncle shakes his head, as if coming out of water. His fist is still on his son's shoulder, the son staring ahead—a soldier. "*Und hier bin ich.*"

And here am I.

Four words, floating on the water.

For the first time, I feel sorry for him.

The *Onkel* leans forward. Toward another cake? But, no, toward the sisters; after all, they are in business as well—and on that score my father has not been obliged with genial exchange. Perhaps awaited? It occurs to me that because my father had been able to sponsor so many—though going out on a limb to do so, but not sporting that, a status equal to *Onkel* and his crowd had been awaited—a whole province surely—of New

York. Because this man—whom I resist seeing as a man—is burning to begin again.

And instead what has he found here—to compare with the lumbering mileage of Detroit, which had "represented" him to his country—all the while he saw himself as performing the opposite? Perfumes and scents—for he had been to my father's office, though not the factory. And now, as coveted—*wirklich!*—by *ein Korporation:* cake? His lips bunch under the nose, but still achieve a smile. *"Die ganze operation—gnädigen Frauen—*how much you want for it?"

My father's turn to smile. "Call it a day, Ludwig. Lewis. These ladies like to dicker. We could be here till doomsday 'thout you close the deal." My mother stirs. If we were alone she'd sigh, "My corns hurt"—which means her impatience has found its usual path. But in company she has no corns.

A head flip, jaunty as a balladier's, that denies the squat bulk below. *Onkel* is nearest to Min. "What you are bid by the Nabisco?"

"Oh—we won't know that 'til tomorrow," she says with that stifled shrug-giggle which was a hallmark of "ladies-come-to-see." And at the resurrection may still be. "The seck-a-terry, Miz Eunice, she gets paid handsome—to answer 'Inna meetin', they inna meetin',' all the livelong day."

"Takes us shopping, for a spell after lunch," Clara says, "which is sent up, but not room service. Catered by Sherry's, if ever I saw...Cake they send—a triple layer, but that don't put us down. 'Tastes lovely,' we say, smooth as cream. 'For a layer, that is.' We don't even have to point to the slogan on our boxes. 'Cupcakes. For folks on the go.'"

"Mr. Riordan, the dickerer, he's a right sweetie," Min says. Her posture is commando, but hearing her from the next room, you would never suspect. "He says, 'Where'd you get that idea?'

I say, 'From you people. One of your ads. Forget what it was sellin'. But those words hit.' A hiatus—" Both Abramses sigh. "Some years back now. But like it was yesterday."

The Southern refrain. My father coughs, recognizing. I smell his aftershave—Lilac Vegetal. In our main bathroom the only rumpled hand towel on the rod will be his. My mother leaves the others, starched board-stiff, hung there for weeks. To test which female guests are still well-brought-up-enough ladies, that is, to leave behind a rumpled one. Not saying how many she is hoping for? "I did try the paper ones, years ago," she confesses slyly. "Your father kicked up a row."

Clara says dreamily. "They don't have to keep tabs, these big corporations. We do. As for holding them to the letter—pooh. Last year's Lord & Taylor bill—I always pay—didn't even come. Tell Riordan tomorrow, they're going to put a stop to that." She falters. "You're right, Joe, about those aigs."

Their family, like ours, would have had a piano, whether or not anyone played. I can see them, standing at it, not scabby-kneed as at ten or so I'd have been, black-stockinged, rather, but thrumming "Chopsticks" just the same. Though in four-handed crossover, probably, where I would have strummed on alone. Their poppa saying privately to their mumma, "Give them music lessons, for the love of—" As had mine, with an oath actually said...

Watching any era whose remnants you have barely escaped, you see only the stuffiness. That day, an unknown one in late 1938, I myself by then married safely, or badly, would have been nearing twenty-eight, give or take a few months, lacking maybe a year. Or maybe, verging ever closer to another "waw" we were into 1939? Whatever I was, all the living of whatever age tend to think that their generation accelerates. (That's why I've never trusted the historians—and no apologies for this parenthesis.) But even with a taste for looking backward, the half-baked classical illusion that early reading—in Alexander Pope, say—had left me with, I never thought of the Abramses as the Boadiceas of the business world, their halberds at the ready, if all too dangerously sharp against their meager chests. In fact, I never thought of them at all. Nor of that hallowed parade of fathers: *"Der Vater kommt"* being the Teuton warning, whether scathing or scared. Or of "the pater," as met in bygone Brit novels stocked with the public-schooled. Neither being a tradition with which my male parent, belatedly come to fatherhood, tenderly grateful, and above all broadly ill-educated, would have had anything to do.

But by now we are well past a millennium I never thought to see. Living as long as I, and with a mind not yet cracked, has its tasks—this one, like so many of mine, being self-imposed. Yet different. Acts of art never run quite clear of the personal, yet ask for attention with another kind of vanity. Here my responsibility is to a mise-en-scène, in front of which, seated as high as I am now, in a theater box surrounded, orchestra to balcony, by the dead, I am its last auditor.

What I may not forget, nor should, is all that stratagem to compromise, those lollygagging to rapscallion unfairnesses—and quiet assents to the murderous, observable by one for the most part without protest—in the half century since.

What I see most is the curve of Clara's mouth, when it said, like a bird opening its beak for air, "As for keeping it honorable—" Or the sweet unreason, humbly proffered, of Clara herself, she throttling Min's blurt of disagreement; "You shamed me, Joe. It'll cost us. But I'll see to those aigs."

In the old apartment the air itself has a simple complicity about it, composed of the creakings from old furniture, the running

footprints of children now lost to adulthood, and habits daily repeated, all guaranteeing that violence does not, will not occur
here. My mother is particularly proud of its "cross-ventilation"
as a corner apartment in which the atmosphere is ever-lightly refreshed. I used to love as a child the hot triangles under the
awnings, when these were extended, one at each window, on
the Broadway side. Safety was there, somehow triangular too—
a rich kind of hiding. What was promised by a genteel childhood was that all the violences, encountered in fairy tales, or
hinted at in the public school, were closed off. Here, in this residence whose pace is intergenerational anecdote, and where the
strict furniture awards you niches of comfort if you know its
carvings and its pillows well enough, no hard violence will
come. All backgrounds will blend.

And, yes, they do. But by then not to merely reiterate what
has gone on before.

The Abrams Sisters, Cupcakes, providers as so listed on their
boxes, are just leaving.

Their mien is somber for a pair so mildly dressed. In their
hearts must they be only visitors here—and each time for the
last? "Well, good-bye, Hattie dear. Good-bye, Joe." Manners en-
sure that they will put her first. From more affection than is
wise, they won't call him "dear."

My half uncle should rise, get to his feet. Instead, he
crouches, like a brown bear. At the time, I'd not yet seen a bear
of any kind, but when I was five, my father, cuddling me close,
often read me a story about one of such a pelt, though both of
us knew that I was by then capable of reading it myself. This
teaching me that the gratuitous act of love is to be cherished?

"What you want for it, your liddle business?" *Onkel* grunts.
On his side of the water, he might not have dropped that

"liddle" but his new language, his new status, has betrayed him. Also his arm remains flung over his son's shoulder, it impassive under his lordly protection.

The Abramses, shrinking back, like to a bit of manure cast at them, have no answer, except to gaze, nostrils working, at the tray on which the larger of their two "items" are studded—on each lemon-iced one a twirl like a cockade.

From parlor chattings between Oakley's brother-partners, I know what broodings go on before an "item" appears, and what "a gross of" is—a value not taught in arithmetic class: twelve dozen, or 144, the gloss of strangeness attaching to a "gross" being that it can be 144 of anything. Ounces of scent maybe, to morsels for the palate. Moreover—it is generally a term allotted to the small. One wouldn't say a gross of—combat tanks. Larger aims take greater apportionment. But though I don't know in what wider-scale terms the greater needs of the world are numbered, there are advantages to an upbringing even modestly mercantile.

Why is everybody so quiet? In that over-itemized atmosphere, that pursuit of the ultimate alchemy, by which the intangible will turn into the touchable, "buy" will morph into "sell," "get rid of" into "have"—one conclusion came to me early.

All getting and spending is a dream process, the cupcakes going down the automatic assembly line in the same jiggery-pokery as the Ford. While the clouds floating in their flirty geometry over the factory in skies blue or gray, in one way or t'other the theorem is Proved.

So I sympathize with him, Ludwig-Lewis. Or the vulgar half of him now rampant, in the squat limbs still crouched...

Maybe so does Min. Even before she speaks, splatting a no-no hand meanwhile on Clara's arm, shaking her head to us, her stance is professional.

"My sister here handles the makings," she says. "She thinks up the flavors, new and old. All the frills. Our nigras love her for it. Me—they get nervous the minute I drop by, 'fraid the sales figure'll be downbeat. Though I never in this world would say. 'Maple sugar—,' I'll say. 'Maybe retire it for a spell? Go for the raspberry crumb; that's flying out the window. Anyway, come Christmas, count on that bonus ham.'"

I can even hear the applause as she bends a brow heavier than her sister's at *Onkel*. "Thank you kindly. But we dickering privatelike tomorrow. A party already interested."

It's as if she's stuck him with a needle. "How much they offer you?"

She shakes her head. Clara's doesn't move an inch. I admire their duet.

"Dicker—," he says, with what he must calculate is charm. "Could be a Cherman wort you get from us."

My father interrupts; he's been looking to. "Comes from playing dice, I b'lieve. What they call down home 'the bones.' Or from just plain 'bicker'?...Anyway, time to let these ladies go."

"Tell him, Min," Clara says. "Go on."

Min looks down at what my mother would call her décolleté, were we in evening clothes. There seems to be no daytime equivalent, but we all look with her. Min has pinned there one of Oakley & Co.'s last year's fancies—a tiny lace corsage, impregnated with one's choice of scents, and meant to be hooked in one's lingerie. And perhaps pursued? My father, who wouldn't admit to designing these objects, was taken aback that it hadn't "gone," but perhaps the erotic fun-and-games of his era can't ever persist in the next, and we in the 1930s, half settled in as "postwar," and about to be prewar, were to be forever severed from the belle epoque, hard as its descendants might try otherwise. Though from time to time remnants survive. "Oh, Joe—," my mother had said. "You're not going to give the Abrams sisters those?" But he had bestowed them sedately, still tucked in the two-inch boxes. Their reception had been properly coy. Clara, the better dresser, had hers pinned carefully to the left of her broad collar, after a brief drama of "Now just where?"

My mother had watched this with the superiority of the once courted, now the wife. Hostessing year after year the two said to have been long infatuated with her Joe. As for him—everyone in my grandmother's extended provincial family would know that he hadn't got the idea for these wee pin-ins just from reading French.

Only I am embarrassed, and grateful at least for my birth in the North. One of his favorite quotes is Robert Burn's "O wad some Power the giftie gie us to see ourfels as ithers see us"—and I have. To be born Southern is to be born coy. (Though with a dollop of sweetness, if one in the key of C sharp.)

But to have one's backgrounds meet—always tetchy. Though not intentionally kept separate, the occasions when my remaining relatives come together are few—and as at "benefits" where the ill-assorted tend to meet either newly or too often, both are mutually bored. But when there's stress on either side—watch out.

Rumor had it (from that famous "unidentifiable source" which with us could only be family) that *Onkel* Ludwig, shown Oakley & Co. shortly after arrival, since as my father muttered, "We have so little else to talk about," on returning to our household for dinner, had made known on the spot that he was in the market to assemble small businesses "for a *Kartell.*" And had suggested, while yet pretending only to speak German, to the translator—my mother—that he "buy in." A partnership. He having wormed it out of his son that one of my father's older brothers, my uncle Nat, had recently died.

My mother might have wished to be prejudicial, but like the few Germans left in our circle and addicted to it, she could not consciously fabricate, though the reasons for this were diverse. *Tante* had a naïveté oddly enriched by experience. In her, the daily round had a humility unappreciated by a decent but remote husband, a conventional daughter, and a son, Elmer, who had been a slightly bad egg. According to my mother, slippery fingers had been the trouble, but he had recovered, in a later occupation selling ad space for the *New York Times*.

All this sifted down to me, a grade-school child sitting cozily in the bay window of the Adlers' parlor-front brownstone flat, mulling what was extraordinary to an elevator-apartment-house child. The Adlers could and did run up and down a staircase to their friendly neighbors in the flat above, who seemed to be their exact replicas, with the odors of German cuisine flowing comfortably between. *Tante* had never evinced any concern at having once herself been immigrant—possibly even as a child? Their circle of friends, who were in turn ours: the Lederers, he a chiropodist, she *Tante* Sophie, a delightfully chattering Austrian, had seemed to feel the same. The Engelhardts, cousins to somebody—maybe even to us, of which I was never to be sure—suffered obliquely, from living not in Manhattan but in Queens, the women however compensating—or so it seemed to me—through their elaborately non-German names, their girl, my age, being Marcella and her mother, Maud...

All of this, seen now if not quite as that chronicler Jacob Riis had, was testimonial—that to be a "German-American," with roots in the 1880s or well before, was a highly respectable affair.

Into this setup, necessarily divulged, our half brother, half uncle, has come, a curious anomaly, both refugee (which none of us seemed ever to have been, I had never heard the word used)—as well as self-styled rich (or high bourgeois), whereas

we were merely the common variety—in the very important
American merchant style to be. Yet my parents, marrying peculiarly, pursuing self-education, had confused all métiers, making
us what he might never in his lifetime catch on to: United States
American.

And now I must interrupt. To mull that "background" which our
household, entrenched in its chosen country, took for granted.
Above our small dining table consider that new night sky. With
the excuse that the small local dramas are the very ones we must
interrupt.

We were a country designed not to have a class system, by
forefathers who at that very same moment deeded us their own.
The image of the good and legal life was spare. A figure with
arm extended, to show inscribed on its upraised palm "I have a
right to" will about do. Honor, truth—in any revolution these
are implicit. If the cry is secular, then add the pursuance of free
will. But a country that declares for "happiness" will ever addi-
tionally excite—and mystify. Even "beauty"—ideal of course,
but no longer fig-leafed—is not barred. While the cage offered
is so large that all citizens may freely range. What's aimed for is
the golden age, its classic restraints unleashed, gone somehow
polyglot. In a landscape forever open to the pioneer.

During Nazidom and afterward, as scholars and other wor-
thies fled to us, the U.S.A., land of opportunity, was judged to be
receiving as much as it gave. *Onkel*, deeming himself such a gift,
did not await welcome. He assumed it.

A photo of that Oakley office he would have met here
shows a row of men in tailored suits seated at their desks, in
high-back swivel chairs, JHC upfront, those behind him all share
the brown-tone serenity, gradually receding in size—a notable
example of how the early lens could show what would later be

called infrastructure, in lengthy articles in *Forbes*. No glass cubicles are yet in vogue. Products, never called such, each evoked by name, were approachable in "the showroom," a customer's entry there usually preceded by a spate of talk, brilliant as to what was in the new "line," but as devoid of pricing as if the conversation were taking place in a club. Indeed buyer and exhibitor had often a long season-to-season—if somewhat jerky—relationship. Rather like 18 East Seventeenth Street's hydraulic elevator cage, which though it might be thought of as carrying canary to cat, always delivered even me with an air of depositing somebody valuable. Lady buyers would have been lunched, hearty women my father might well charm. But even my cousin Grace, a sexual chatterer, admitted that "Uncle Joe" (his family moniker) never mixed business with pleasure—"even on the road"—as her father, my uncle Clarence, could attest. "But he was a stage-door Johnny, from beginning to end. Which ended with your mother. Never saw a faster fall."

In the showroom was where the firm's Edwardian tastes emerged more usefully, with a foppish, Europeanly masculine understanding of the female. A mustache with points after all inclined the wearers to pomade, cologne wafting from their heavy vests. As well as for what the newspaper called "evening attire," in ads as decorous as what they puffed. Oakley did not stoop to "a full line of cosmetics"; rather the items purveyed were prophetic of articles the museum shops would one day sell—little pieces of "art" or allusions to art's history that you could take home, in this case to the boudoir or dressing room. Pats of rouge in rose-satin boxes, roundels of soap in pleated tissue, the cologne in decanters by Lalique, of which J. Henri was proud. Even the firm's address, on Seventeenth Street, was an allusion, perhaps by old Austin himself, to its founding in 1817. A prototype of the old gentlemanly business style that in those days infused even the corporate, under my father, Oakley's would heave itself up to 339 Fifth Avenue: "opposite the Waldorf," pushing northward, along with the vanity trades, to what would be Midtown. Until—(that signature of all eras), under the pounding of the labor era: unions, strikes, union heads as prominent in the news as prizefighters, the "gentlemen" would bow to the go-getters; the merger millions would deride the small. These as to be consigned to the back shelf, as surely as my father's silky black collapsible opera hat.

Whatever was it our "import" saw?

A smoothly running office afternoon with my father just ushering out a couple of customers, and a below-desk cabinet open to a bottle of Chivas Regal and glasses. A secretary no longer young but curiously charming and competent, putting on her hat, and fluttering good-night to a place of work she must cherish. A scene all too well set for the outsider, his own situation tight in his throat?...A fat little operation, to be plucked.

Onkel must have assumed himself up to it. First offering my father condolences on the death of his brother—in German, but lowered voice and bowed head, and an escaped *"dein Bruder,"* surely conveyed he had observed a decent interval. Then, in "American" garble, touching a dog tooth with his tongue: *"Ganz gut für* both us guys, yes? I buy in his partnership."

Neither my mother nor I had been present, but overhearing my father's report to her, I'd had no need to be. One never saw him in any nonfamily rage; the indoctrinated courtesy of his region simply could not let go. But his voice could shake. "I told him no partnership existed. I took my brothers into the business, that's all, when they came Nawth. As all Richmon' at the time knew."...

Once, unaccustomedly alone with me in the backseat of a hired car (would it have been on the way to a family funeral?)—

he had pointed out the building, an imposing crenellated pile: "A set of apartments," in which the family had first lived; he did not say for how long. It rears there yet, in my remembrance, somewhere in lower Harlem, in color the then-familiar gray-green of what was refusing to crumble and looked it—"old New York." "Harlem?" I'd said—only the intonation needed. My parents, goaded by my mother, had long since left the fresh air that Washington Heights had offered a marriage, first for one of the curved, small buildings on 116th Street, near a frat house, then for the new red-and-white Paterno building at 114th Street and the Drive, where we had lived from when I was fifteen all through my college years, and he still did. As with everybody's youth, the snows had been vaster then. One winter, when the battlement of shoveled snow lining the pavement out front was not to be the highest yet, he'd said suddenly, "Lost my pet greyhound, in the blizzard of 1888." He would have been in his late twenties. His mother, in her sixties. And where was "Paw"?

It used to shock me in later years, that I had not asked him more—about the migration from Virginia. About who came when—or, like Julius, had maybe been left behind? The weight of elderdom in our family was like a drapery to be taken for granted. In which anyone could at times gratefully hide. Yet he was my earliest confidant—on a merry-go-round where I listened, he spoke. While reminiscence, a horse fixed in one place, rose and sank. Did he merely appear to have more of the past than the rest of us, bidding us to prod? I can understand better now. Now that the past is accumulating in me.

All this time *Onkel* has been shaking his head, left-right, at the benighted state of office affairs there. Or of ours. Antiquity gone rotten? The country is not old enough. He swells with the importance of the international trader, confronted with this poppycock bag of tricks. "*Ach,* Cho." *Onkel*'s gift, spurred by crossing oceans constantly in his head, is that whatever language he has a smidgen of, as long as he talks money people will understand him. So no further need to interpret the syllables. "*Ach,* Cho. You have to say that, *jawohl.* For tax reasons. So—I tell you what. This *komisch* liddle"—he pauses to find words for it—"upperation dot fits a voman's knitting bag—*und warum nichts?*—I buy you out. Altogezzer. *Und* we put the Oakley name—cholly goot, *zo englisch*—on my *Kartell.*"

I see my father take off his pince-nez, so as to view less clearly this thorn in the side that history has tossed him. He often does this whenever the present, that eternal foreground, does not quite please; the bridge of his nose, rubbed at these intervals, is always inflamed. Worse, there's one word he apparently cannot say: "No." The nearest he gets to it is, "Forgive me, if I seem to contradict." As he'll explain to my mother, when she complains about his handouts, from tipping largesse to charity, "Talking as a salesman all day—takes agreeing. But, Hattie, m'dear, it does bring the orders in."

To some he has been more slyly elaborate. Saved from his happily blighted schooling, he treasured a rhetoric manual, that day left providentially at home. I was present when he was being plagued by one of my senior aunt's "followers," she being flypaper to bores after dear Clarence departed. This one protesting to her brother as to why, though her boarder, he could not marry her: "I'm the prisoner of my psoriasis." The "Pater," as he suddenly seemed to me, had tipped me, his college daughter, a wink, a smile of satisfied literacy whelming him. "Pity. I suffer from exegesis myself."

Indeed he did. Every object, in house and office, merited explanation, as did nuances of behavior which for the rest of us were the norm...And in a nation groomed to be "individuals," in his view, perhaps we most definitely are.

Our *Onkel* wasn't one of the refugees who had historically fled to us for just that: freedoms, from worship to political. Instead, used to all privilege, he had merely lost that. In the stilted regime where he'd practiced, the business autocrat might in effect "buy" people, their blind fealty as well as their services. Now, in the new autocracy, there'd been a price on his own head. He couldn't want Oakley for either its prospects or fancywork. But individual it was, almost to eccentric—yet with a tradition of what this country had labored 150 years to attain. But just a figurehead, for this entrepreneur to be. His need to be that again had already blasted him out of the punctilio of manners which still occasionally clung. As for the scam by which he had profited, by bringing in his cronies in trade, surely it had been a pitiably small one for this boasting tycoon. Yet with the Nazi world echoing at the corners of our righteous one, and its worthier victims on our doorsteps every day, even such a man's compromises could seem sad.

"Not for sale—," my father said. "I told you that before." Which very ploy was on *Onkel's* part new. "Not ever. Put that in your pipe—and smoke it. And go buy your piece of my country somewhere else."

From *Onkel's* face—as reported later—that was the value he was after. "You would sell, yes? But not to me? Not to a Cherman. *Und* who has serfed in uniform his own *Volk?*"

The French say *"Pays"*—a defiant shriek. Once for *the Volk:* We have only what—turf? "Not for sale to any one," was it now a brownshirt monosyllable?

"The man's so double," my father later said. "Doesn't see his own inner works. I couldn't resist."

"Must've treated you pretty well in camp—our team, Ludwig. For you to want to join up. But—sorry. Not for any amount of money. There's no price you can pay, understand?"

…"Trouble was," my father said later, "I was beating him down on all scores. I didn't realize."

"Who's your banker?" my *Onkel* said.

"Trouble was, Hattie, I was so surprised, I told him. And worse, 'Why, Ludwig, you need a loan?' And that must have done it."

"Hah" was the reply. "*Du denkst. Aber* maybe you borrow big, hah. Maybe. On this—" The offending quiet; he had no word for it. He waved his paw, circling the office. "Hattie, I don't recall the word he said but I damn well caught the implication. This—pack of cards. This—what's the Hun for outhouse?"

My father had never in our lives used that word, for the German enemy. "Sorry, Hattie. But know what he threatened to do? Go to the bank and offer to buy in my loans...Crazy. But gives us some idea of how he thinks he can do. There's no call he can, a'course."

My father hung his head a bit, as debtors may. From "shelling out" (his phrase) to his brothers to keep their families afloat, more than he would ever have paid an ordinary employee, Oakley was often on high-interest credit issued solely on the bank's regard for him. For by then he had attained that isolated, even lofty credit rating awarded the frequent borrower who never failed to pay up, on the date the reckoning was due. Since his borrowing always came at fixed points in the calendar, his promptness there even added to his reputation, consistency as well as profit being what a bank likes. In his anecdotes about Oakley, he had pointed this out to me with a wink of mischief: "Not that it's a rhythm I recommend." (Indeed it was one I was never able to manage later. Excusing myself on the grounds that my mother's frugality had tamed me. To her such fiscal sorties were "lowlife"—and exclusive to men.)

Perhaps for this reason, my father's account of *Onkel* at the office had stopped short, with a shudder indicating that the man was impossible. Also dinner was due, as usual shaking all those who might be dropping fortuitously by—into their family positions for the evening. My father's time-sense was a forgiving one, an ally helping him to clean the slate, while *Onkel*-at-the-office, as the incident would become in his annals, had taken place "last week."

My mother has had to glean the rest from Miss Eadie, the office assistant and Mr. Joe's "right hand," who had witnessed the altercation while about to leave and putting on her hat, a protracted daily occurrence that earned her some office ridicule. Her response being, "Most important things in an office happen at the end of the day—and we always run late." She tactfully not adding that this is because "we" begin when half the morning—so vital to hardball trade—is over. All the staff know that though Mr. Joe prowls his house at dawn after no doubt mulling Oakley's welfare, as morning proceeds, until after ten he is slow to get out of its door. Yet they must await him, lest anxiety suddenly bring him in on the dot of nine. "Oh, we don't begrudge him," Eadie assures my mother. "It makes the place more convivial."

An odd assurance perhaps to give the boss's wife, but proffered as from the sole woman there. When the wife not too often drops in after shopping, Eadie considers herself to have a responsibility. To interpret the place, along with a cup of tea.

"Part of Oakley's style, eh, Mrs. Joe? Which the customers come to appreciate. Leisurely, for those who buy leisure goods at a leisurely pace?" Slogans were just then the advertising pitch. You'd "walk a mile for a Camel," or "Reach for a Lucky Strike." While a policy of leisure was one with which all those in that office would agree, as after all, compounded between Mr. Joe and themselves. And a mild sort they were, the pickings of a boss who, true to my mother's lamentations, was a notably soft touch.

In the line of desks behind his, one was never sure of the succession, since except in that photo, those were not always occupied. First, probably Clarence Winstock, who, tall and majestic as he was, had fitted his pace to my six-year-old trot without ado, between alternate jokes and silences most comfortable. Though from "old" Richmond, a stranger would never hear that from him. Likely he had come North with the others, as my senior aunt's husband, though one never heard from him an ounce of the personal, say, as to what profession or job he had had before. He did have rather an air of resignation at finding himself where he was—mate to a dominant female, father to a silly one. Though the young are often quick to feel bitterness exuding from a person, I never felt it from him. During his final bedridden spell from a stomach cancer, I would visit him unprompted, from my college nearby, never to find him what the other elders whisper: "long-suffering."

All his life he had been my father's office deputy. One sensed martial values in him—the same heroics that flags were still clapped for. Values that would never be drawled aloud by him. As a brother-in-law bird, who like the real brothers had been awarded a nest, he never feathered it, emotionally or otherwise. I thought of him as the paragon of Southerners. Whose emblem was perhaps: "Though."

Miss Eadie, when hired, had already been a veteran of other select places, each of which she had confirmedly left on her own. On being hired she had asserted that Oakley's would be her last. Devout service to the end was implied. Date of leaving would be left to: "Well, temperament."

More likely, an office anywhere being the best of sniffers, that date would depend on circumstances of a very particular sort. An attractive woman "of a certain age," her own phrase, she would add, as she must have many times over, "Not that I haven't had my certainties."

In the meantime, one of those New York happenstances had occurred. My mother, squiring me to an opera-benefit rehearsal where I was to dance a solo "on toe" (a ten-year-old arabesqueing to the tune of "It's three o'clock in the mo-orning, we've danced the whole night through"), after identifying herself by name to a woman next to her, in the array of those gold chairs such mothers used to perch on, had been answered, "Calisher? I get perfume with that name on it. I never use anything else, get it for Easter and Christmas, regular, from a dear friend. I used to sing in the Dessoff Choir with—know it? Haven for voices not good enough for concert, but who have to sing, mostly just *oratorio*. I was just a routine alto, but Eadie Eardley? Soprano like a lark, but not fitted to go beyond. No real training—on maybe anything. But could do solo. And kind of religious, from all that sacred music maybe." The woman talking to my mother hadn't been one of the mothers but the social secretary for the Goulds, in whose Fifth Avenue house the rehearsal was. "Skinny little thing," she said. "But the last night we sang together, I'll never forget. She wore amber velvet. The voice sure was. 'She'll end up a mezzo,' our conductor said. Anyhow, she and I had used to go lunch from our jobs. She was always changing them, but that was the last time I saw her, though we all know what happened to her...What?...Picked off, to be his mistress, by one of those so-called patrons. Of music, opera, museums—you name it."

"Stage-door Johnnies, most of them, if you ask me," the woman had said. "I used to work for some of them...Rumor had it that she wouldn't take money from him. Still worked, so as to keep it an affair of love. Their only social life being the benefits he bought tables for, where they could appear to meet by accident." It was at one of those that the social secretary had met up with her again. "'Do you still sing?' I asked her, and she said, 'Only privately. For someone who doesn't mind that my voice has gone—that conductor was right.' I said, 'I can guess the person you sing for,' and she smiled. And it was after that the perfume started, came on the button, twice a year. 'Anonymous.' But she'd know I'd guess who. That perfume was her and my favorite, Triple Essence of Rose, it was called. Crown-stoppered, in a little squared-off glass bottle, with tiny flecks of gold dust scattered in the glass, that made it magical. They haven't had it in the stores for years; she must have a source," the woman said. "She knows it is my favorite. And the label and the band around the stopper, yellow and printed with kind of a clumsy of roses, has 'By Calisher' on it."

Waiting low level between the two women, I have been rehearsing my dance to come in my head: *Battement*, deep *plié*, *attitude*. I was not good enough for *pirouette*. Scared at what I've let myself in for, one of the tangles that being my age involves, I opt out of the exchange going on above me, unaware that I have recorded it. A quarter of a century will be spent at this kind of idle imprinting, before I realize what my own "voice" is. A recording one.

At home that night, I overhear my parents, the sensation more like being underwater to the dialogue. It is four years after the birth of my brother and the mental depression which after that sent my mother briefly to a sanitarium, but the irony in her voice, that heavy layer which I mistake for Teutonic, is still strong.

"Yes, of course, Joe. Can you blame me? A woman who sang as a girl. Our piano bench, still full of your old opera librettos. A stage-door Johnny—once. But above all, the bottle, from that dusty hoard you won't sell but have in the office in plain sight. Bottles you put your own name on instead of Oakley's. Why wouldn't I think that you might be the man who once picked her off? You feeling bound to keep her on, in her nutty way."

"Her antiseptic way, rather, Hattie. That's in part why I hired her. She's such a good front—even for herself. All those party guys our trade attracts, in from Podunk. Or hotshots from Dallas, and staying at the best hotels. You don't often get a secretary with dignity. Because that's what she has, really. Which we all ignore. And I'd a hunch she'd stay. Not getting any younger. And the job history was as tatty"—and here he must have spread his hands—"as all get-out."

"Antiseptic" was a slogan much in use then, by proper parents. Though entailing little more than Mercurochrome dabbed at once on my bruised kneecaps, while boiled carrots faced me at lunch. Yet thanks to the household's germy interests in real food and the city streets' contagion, I mostly escaped, into the norm.

"*You* somehow attract, you mean." I can hear my mother's smile. For that bond between them, which I will never be able to name. Neither sex, nor glamour, nor money alone. Family? Not its "values," in the cheapie slogan of my era. Marriage maybe. Not theirs alone. A marriage of a couple—with their era. That's more likely. My parents were a couple who married their era.

"You somehow attract, you mean," she says.

He must be shrugging. Taking that as given. Which he always will.

"Ever find out who the man was? Gee—maybe still is." My mother never said "gee"; forbidding it for me. All the inner vocabularies are coming out. Overhearing—I begin to sense what a privilege it would be to have such. In the era that will be mine? Mother is melting—kind of.

"Inevitable. That stuff gets around. And with her in our showcase."

"I know. I well know."

"Ah, Hattie."

She's thinking of the modeling she once did. Referring to it. Once she shrewdly estimated its effects. Now, in middle age, she is proud.

"A name to whisper," he says.

After a minute she says, "You don't say."

"A name to conjure with, yes. No wonder she had to sing for him privately. Or maybe they knew it would get out, either way. So did as they pleased."

"He couldn't have left her anything in his will, Joe, could he. Too exposed. Or she wouldn't have accepted it? So she has to come in to work Oakley's, every livelong day."

"We're first-class employers, Hattie. More than the competition requires, our benefits. And if the salaries can't compete, at the top that is—Aaron and Nat never faulted us even if their wives do—in the factory we do as well as anybody. As well as Chanel. And that up-from-nothing Bernie Sallick, who's always imitating us."

He's fallen in again, into the trough always awaiting him. His status as "manufacturer," as early American citizen, even one bound by the ancient family atmosphere which might deaden, and never had as much money safety as would seem—all that could at times still seduce her. But it was his benignity she couldn't neglect to fault. "That bottle," she says. "When in hoot did you put your name on it? Instead of Oakley's. I never asked."

"When Aaron and Nat came in. They wanted it. Old Austin was dead by then. Retired, he'd still kept tabs. I'd damn near saved his company for him. Suppose I wanted—a little boast. But the customers kept hinting the name Oakley had more dash."

A little boast. I crave it for him still.

"Eardley-Oakley. I suppose she likes that too."

"You jealous? Come on. And you two—I thought, she and you had such an affinity. On hats."

They laugh.

"He did leave her something," my father says. "Or maybe directed it to be? You'll never guess how."

"How?" In these gossips she is always the shill. Complicit.

"The wife did. In her own will. One of those 'faithful employee' clauses. 'For services rendered.' That gobbledygook."

"And she accepted?"

"May have. She runs a small benefit every year, she told me. Something musical."

"Maybe I should tell her, Joe. That I met her friend. That would be the day."

"Don't you dare. In business that kind of intimacy is out of order." An axiom he is always abusing.

I think of the one chair in the line of desks always now faithfully occupied by Harry Lehman, brother-in-law of Nat's wife, Belle. Hired as bookkeeper, and just barely experienced enough to steal from him. Who, reinstated, on his or maybe Belle's plea, went around hangdog until the boss—a word no one at Oakley's had ever used—not my father, certainly not his brothers, said, "Buck up, Harry. For God's sake, show some backbone."

"Ah, your stories," she is saying now. "Will they never cease?"

That's unfair. Storytellers give off a kind of ozone just short of funky, but enough for demand. Or like man-eating flowers people can fall into, there to be thrilled by that ambivalent boredom which revives them to a second life.

"Fresh roses," my father says, half to himself, his voice deepening. "It started before my time. As Triple Essence of California Rose."

I would get too interested in Miss Eardley, both then and now. We as a family were always paying too much attention to those

who were supernumeraries to our stories—or should have
been? While she, whose fate had been to evoke one man's interest supremely, was now content to be in a minor role: "as a person of interest," merely? I think so. And I suggest that she
changed jobs for that purpose. Looking back can tell you a lot.
(And one needn't promise not to improve on it.)

At Oakley's offices, where *Onkel* and the head of the firm
were engaged as so far reported, she was of course on hand,
moving with that ever alertness the good assistant manages
to convey. But that week, as she would tell me, had been
"fraught"—being the last before the move to "Three Thirty-
nine." My father had asked her well before if she would go
along: "That woman has as many stipulations as a musical
score; like that voice-exercising singers do; there's a name for it,"
he said. I knew the term: *Solfège*, but didn't want to come up
with it too promptly, to a man who pretended to more French
than he had…It warms me now, that I never let my education
lord it over his.

She'd agreed to stay, with the crankiness that complete
devotion allowed. "Be a nuisance, getting used to not saying
'Eighteen East.'" Always said with the same air of fashionable
aplomb as when she put on one of her just-on-the-edge-of-
extraordinary hats.

He savored these exchanges, the way a long marriage can
enjoy its spats. Those at home being more serious, as based on
what my father thought generosity, and my mother—though so
much younger—witched into extravagance. Besides, Miss Eadie
was always quotable. "You could just say 'Oakley' in the new
place,'" he'd said. "Oh no," she countered, "only the owner can
afford to repeat it as often as you do, Mr. Joe."

When she was hired, he'd been careful to check how she'd
prefer to be addressed. "We run to first names here. Would you

prefer your last?" She'd recoiled. "No, one place, the manager called me that, without the Miss, all day long. 'Eardley, Eardley, Eardley.' Sounded like he was gargling." Why not use the Miss, Mr. C, but with her first name, Eadie?...Which, spelled the way it was, would do fine. "'They're both Staten Island patronymics,' she said...Was it any wonder I hired her on the spot?"

"Beats me," I told him, when I came of age. "How you always get employees to match the old joint." I'd waved at the cabinets in his office, rows of bottles behind the glass, mostly clear ones of dainty shape rather than the new weird French ones—of onyx with fan-shaped stoppers and sueded boxes in fawn—that the 1920s had spawned. These eliciting the adage handed me quizzically: "Always remember—that the package may well cost more than the perfume. Nobody now uses—or can find—the precious old essences. In people as well."

He gives me the quizzical look that often passes like a key between us. "Well, I purt near match the old joint myself." He would have been pushing eighty at the time, depending on whether his birth date had been '61 or '63. "Our goods, these lean times. Need all the atmosphere they can get. People like your uncle Clarence, say, when I'm on the road." About Clarence's worth, not clear to some, he would always be staunch. But in business, loyalty can be a monkey on the back. As he was not bred to see. I wasn't worried that he might want a daughter to match his own era. Apart from him, from both, I was my own; sullen, with sass. A Martha Graham acolyte, dizzy with dance.

But he'd placed certain books in my hands, like stolen melons, and had inserted the old battered slang words in my ear. A practitioner, counseling a bit of skulduggery. And though I keep digging myself out of that *down derry down,* the onomatopoeic murmur of the nineteenth century must be in my genes.

Oakley's? Only a long-gone decibel, which can sometimes amuse. But the torsion of the years stretches a person. Toward that aptitude the elders thought never to see. Wish he could still read. To bend over this page. The way I can still hear his "Miss Eadie, she did give me some moniker." He tosses this at me like the deadbeat riddles we used to: What's black-and-white and red all over?

All those monikers we kept awarding him: Mr. Joe, Daddy Joe, your father, brother, Uncle and Cousin Joe; what more can there be?

A tucked-in smirk of mischief. The handlebar mustache was almost thirty years gone, exchanged for sedate pepper-and-salt with just a fractious hint of twirl. The torsion of living with us has shrunken, then stretched him. But the brown eyes above, crinkly with earthy wit, will one day belong to my son, then not yet born.

"Mr. C—," I cry.

That ghost—have I punctured him!

With a poke into my childhood, no—he revives. "I collect them. Monikers. Like cigar bands."

So, on to Miss Eadie Eardley. The day is fraught.

I'd come back to "Eighteen East" to say good-bye to this other half of my father's life and, to a degree, of mine, where since the age of six or so I had been petted and cajoled, and the teasings, repeated, were like windup toys. Formality ruled, with everybody in the office sharing a piece of that. Courtesy prevailed, and a kind of *masquery*, in all the shades of bargaining that business entailed. My father acted as if this enclave wrested from oblivion would last forever, and the small staff of outsiders (even the errand boy was in his eighties) took the cue, in an exercise of permanence with which even our family could not compete.

Many of the small businesses of the time had similar egos. Since my father often consorted with the heads of firms who paraded the same vanity, this sector of the business world seemed quite normal to me—and perhaps then it was.

Miss Eadie, who had been there for only fifteen or so years, was alone in the office, as usual on Friday afternoons. I knew its habits. Once grown and in college, dropping in here had little disturbed those and had helped make me feel a citizen of "downtown." While if my father was there, we'd go home in a cab.

Miss Eadie always greeted me as a conspirator: "Hah—our newest employee"...Even perhaps seeing me as a successor here, though my brother, still much too young, would be first in mind...But "the office" already loomed for me as where such habits—all to do with employment—groped for you, and held you in an everyday vise. Saddest was that she took this negligent greeting for flattery.

While there often would follow some minor confidence that made me squirm—a bid for intimacy, with the powers that might be?

"Thank God you came. I'm in shock."

"My—"

"No, Mr. C's okay. Left for your house about an hour ago. With—that person he was showing the office to." Her mien softens: she believes many think Oakley a showplace, worth their time. Though I am only now beginning to see this quiet corner, which fed us and did send me to college, as an artifact. "He's a relative?"

"Oh. Him. My mother's half brother. They hadn't seen each other since she was sixteen. He—" It's a trial to hold back what to me is the most salient about him. Not that he was a "leading industrialist," like the papers say. Or thinks he was. But that he fought against us, in a war that for once, according to even the more pacifist of my teachers, had been about what its champions said it was about. Or nearly. The war to save the world for— And here we were again. "He's over here as a—you know."

"'Deed I do. I did all your father's busywork on that…He's a saint, your dad. A saint. But thank God, with a temper has a short fuse. You'd been here to see him under assault, daughter-girl, you'd been proud."

"Assault!" I revert to those gangsters who, Prohibition or no, coveted the permit for alcohol. The building would have been near empty, this afternoon—only the switchboard operator still in her cubbyhole. "Somebody try to get in?"

She draws herself up. A woman of the one circumstance. The face blunted, maybe from what had been charm, the head high, "You may well say."

She is almost incoherent. "War brings out the worst in us. I know all about that; I'm Presbyterian."

Does she mean the worst in them? Or that she's immune?

"Well, your uncle. Imagine. He stands there, watch chain draped on that belly, however he came by it."

The belly? Or the chain? My father also wears a chain but is trim.

"He wanted to buy the place," she says, exhausted. "This place. Oakley's, I mean. The palaver he put on—I can't tell you. Maybe Mr. C will. Your father, I mean."

The trouble with offices—she helped me to see that clear. You're a member of a pack, even to the tongue-twists. The dignity you assume—no matter how high you are in authority, belongs to the office itself. Is never separate. You do not practice alone.

"He wanted to buy in, that greasy—well, no, he wasn't. Just nothing to fight another war about, if that's what they say we are going to. Your father says, 'Not for sale.'" She laughs, sort of. "Bankrupt he might go, I keep telling him; he's the only one of your lot who works, I might as well say... So then that man makes a dirty—well, a threat... Could never come to pass; I've been in enough businesses to know."

She's tiring, she begins to cry, but without grimace. "So, then, that—villain, that bloodsucker, that grabber—" A string of like accusations, high and romantical. No oaths. I'd half forgotten, or never much registered that her history was said to have centered on someone. But I swear it does seem to me that she is vilifying somebody else.

"He said—," she chokes. "He said—swelling out those smooth cheeks he has—not a vein in them, but you can see the good living. '*Ach,* Joe. I can buy you and sell you.'"

She blots her face. "And your father, dear Mr. C," she chokes again. "He says, 'Try.'"

"Took it upon myself to show that pig out," she tells me a few answered phone calls later. After all, she does have a job she's paid for. "More than one person around here has to save your father's dignity. Since he won't bother to himself—" She stops short, smiling to herself. "And was I glad, *la la,* that we are still at Eighteen East. Because... Know what I did?" She settles into herself. A physical maneuver older women manage even when not overfleshed. Satisfaction of some sort did it. Though I hoped to find other ways of demonstrating that.

"I put that man in our old hydraulic elevator cage. There's a safety button you press, to lock the door. So, bowing and scraping—I do that. There's a bench inside you can sit on. 'Case the elevator jams between floors. And a button to press, 'case you can't open the door... We had to have the super install it; sometimes it works, sometimes it doesn't." Parting her lips, she emits an *ulla-ulla-la-la-la,* with a slight whoop in the middle; that's *Solfège* all right, and since we're both sitting by now, reaches forward to pat my knee. "So there he is, that pisser. Hung in his cage."

And at that hour of the day, the telephone operator was sure gone.

"Knew it wouldn't last," she says, leaning back. "Retribution never does. As I know from another connection. But sure feels good while it's on. Fridays, though, Mr. C goes home early, leaves me to shut up shop." She makes a face at me. "And you've gone and missed his cab."

Onkel did not. As my father later would report.

"Came out my office to go home, Hattie, there he was, hung in the shaft like a sitting duck...Heh. Heh-heh. Opened the door. Sat myself on the bench. Pushed that button. And we rode down...Outside, Abner was there as usual."

Abner was a black cabdriver whose conversation he had once enjoyed so much that he had helped him to establish a car service. Abner is as special as all Mr. C's servitors turn out to be. "Late again," he'll say, nightly appearing. "My wife will have my head." Mr. C's nightly response is, "So'll mine." And is driven home. But Abner has one rule, for a service on which he insists, but for which he will not charge: No guests.

But this one time a request was made. "Hattie is expecting him." The wives had met, exchanging latenesses. So Abner has granted the request—obliquely. "'Nother one of your charity cases, Mr. Joe?...Okay, fella. Get in."

In reflection...

...There was a kind of playacting between master and servitor that attached to any of us from the South—an almost jokey intimacy, enabling white to accept that his most private details, from his underwear to his silver, were being handled by an untouchable. The servitor, playing adroitness, and a serenity to match a bishop's, could retain his dignity. And both could wink at the real.

An overbearing heel-clicker like *Onkel,* steeped in authority versus subservience, would merely think less of the man to whom he owed his arrival, and of us, his entourage—who existed only to be patronized.

At least the cab had got him back to us. Obviously a daily service, though a humble one, did it perhaps remind *Onkel* of his former chauffeured limousine? Spurring him on to a further excess the Berlin salon might have restrained? One can't ever be sure of what one witnesses—as those faked incidents staged in psychology class tend to prove. But my double household will be teaching me. What later my life will confirm. As a child, hobnobbing with the help, I saw without question that the playacting I witnessed was being initiated by the blacks and cleverly adopted by the whites. Gullible as my elders, though not yet as wishful, I took the acting to be natural...

...To be a refugee? To be an "import," more recent than the rest of us? And awash in our political pity?

Tonight, which will be the last *Onkel* is ever to dine with us, or be seen by us, I am seeing how hard both roles are. Taught so by the home country, however embraced. Each of us, bestrode like any player, by his or her own temperament.

Back now, in apartment 5A, my father was smarting still from what went on at the office? Or writing it off, with that indulgence which makes sense to the head of such an extended family, and must steal over him at night? Conversation is his loophole, and tonight maybe is being his mild vengeance; he has just coached *Onkel* on what is "dickering." He will never keep an enemy as faithfully as I do, or be as faithful to that avowed enemy as I will be, writing this.

Back there, I regard the sisters. A family is willy-nilly judged by its hangers-on. Those it attracts, accepts, rejects. In whatever order.

In how they do or do not commingle, we judge ourselves.

"Tell him, Min. Go on."

Yes, it was Clara said that, and what happened then will be forever in recall. The small brutishness sometimes survives best.

"Go on, Min, go on. Tell him."

"One twenty-five." It's unlike Min to whisper. She and her sister swap happy glances.

"Vun—? Vun twenty-five." *Onkel* mutely asks us all to assure him. "Hattie?" I hear him ask the word *"Spassmacher?"* That's a word I know.

"No," my mother says. "She's not joking."

But *Onkel* has found his English. "You kid," he says. *"Das ist alle?* From such a company, that is all?"

I am used to my father's business reportage. In from a trip, my mother, qualified or not, will be his late-at-night—or even at dinnertime—first recipient of how he's done, at say, Hochschild's, Neiman Marcus—the great department stores, whose names I imbibe along with the hotels he stays at, yet. And as with what "gross" meant, I know what's meant when he says a store will be "good for" an "order"—totaling "One five." The "one" means, in Oakley's common sales parlance, a hundred thousand (dollars). One five would be $105,000—and so on. The same for the value of such stocks and bonds that might be accumulated but rarely retained. "Ten," meaning ten thousand, being more likely life insurance? Well, maybe.

So the sisters reply—I take it as *Onkel* must have. One hundred and twenty-five thousand.

In a mix of both German and English, he conveys how paltry a bid this is—how unfortunately suited to our pinched ways, and to this establishment. Though with a bow to the sisters—and to their fine product. Then to my father, with a head shake. "*Wirklich*, Joe?"

There are some words everybody in our house knows. "Yes, really," my father says. "Saw the bid myself. Well, seems more than appropriate. Not a franchise after all. But that brand upholds a long way in the South. A known brand. And one of us."

Onkel draws himself up, fingering his jacket's center buttonhole. One can almost see the shift, to boardroom, or law office posture, wherever his business would have taken place. He leans forward, to a spot unseen, equidistant between the Abramses and him. Such spots demand a soft voice. "How about...*Eins fünfundvierzig*. One forty-five?"

As half affrighted, they ward him off, his bidding increases, topping itself, refusing to take their squirming refusals as unequivocal. Or my mother's hiss, "Stop. This is a dining room."

By what sum he reached, and by what increments, my father will confirm later. It was at this point that his son, my cousin, unhitches himself from his father's arm, under which he has been staring forward like a tin soldier. He sits up straighter. "*Vater. Wir hatten es nicht.* The money. We don't have it." Said in English. With a slight smile, one would swear.

In a torrent of back-and-forth, we are made to understand. My cousin had indeed been trusted with a sum, more than sufficient. He no longer has it.

"*Bummler—,*" his father shouts. "Loafer. How much did you spend? On your women." Unanswered, he rears back. Cajoling, he says softer, "Or did you invest?"

"*Nein.* I sent it away."

"Away. *Mein Gott.* To Switzerland. Fool. We'll never get it back. Idiot...How much is left?"

"*Gar nichts,*" my cousin says. Nothing. But why is he so cocky?

"*Gar—*" *Onkel's* jaw drops low enough for a vis-à-vis to see his gold inlays. He covers his jaw with a hand, maybe to protect what he still has? Through the fingers a whisper, "*Nichts?*" And again, "*Vier hundert Tausend...Gar nichts?*"

If my cousin had just shut up. *Der Vater kommt.* That is the old expression for fathers, important fathers. Or was. Meaning: *Watch out.*

But my cousin speaks. After all, he's been living with us.

"We can get along on *was Ich mache.* On what I make," he says, in the pidgin German-English he is getting good at. "*Und du, Vater.* Like an *Ochs* you are. Like *Grossvater.* You could work *auch. Am* fecktory."

Too late quavering, "*Besser Mann lernt* English so." Better one learns English so.

"*Schweinhund.*" Pig-dog. The father's palm raised, swipes my cousin across the face, One— Two. And again. From the right, slap, and reverse the hand palm upward. Slap from the left.

Blood spurts from the nose. A red snot familiar to most from school fights and their own falls—and easy to stanch. The forehead's gash above seeps, broad and slow. ("That one, on his forehead, will last," my father says later: "From a signet ring.") My mother, snatching a couple of napkins from the table, rushes forward to slip my cousin a napkin for the nose, meanwhile stanching his forehead with the other. "Only the skin—," she says. "Where the skin is gone it bleeds worse," and we take for truth her housewifery.

Whether there'll be a scar on that forehead, we're never to know. But that wound, if later evoked by an idle word or a stray flash of light, will hang forever in our atmosphere. A red weal, emigrant from a war then not yet arrived, always to be arriving, its railway cars clack-clacking with their burden of proof.

My father moves toward *Onkel*. "You better go. Somewhere else. The friends you brought here, maybe will help." Does he know that *Onkel* has profited? If so, we shall never hear.

"You are welcome," he says to the half-bent head my mother is still holding the napkin against. "You are welcome to come back here. It's hard for a son. As I know."

My cousin, taking the napkin from her hand and pressing it to his forehead, says "*Danke*. But it dries okay. I go with him." He clenches and unclenches his own hand toward his father, whose back is to us, bowed. "*Der Vater*. He has nowhere else."

My mother moves toward the Abrams sisters, from whom not a clack has come, all during. They come from war country, I tell myself. Old maidens, married to history. But why is my mother, so undeclarative, pressing each to stand nearer her, holding each by a finger on a wrist.

"Tell us—," she says to my cousin. "Tell him there. Tell us all. Where you sent the money." From her tone it is plain he has told her.

We've never called him by name. Only "cousin." That comes now to me.

The father has turned to stare, lip snarled, nostrils wide. What he imagines, or does not foresee, is not up to us to wonder, or so we thought. When my cousin does speak—that we have not thought to wonder where the money went, will be the shock.

In the ski hut, with the wooden bowls incised in the table and the liners to protect them, my cousin's face would have been sophisticate, with his ice-world behind it. Or even striding down the gangplank the day he came, luggage of pigskin, girl on his arm.

His face is simpler now. Worn, but rounded also, in the innocence of those who live in the daily expectation, the terrible hope, of having to re-earn a name.

I know how that was. In marriage I had done that. Living in a new country, under whatever name, must be like changing one's own soul as well? Or turning the old one in—as part-pay?

As we wait, I see that dining rooms distribute people badly, unless they are seated already, or standing beside their chairs. Seating is rarely designated with us. Each night the family dinner appears, as if, in the interim, the table had never been wholly cleared. Such casual rhythm is sustaining. A blockade against harsher event. No wonder the relatives and other hangers-on, they all keep coming, exclusive of other reasons. And I.

Tonight however we squirm uneasily at random, as if stage-managed. By an inadequate director. We are a scene moving inexorably into the remembered past.

My mother has annexed herself to the sisters. My father stands alone. So do I. The air smells of that patchouli which may be blood, or theater dust. Each of us stands in the patch of half-illumined dark that will be his or her history. What audience there will be is as yet invisible.

My cousin is tying the two bloodied napkins together. Big linen ones, folded dexterously they form a band he applies to his seeping forehead, and knots at the back of his head. So bound, he stands up, soldiering himself with a shake. That bow-mouth, the pedestal of his good looks, is turned in. As he nears the father face, will he spit? A knife should be rising through our tidy floor, warning us, or the walls be pressing in. But all holds.

My cousin stares into that face, a son worthy to it, and to the grandfather who knocked down an insulting man. The right arm with its new biceps lifts, bringing the factory with it. It slaps. Once.

Don't broken noses always bleed? Or only hemorrhage from within? A hand with a signet ring touches it. The face it belongs to has come to a standstill. Who speaks?

It is the son. Gerhard does, cousining us all. Shaming us.

"I sent it to *Mutti*."

In rooms like those, like ours now, electrically lit ever since the Pearl Street power plant of 1881–82, rooms pretending that their like covers the earth, the light beam sometimes shivers, begging to be real.

Early morning, just before waking, I had one of those pursuit dreams that, I suspect, replace for me anxiety dreams of youth. This time I am visiting some mildly organized locus resembling college. (In real life it is indeed graduation time—to which as an alumna I am often invited, but must always refuse.) I have passed in dream through a dorm nighttime accommodation, then classrooms—now empty. Most of my 1932 class is indeed gone? Now I am dream-seeking the small handbag, a fat and cheerful black leather pouch, bought years ago in Italy, which is my favorite. In the lost articles office I draw its outline for the person in command. No one has seen it...I wake.

How grateful I am. The bag and all it must contain remains on the high closet shelf I stretched to place it on, in our city bedroom. Though I never keep a diary, here I am, indicting this entry. Up in the country. In a small house that for brevity we call "the farm," which it long ago was. Water has been dowsed for, and now flows again. The small farmhouse, circa 1840, has four "eyebrow" windows, spaced 1...2...3...4, just under a slate roof that has lasted. House and land are owned by my son, but since he lives now on the other coast, we tenant it. Perhaps I am writing this account for him, so that he and his may know what I often think of as the *tenebrae*—Latin for "shadows"—of parentage.

For we are all half-and-half persons, are we not? Somewhat as we of the city are half-tenants here. As humans, not amoebae, we each of us have two distinct lines of ancestry, running back into the Eolithic distance—when our instruments were flint.

I do what I can with mine. Households, those bubbles atop the human condition, disappear regularly. Ours will do so like most, according to its rhythm, minor but unique. But with one note finally taken. A small revelation, at last written down.

Herewith a record of what might have happened, in part must have happened, in the State of Virginia, circa 1852—and on? To a Declaration: 18—?

As written by the undersigned, using the eyebrow windows of a descendant's recall: ...

And what did this teach me?

Not much—literally, that is.

In college, I took no notes. I myself could not understand those who did, or why; it wasn't intransigence. But I seemed not to want anyone else's exactly phrased thoughts to enter that brooding orifice called "the mind." Mine. I would welcome this later on, perhaps. But wanted not to be beholden to other's ideas while my own portion of those might be forming. This was not rebellion. Rather, that I belonged to a crowd, like me, as yet unidentified.

Though I was left with no record of lectures, this was not to trouble my progress. I seemed to recall their import, by some process, akin to digestion maybe, that went on while I was unaware. Taking place in the soma—the biological word for undifferentiated flesh of the body—but in that extrasensory organ called "mind." For if I'd been told—in zoology, perhaps—that "mind" was flesh, I'd have replied, "So that's it—the way the world comes to me. Of course."

So there it was.

I could not be taught. Or not rigorously.

But I could learn.

Oh—how intently I could do that.

Soaking in the very architecture of dream that was the world surrounding me.

There's a name for what I am, in most languages.

Offhand, as for a species of clerk, with a bit of sneer. Or lately, dipped in foolish glory, envy-attached.

My preference for what I am is simpler—and from my own dictionary:

Scribe.

Verb: "To mark or score with a pointed instrument the outline of a piece to be shaped."

Or as a noun: The person who sits in the marketplace, horn-tipped quill in hand, tablet on knee, ready to interpret to all and sundry, whatever the hierarchy, royal or scholarly, does not have time to listen to. Or to record.

The account of my Southern half seems to me indulgently long; I had caught their rhythm again, and the divagating style into which I was born. Also their self-approval, which when contemplated, offends. Yet it is a folklore style really, in which divagation, the power of the added subjective clause, if never quite innocent, has its place. Though I was chartered early to the South, the North would save me from its prejudices, enough to understand my father's paternalism toward the blacks, in a story ("Mayry") whose opening sentence read: "My father was a Southerner, but a very kind man." At that time, public reparation must have seemed enough. But it was merely a particular one. As the discovery of a small item from my steel-engraving grandfather's papers would one day prove.

Meanwhile, those slaps exchanged in that oasis of the daily called our "living room" had caused a shift in me, somewhere in the soma of the writing flesh. I saw a family existing like all in the world, on our "war-torn planet," yet we had almost entirely escaped such violence for an extraordinary length of time. In our case comprising at least three generations, including my own. Violence in person, that is: via war service, civilian bombing, or others subtler; starvation, imprisonment. Et cetera. Richmond under siege was the nearest we had come. My grandfather had been too old to fight in the Civil War, his children too young. Almost repetitively it would seem, my father had been too old to fight in World War I. In World War II—that neatly grammatical phrasing of horror—my then-husband, five years older than me, married, and so relatively ineligible for the draft, but an engineer, did serve in Army Ordnance, submitting us to the mild hitchings that "Army" imposed: sudden changes of residence, or his absence while he served on board ship. While at last, in World War II, we would have a conscriptee—my brother. Who "objected" to service, apparently did serve, as medico, I believe, though I've never checked, but surely never went "across."

As for me—one could even get out of jury service in those days by stating simply: "I am a woman." That I was never to do. Meanwhile, any "contribution" to the "war effort" could be in rolling bandages, knitting what in an older war had been called "balaclava helmets," dealing with food as rations—all volunteer.

I began brooding on such family exceptions. Many surely not owed merely to the peculiar age stratum in which we had traveled, but perhaps as caused by other similarly "petty" circumstances. Money differences would "contribute"—that ever-useful term: Business executives, say, who couldn't be spared; college-trained professions that, like my college students, shouldn't be interrupted. So, except for a few needed-at-home hard-hats, the poorer seem, certainly, the first ones to serve. I say "seem" since I know of no study in which all this "circumstance" has been calculated. (Or could have been? The sociologists, who brood by methods they believe to be nonfictional, will have considered such disparities. Or, as in the first primitive stages of their methodology, made a graph?)

But our greatest protector, and alike for all, has been our country. Power, yes. But wasn't there a fuller reason, a truer story, this time quite literally bottom line? What other great power had had such few foreign border irritations? Not even Asia, certainly not Europe. To the North, serene as a pendulum, we had: Canada. (One little aside—that fuss about the Pribilofs, scarcely remembered, seldom correctly spelled.) While down the other way a great continent, the other America, lay, like a volcano, ever busy at the rumbling in its own innards. One island, Cuba, troubled us. Others solicited. While Mexico sweetly gave us our divorces. (With that pragmatic head shake toward heaven which a state religion allows you, the judge in El Paso would one day *tut-tut,* as he awarded me mine.)

I never reread any of my back books, in toto, though now and then, for a quote, or to verify some point of reference, I have consulted them, always to half surprise. They are like multiple personalities, each working at its particular job, and at finish discarded from focus—in the steady drive to pursue yet another temporary idée fixe.

Once, however, in the novel *The New Yorkers,* I seemed to be operating under an overview of what its total import was to be—this ordinarily an overkill as likely to produce blight as disclosing tomorrow's probable chapter to your best friend. To a writer, one's best friend is oneself, but let each day's urgent swash of impulse first take form in print. Wiser by far to expatiate on what you are going to do after you have done it. In *The New Yorkers,* somewhere along I knew I was writing about the middle class, and indeed with empathy, having discovered not long before that I was willy-nilly a born member of it, and would likely so remain.

Back in the lean early 1930s of my youth, R.H. Macy & Co. functioned as a postgrad study for so many BA's who either could not afford to pay for such or else like me had found further university nitpicking impossible, that the wonder was as to how Macy's could absorb us all. The atmosphere should have been collegial but this the gorgon female "merchandise managers" prevented, at least on all the major clothing floors to which the young clerks like me were doomed. Rumor was that Furniture was an ambrosial Eden, presided over by an educated, even artistic man, but Garments appeared to be our blocks-long doom. On the ground floor, where I spent a stint in Gloves, one was totally exposed. The real hazard was that after kindergarten on (I was now twenty) all the pastures of education had been in company. Now, from 8:30 AM, when one's last communal move was to "sign in," until 5:30, when the employees' doorway delivered you to the thronged street, you were in a severe state of isolation from your fellows—one almost clinical.

While if you were a budding section manager, consigned to a queue of complainers ever renewed at your stand-up desk, your responses, trained to keep within the genial company policy of Return or Exchange, were at best automaton. At worst, "Sorry, madam, sir, this article is not ours, has been worn; kindly see the head manager in the office down the way—just beyond the jewelry counter and left to those parasols"—you deny both the customer and, humbly, your own authority. Twenty-odd years later I would write about it in the story "The Woman Who Was Everybody"—that period of supposed nullity had allowed me to admit that she, or indeed "everybody," was not me.

This scared me back into the grad school at Columbia, planning to enlarge my junior thesis on the Pre-Raphaelites, but met the prof in whose class I enrolled, he on opening day declaring, "Ladies and gentlemen, you are not here to wallow in the beauties of medieval literature but to be examined on what is in the syllabus"—this handed us the first day. Syllabus would be a word I would have trouble with the rest of my life—it would erase and return—as it has just now done. Why? I think it must mean for me a collected, maybe petrified body of fact, respected at large, academically certified—but not personally or psychically mine. Rather with that bombast which attaches to canonic certitude.

In a department store, the clerks, male or female, passing through as extras or stuck there for their lifelong duration, are the *Untermenschen* of that arena of workers. While there, I was also a college girl who on campus had been an individual, active extracurricularly in the drama club and as a dancer as well. Yet marked by the faculty as of superior intelligence but "untrustworthy"—in that I would keep questioning the rules—whether this meant unconcernedly peeling naked in the locker rooms (which shocked the elderly attendants) or, when our prof in philo—the distinguished William Pepperell Montague, disciple of Peirce—demonstrated "the continuum" of space by voicing his intent to move a grasped ruler in a high arc circumscribed from a low point at his left to a similar point on his right—I recall even now the bubble of puzzlement that swelled in me...

"But what's outside?" creaked from my lips. "Outside what?" he croaked, a benevolent man, but with ruler still in the hand.

"Outside the continuum?" I did not know that this was to be perhaps the abiding query of a lifetime. Indeed he looked at me hard, but did not answer me. Then the air in philo class, bumped for a sec, resumed its proper course.

At Macy's I had felt myself an overcomplex plant in the wrong forestry. In grad school it appeared that there, too, their tape measure found me impossible. The real clutch was that in college we, and I, had been urged to be individual. In the working world, at least in the lower echelons, this was not the case.

Yet the world of "the Depression" was about to give me a great gift. It was going to award me a ticket of entry to the arena of real *Untermenschen*. A rabble that covered the earth, apparently. A fraternity for which the sole required bid for membership was poverty. It would be a translucent otherworld, whose inhabitants could acquire lineage, and the ultimate royalty was at the bottom.

One day my kind, breezy girlfriend from college—who had coaxed me into the glee club because I could read music, if not sing, and into a group that dubbed itself "Friends of Music" (and whose brother I was dating)—telephoned to alert me. The city's Department of Welfare, overwhelmed with Applications (pleas) from Clients (needy persons) has allied itself with a state agency called the TERA (Transient Emergency Relief Agency) and is hiring like mad, college degree preferred. Her good alto voice is a prospector's, seeing gold for both of us. And so it turned out.

The job is called "Relief Investigator." In the main we are spies who trample the slums—and in a Depression not always "slums," visiting the homes of those who had got past "First Interview," which was held in the "Precinct" (office) in order to

"Verify," i.e., "Substantiate" in the "Case Records." What has to be bona fide was "Residence," "Lack of Income," and then an amorphous, nameless catalogue which might have been titled "Misery," for which we found some misnomer like "Situation" (sustained by such excuses as "No Food in House" or "Furniture on Street") after which "Procedure," we investigators (many of us from Macy's) must write a "Recommendation." If it was "Deny Relief," this left us vulnerable, afterward, often when we went out, "into the field"—as the social work lingo called those pummeled streets where our "Caseload" was—or at the "Precinct," where only one policeman was on guard against the incoming rage of the "Denied." But mostly, aided by the actual Situation, and the empathy that clotted throats more used to song, we turned ourselves into gods and goddesses with the one word that could illuminate an Application like a built-in flashlight: GIVE.

Midway during the few years I "investigated," I would marry—that same girlfriend's brother, my then date—and for a while would live in the pleasant myopia of the newly married. But wait:

Once I got the job, and while still single, I had moved out of the parents' aegis, and into a tiny flat in the loop of the Second Avenue El, as recommended by Bob Daker, a fellow worker. He and his wife lived on the same floor. The building was one of those miniature restorations done by a landlord new to the ownership, and almost as amateur at entrepreneurship as his tenants were as employees. But it seemed to us that our lives were in excellent balance. Bob's wife, Helen, did not work; she was having a baby instead. He and I each earned $27.50 a week at the Relief Bureau. Our rent—on Twenty-third Street, off Second Avenue, was $27—yes, twenty-seven dollars—a month. No Nobel Prize economist could have allocated our finances any better. Whatever Bob's "other" profession was, or could have been, most of us on the Relief Staff, young or old, either hadn't any other yet, or no longer. But both he and his wife had a talent for making the most of a minimum—and like any entranced neighbor, I imitated. My parents had been disturbed by my moving out (not usual when the parental home was available) but not alienated, though in our crowd, or level rather, it was not done. Those of my first cousins, grown women who had not married, still lived at home.

In college, several fellow students had been debutantes, or of that set; the men they would meet were predictable. But for many a city girl with no small-town structure at our backs, that could be far chancier. College, of course, held sway, but so briefly, and likely in the mazy realm that was neither football nor intellect. Both geography and ethnicity were so scattered; couples who were "flames" while at university often deserted each other for wherever or whatever they had been brought up to. Or foraged out into the world for reasons far removed from finding mates. There of course—often to find those.

My parents: that delicate, winsome Hattie, that Joe, whose alias, J. Henri, was for the poems he admitted to authoring but never showed. They would not dream of saying that I must be leaving them in order to have sex with my boyfriend—though they must be thinking so. I myself was half in shock because, though I was a virgin, "petted" mildly in the fashion of the day, and craved more, sexual opportunity was not why I was separating myself. What then?

My brother, six years younger, whom the entire clan called "spoiled"—either among themselves or directly, "You're spoiling that boy rotten, Joe," from his sisters—had when a kid been slightly more than a "Peck's Bad Boy," from whatever story that had once set this benchmark. Naturally he would have innings with big sister. Climaxed once when he'd bored holes in the door to my room, not as much to view me unclothed, as to pester—and make his action obvious.

I could almost sympathize. An older sister, in full flair at college—acting in plays, writing a column for the school paper, could be a prig. What a younger brother wants more than anything is to be *obvious*. (And objectionable.)

But even this constant harassing was not why I had felt the need to leave. To be secret. To be alone, yes. But for what? I knew only what I did not want: Vocation? A word not to be breathed.

My first night in the little one room that was blurred by the curve of the Second Avenue El (elevated railway) that nuzzled us, but had a kitchenette as neat as a theorem, I found out why. In the corner was my new bookcase of orange finished maple shaped like a half wheel: two shelves stuck into a waist-high arc, the undersides enameled black. For eight dollars, it has spoken to me from an old-bones shop, in an eye language I have never seen before but with a buzzed sense of design have somehow recognized. The dusk, as it comes in, is "art deco" too. On the floor, for my plumped feather bed, are quilts patterned with childhood. Donated me, they kept their distance, but are as comforting as arms from home. Being a constant eater and kitchen stealer there, my nickname had been Hungry Henrietta; in faith to that, I have stocked up. Curtailing my budget, or trying to, I learn in one gasp that I know nothing of what food costs. My mother had been queen there, always to suffer from her nation's tug-of-war between the frugal and the lavish—she had set a table alternately spare and given to bouts of display, over which my father had both fretted and laughed. If, as J. Henri, he was a gourmet, the New Orleans interlude had merely elaborated on a cookery that he had been groomed to believe was his birthright. "If there's one thing a good black cook knows from the heart, it's quality." Adding, with that chortle always emitted when he was condoning human frailty, "And do they have ways of insisting on their standards." That throaty gargle doesn't take to being written down; too many consonants packed around one elusive vowel. "And not their masters' standards. They gave us theirs."...It now comes to me through that angle of time-scope which no Hubble Telescope will vanquish, that his way of lecturing me on the major honor code is to comment negligently on the minor ones. From my own closeness to our black help when I was a child, I know that method well, its evasions and insistencies. And "heartfelts." So I would come to understand that his vaunted birthright was both black and white. (With any aristocracy that might adhere to the born Virginian, whether Episcopal, Jewish, or Abyssinian Baptist, governing or governed, each and any having likely to wait for final annotation by God.)

So I sit there, that first night in the first space I myself was paying for. Or am working for, still ignorant of the go-along perspective that will be forced on me as I trundle day after day to the lives that city, state, and country are pushing at me. A rap on a door, in the door and out again. Sometimes a sit-down and a heartfelt, in between. Other times the door pushed in my face. Or even a threat, though so far no blows. Fortunately, the handout comes in their mailboxes, not from me. In which case, to my mind, humbled as much as the recipient by having to "give" the handout, I would have had to quit. But my nation, my slice of the century, no longer gave baskets to the poor. It "issued"— it gave—"Food Stamps," a bad phrase but cashable at the store. So that if you were "on relief," only the mailman and the grocery clerk officially knew. Or, sub rosa, your neighbors, as they watched me trundle in. And perhaps waited for their turn.

I learn at once to think of my cases in category, in terms of which lack or need most obtrudes. Under *Health,* the woman with the huge diabetic leg that looms cartoon-like when I enter. Under *Hospital,* those clients who have either just been there or refuse to, saying more prophetically than I yet know, "The hospital—that's where you catch things." Or *Care*: Four children left without adults, under the care of the oldest, who is a pathetically smart six.

She—the investigator who is my doppelgänger, will come to see that the initial query her forays have to answer: *Need?* embraces everybody on so-called "public assist," including herself—who as the viewer and quasi-collaborator in the dole process will be assisted to change her life. What did she want when she left her own family? Less of it, of course, like any young insurgent who knows only that she is rebel, but not her reasons. In middle age she will mourn the loss of the clan, that worn grotto so full of character—and lost to her own children as well. Some countries foster the clan, out of veneration for a religion, a language, a past—or the consanguinity that comes from lack of space. Her continent, vast enough for laissez-faire, and addicted to the changes it calls modernity, disseminates the family more often than not. And in her family's case, age difference has given that an extra boot from behind. Or salvo?

How is it that now she sees everyone in terms of food? So much so that years on, when her own kids, shifting from public school to private, on scholarship and rubbing elbows with the privileged, ask, "What is rich?" she will answer, "If you always expect to eat. Never seriously worrying where your next meal is coming from. That is what rich really means." I adding: "This is a naive analysis of the class system to which I still cling."

That night on Twenty-third Street; I can still recapture it. One has merely to be breathless, yet breathing. I eat no food, nor feel any want of it. I am eating my privacy. Taking it in, in great gulps, then in gradual evenness. I acknowledge the privilege in being alone—and am satisfied.

Tomorrow, from this eyrie, I will learn the better to observe the great swollen leg of the other world, or in another corner, that boy, who, handing a cup to a four-year-old, spooning to a two-year-old, and warming the bottle for the baby, is trying to feed them all their milk.

...I have taken the first step toward a profession. The fire that burns, yet does not consume. That will require a lifelong haggle, between the separation of the observer and the life-plunges of the observed.

A calling that was no military arsenal—even decrying those. While offering only, from its civilian rucksack, the arsenal of words.

Finally...(*Oh? Is that final down there?*) ...some star may have bugled to another even more elite. Or may have not. For in the groves where maybe a baboon mother is checking her nursling's bottom, to see whether its tinge is properly rainbow, or in that fashionable ravine where an ape-wife who knows her etiquette is picking the nits from a mate's matted skull—suddenly a lead male elevates himself painfully from the stumpy crouch his bowlegs hold him to. Beating his chest in the *thrum-thrum* of his ancestors, he intends as they have always done. To roar. But compressing what is not quite yet a glottis, yawning wide the raw pink gulf at the base of which is a bobble nearly a larynx, he, the first of scattered firsts of his kind...articulates. It will have been a small sound, akin maybe to what girls in a circa 1928 dorm would shriek when a plumber was doing his rounds, or a swain down in the date parlor had sidled up the stair: "MAN coming!"

And there we were; we are. Beings like me. Grand finale to the earth's zoological tricks. Angels of unique intelligence, who either would not or could not "clear" or merit those ruined cubicles that came under the interviewee's query: *Housing?*—though many tenants scrubbed and groined those tenements to tolerable.

But above all, custodians of the planetary food line—to which no tickets should ever be necessary.

Devils of intelligence? Steeped in biologica, mathematica, philosophica.

Who yet never stop setting their life-clocks by its distance from a "waw."

So I nuzzled into my innocent quilts, nibbling after all (for who is not a compromiser?) and rose the next morning to scramble for the answer to the summing-up in each day's roulette of charts: *NEED?*

...History...

The battles of young women—of those gawks with the beautiful cheeks, and all too often iron-muscled abdomen that inhibits giving birth rather than easing it—are often ignored? While the initiation of the male is a golden-gloves boxing ring, on which the race depends. "You danced too much," the grinning gynecologist will one day say to me. "You won't pop easy." True, no I won't. Second time, yes I will. Women carry the energies of the body under a cloud of secrets, half a nun's, half a whore's. In our own tournament. Whether or not watched...Often, not by us.

The Relief Bureau opened that young woman's eyes to the true condition of the human condition. Each working day my long legs strode the portion of the "Precinct" allotted me (about ten square blocks), a whole cathedral town of mostly five-story tenements and their occupants, whose livelihood depended for the nonce on me, their not quite twenty-two-year-old *demi-vierge* listener. To deliver an "Emergency Ticket" I pumped up those stairs all the harder. End result? My legs have grown shapelier. But when the eyes are opened, there is so often too much to see. An unseemly corm, pitted with doubt, even horrible, had reared in the sole of my tenderfoot mind. Hurting the more as I walk, listen, dole. It is my vision of us.

We were stuck with our planet. Barring those stay-at-home scholar-voyagers, the physicists and the astronomers, who dream of appropriating one or two more—or at least hitching a band of us, ripe with all we (and they) are, alongside.

Our planet. The Planet is meanwhile stuck with us.

For how many millennia must it have managed without us. A primordial mud. Yearning toward chlorophyll. Then those one-celled lovelies, urged in from that green stratosphere? Or from air a million-weight heavier than air? The five-syllabled paramecium, a fishlike outline, floating on its vowels. The amoebae, stretching their spots to herald: "We split!" Then the species marching in, fish fitted to the sea, the legged to the land, as in some social register. While the variants show up the system by the very lisp and hiss of their spelling: *Pterodactyl, Coelacanth.*

Then, up from the ragbag of variation, everything is going on all over: be warned. The primates, hemoglobin is in the veins. The old ball spinning in the calm red balance (an ecosystem they'll be calling it) of tooth-and-claw.

A young first marriage, freely entered into, can make one feel that "everything" is solved at once. Depending on the everything: a cloud of expectations intensely suffered, almost entirely unclassified. A voyage, say, for which an undisclosed travel agent, neither dotty nor evil, but too experienced to care, has booked you to Paris, while providing you with all the maps and reservations for Indochine. Plus a handy list of the stops on the Autobahn.

The elders, if well-intentioned, keep mum. The "new couple" lives at a giddy height of illogicality, politely deferring to one another, until whatever decision slides to the floor like a dropped key. For a time lying there, illumined.

House-seeking was like sex; you deferred until satisfied. In lean times, benefits lurk. (If that improvised rhythm takes over like the doodle of the "vamp" scored on a tattered piece of sheet music.) At Four East Ninety-fourth Street, we found a one-and-a-half with kitchenette, top floor of a former mayor's mansion just renovated—which mayor was not disclosed. Roof-top privileges (to half of it) as well. A "concession" brought the sixty-five-dollar rent to just twice mine. But we had about twice the income now, he earning a little more than me. We were off!

I had two personalities now. The top one? College girl, translated as if by one lightning stroke from a fiduciary god, into homemaker, responsible for all the domestic: cookery, to decoration, to the psychological and physical maintenance of all children-to-be.

Secretly, at graduation, I had envied most those in my class who, destining themselves as lawyers or doctors or research sci- entists, had a prescribed path. Meanwhile, those of us who had no vocation—or like me, one buried so deep that it could not yet be phrased—took jobs that had turned up like dancing partners all too willing to show you certain steps. If you had married, in the life left to one "outside," intellectual though you might be, you tend to follow the conventional mother- prescribed path—much of which could be enjoyed, the way men of the most searing personal ambitions, far removed from derring-do, still went for sports. Out of choice. While for serious

women, to observe the vanities of fashion and appearance generally also relieves anxiety and doubt.

...So, see me erupt, late for "work," from my minor
mansion-top, five-story, formerly a mayor's mansion, built of
what resembles Britain's Portland stone, and may be it. Intended
surely as a single residence, it is by then, a tenement for the
elite—i.e., those who from birth are never to question whether
they will eat—only contemplating what a meal shall be.

Our block, though just off Fifth Avenue (if a mite too
"upper" Fifth) is still a "top" one, if like all such neighborhoods
in New York even then, beginning to soften in outline, though
the edifices have not. Like all such neighborhoods in the city,
even New York's most exclusive and sacrosanct, it is becoming
quasi-posh. We, the tenants, are the most quasi. The location
does what it can for us. And is, of course, a sociologist's dream.
Just put some things in quotes.

For I am loping to the "Precinct," at 110th Street, which I do
every day. Going home I will shop at the pushcarts for fruit and
veg—those who stock fresh produce from the city's portholes
ever on the intake from Jersey's market gardens, say—miles of
berries and lettuces. For this I have only to go ten blocks north
to 104th Street, where in fact my own caseload is—as well as, I
am told, the highest incidence of TB in the city, the state—or
was it the world? Anyway—Harlem. Spanish Harlem, Italian
Harlem. Vito Marcantonio, the politico, has his base here, black
Harlem—and white. Like the banks are, and the police, and like
me. All the authoritarians.

Once at my "desk"—which may be either a long plank at
which others are sitting on stools like mine, or else my knee, I
write up my histories, patch by patch. Each family is a problem
almost medical in analogy: swollen, tumescent, about to burst.
Or deliquescing—whether alcohol from the brain, urine from

the poor old kidneys, or blood from the too-feeling heart. Then, of course, the "mentals," not always distinguishable from plain misery. Or from that famously missing gene, intelligence. Or from the simple anorexia of shame.

Afternoons, I go by shank's mare again, "into the field." This is the too-marvelous social-work technical term for home visits, interviews in the sorry flesh as it were: *Live.* A sadly do-gooder term, to my mind. There being no dandelions. Plus a trace of Lady Bountiful hogwash.

Yet I am trying to hold on to my empathy, though told by the trained higher-up social workers from the private agencies that this isn't wise. "Actually it incommodes you." And indeed it does. Though it helps that there's humor. Like when I said I couldn't keep a gangster of the Dutch Schultz family "on budget" unless I saw he was actually living there. He wasn't. "He's away." I had learned the lingo—this meaning he was in prison. "Sorry, I have to see him. Otherwise, we can't feed." Meaning the money allowance. His mother smiles at me with the sweet forbearance of those who know how to con, toward the untrained. At the same time, she is kindly giving me, the un-trained, "the dope." "We could take you to see him," she says.

In the 1930s there were already two other "fields" whose re-cent graduates awaited you, both theological: "Communism" and "Analysis." When a single person went for both, the combo made him or her conversationally bulletproof—while the rest of us uncommitteds remained pitiably at the gate. The trouble being that if you were merely a "committed" young American, that is raised to believe in freedom of thought, you likely had acquain-tances gamboling in both camps. Their resemblance was striking. Both being out to proselytize, one could scarcely tell them apart.

For the Commies, "committed" was taken to mean the same as the popular French term "engagé," which, though it is the antithesis of "passive," does not require the goose step. The Freudian fields being broader, or to some all-inclusive, its "elected" (that was their aura) when confronted with us candidates could afford to smile at us patricianly, and lend us books.

What would save me from the Commie "organizer" at the Precinct—a staff member, obviously using Party pressure— would be my old freshman course in logic, that had bored me into what I had believed to be inattention. Our working conditions, improvised on the ground floor of a former public school, were indeed minimal, if not insupportable—but even quirkily reasonable, given our daily influx. Desks had been removed when found peculiarly vulnerable to bedbugs; upholstery, and even window curtains, had harbored lice. It did seem that being a social worker involved being as short of amenities as one's clients (along with suffering the contention that we could be paid less than average because we were "doing good"). "What about work overload?" I asked. "Seventy-five cases to be seen once—a week?" Impossible. Some had more, including me. "Oh, they're getting to that on their own," he said. "So it's not winnable. They're hiring even more." Whom he presumably could then organize? But about to sign the petition, I saw it averred we had holes in the floor. "But we don't," I said. "Don't what?" I pointed down, to the oak that in schools was once decently common, if here abraded, even gouged, but still solid. "Have holes in the floor." *"Tchk, tchk,"* he mocked. "Wuddya know...Listen, kid. If we're going to win, we have to make it real bad, see. That's how it works." It was my first lesson in Ends versus Means. When I quavered the word "honest," he left me in disgust. "But what if they send someone to see?" I called after him, to no avail. But I was yet to be treated to an example of how self-delusionary some of my own friends were—and perhaps all "politics"?

If one is sympathetic to people and interested in their dog-
mas, one will often be assumed to be convertible. I used to be
lugged to cathedrals by my Catholic friends and to rallies by my
Communist devotees, until I learned to stamp down any misin-
terpretable glow. What depresses me most is when the kindest
of women, asked to expound on the Spanish Inquisition, alleges
that the spirituality of the church is quite separate and not to be
confused with the actions of its practitioners. With the Commies there were opposite considerations—like private hilarity.
As at the rally to which I was invited in the Rockland County
where I would soon be resident, where we were led in song by
the daughter of Mother X—a Marxian monarch of symbolic
heft—to the tune, roaring in conclusion, of "Landlord, landlo-
ord"—a right good chorale against those oppressor lords of the
slums. "Dichotomy" was a very fashionable word in the 1930s—
much batted back and forth. That day, there must have been
sixty or so singing "Landlord" lustily. Every one of them there
owning his or her house. While because of the low incidence of
mortgages during the Depression years, the drop in real estate
prices, and land teetering between the Hudson and the Rama-
pos, in this bright array of eager-beaver talent and energy going
domestic before it went public—almost all these houses were
owned "free and clear."

By then I would become cynic enough to laugh—but also
much wiser in the varied psychology of these turncoats: some
"pinkos" yearning for community, others for the unrestricted authority—while Eden always lures. But that was to be years ahead
of the young city investigator who each day came home from
the seamy underworld of her country to the wedding-present
comforts that should have made her feel guiltier than she did. By
day the vision of America the Beautiful had become unalterably
frayed; by evening the lamp-lit parkside streets returned that

image to me, glorious in "declaration" for "happiness" still, but forever compromised? This was the "way of the world" for sure. I knew myself to be both too stiffly opinionated on some scores and too laxly tolerant on others ever to cope with a life of social reform. Yet a kind of termagant insistence on honesty, and this woeful mourning at what I saw, would have had to go somewhere.

It would be my "families" that saved me. At night they return to me in a waking dream, a zoo world in which each inhabited unit loomed at me one by one, each in its single circumstance, yet trundling the city like the circus elephants come to town, parading in sad, meek tandem, trunk to tail. Although an "investigator's" obligation was finance merely, a case, often of years duration, must be reported in toto, our supervisors reminding us, "In these times, with the private agencies swamped, you may be the only point of refer." Meaning that I would literally be the only one who "saw": The aging Yorkville couple who showed me their bank books, "Four thousand, miss," in savings exhausted slowly away over two years... They now arthritic and cancer-ridden, immured on a fourth floor with no relatives or friends to shop for them. Or Mr. X, tall, bland replica of a policeman in starched-shirt mufti—whose record confirms that he sleeps with each of his several daughters as they attain puberty. Or the skinny black charm-girl and occasional "pross," who reports the result of her Wassermann test for syphilis with a skiddy grace: "Positive, hunnah. Pos-i-*tive.*" They were the real world. So was mine. I was never bemused enough to pretend otherwise. Their world throbbed, without perspective. Mine glided between savannahs of those.

One day the two would merge. Pushing past my fearful ego—onto the page. In that crisscross, where empathy can steady itself, and judgment throb... And where I might be "the investigator" still?

Should writers have to accede to a general sobriquet, I suppose that would not be the worst.

Now comes the patch all too easily titled: The Provinces—a domain of many smaller patches as I, fretful yet wondering, am moved out, and on. An engineer's wife is not the tail that wags the dog. For a while this will suit my own inner fright—that as yet I am otherwise expressionless. Unwittingly I will be having my Grand Tour—reversed.

A city girl is soaked in variation, no matter how many relatives hem one in. A city person is half street-person, one's very body outlines melding with traffic, stretching high to meet that airy dimension ever quivering, ever counseling: "Up!" A street-person, if used to the freedom of great architecture, tolerates the small expectancy, consoled by the grandeur of the backdrop. Or impelled.

Now, for some twenty-five years I will be learning the sweet erosions of small-town life, in which morning is the great push of the day, consuming father, mother and child, and workmen alike. Threading out to the afternoons that are the women and children's perks. Then night falls, and falls, and falls.

Neighbors reign, minor characters, picked up at lost-and-found. These allegiances empower, if already cut-and-dried into communities, bridge clubs. Gaiety twinkles, borrowed long-term from "what you belong to." There is "the garden," with its delusory touch-of-earth. Where the slug oozes, proper monster to the minor life, conducted low-key.

I begin to know what I am, though I will not yet tell anybody. A provincial New Yorker, turned loose on the land beneath the cement. Carrying my "background" strapped on my shoulder like an invisible "sandwich board" as those were once called—though the city waif-men, who still hand you the paper flyer selling whatever, no longer wear these. My "board" is an invisible mural of people of the walkie-nontalkie crowd-stream, of neighbors nameless, but schooled to the streetlight pause, to the silent conduit of metropolitan convention that was my habitat.

What I cannot forget is how the piano floated again out of that top-story window off frilly Fifth Avenue, its hawsers as if held by a host of unseen angels—though I could see them. Primary-book angels, or at best those that seem to hover, unpainted, in the folklore colors of Chagall. In kindly complicity they are ushering me away from the urban complexity I don't yet know I will crave. The crew of movers, their jaws agape, know better. "By Gawd, she's down."

The piano, like any mute instrument waiting for some finger or breath to evoke it, perhaps knows best of all?

What did I crave? (Now that I know.)

To walk the museum barefoot. So that I may absorb through the soles?

To be so swallowed up by art—the huge, raw orifice, that stuttering like some biochemist on a blow horn, I can report the whale's every nerve?...And be blown out, mauled—but sacrosanct?

To listen so hard to language that I may describe the uncommon to the commonality?...(Squawk "hubris," if you must: I never studied Greek.)

What I craved most was to learn how to live, in the large, but righteously. In a land so free.

You learn most about freedom when you don't have it? A paradox, only as elastic as a stale rubber band. To which I would learn to reply:

Here's the Itinerary taken—as if by happenstance, coupledom, and choice. Or in more realistic terms: By Conscious Accident.

———

Wilmington, Delaware: My college roommate, Jo St. Mary, by then working for the DuPont Corp., suggested their "Experimental Station" as a possible leg-up for my spouse. So began the first of many such posts. Suburban or small city, they would all resemble each other in their convictions, fringed with envy, that they were God's country, as opposed to big-city evil, particularly as centered on the East Coast. Wilmington had less of that, being so near Philadelphia, and flush with money that could help sophisticate.

What I was learning, nevertheless, was what it was like to live in a "company" town, here also a one-family affair, whose Frenchy surname hiccupped in and out of almost every conversation and communal activity; their influence, as main employer, roweled deep. Here the "corporate" image would be presented me, singled out, long before its perceived aspects would be disseminated nationally, globally. While whenever I see or hear the phrase "tax break," I am back in a neighbor's law office, its walls serried with the listed names of companies in no way necessarily local, who had hastened to incorporate themselves under Delaware's beneficial tax laws, status officially displayed here in tony Jacobean script. In fact this function office, so printed-up, appeared to be his sole business. Suggesting how magisterial the legal life could be, exclusive of the courts.

Incidental to this or so it seemed, or meekly parallel, I was learning that such trains of observations were oddly subordinate to, well, motherhood?... The gynecologist, appropriately a Dr. Handy, was a braw woman with an impressive manner, who when visiting me in hospital after the birth wore a large clubwoman's-style brimmed hat—perhaps to confirm what together we had done? Or that she was known to attend only the best? This left me with some budding thought on how social structure could weirdly interpenetrate even parturition—or maybe

always had? Much later even to note a surprising difference between the childless and the familied, in the work of women
who write.

Not an observation that will hold water, of course. And
snotty of me. Yet—that effected knowledge of violence which
can depend on body detail: and absorption of it—compared to
the emotionalized slashing, more especially blood dripping,
down the paragraph? The latter does often seem to be the
tender-minded perk of those who, in at least one common circumstance, haven't been there, or done that. Or whose preoccu-
pations run to the uncommon circumstance? Which they
identify with "raw" life.

Rochester, New York: (back then) was where I learned most
about how categorized, in terms of religious, social, and professional groupings, American "culture" could be. Three country
clubs, the reigning Genesee Valley Club (Protestant) and two
others, one Catholic, one Jewish, symptomized levels everywhere orchestrated—even the American University Women's
organization, where a member questioned naively whether my
college, one she'd never heard of (Barnard), could properly belong? The attitudes, not at all murderous, were all the more
dulling for being so mild. And on other occasions, so ignorant of
the cultural world. Yet a vast crowd in my country?

Here, in this blandly organized city whose goodwill expressed itself in groves of magnolias in an admittedly chill climate zone, was when I surmised that college, where zoology
had taught me I was one of a species, and the city, where I had
rubbed shoulders unconcernedly with all kinds, had together se-
duced me, and for all I knew, done me in. Was I always going to
be churchless in the arena of the churched? If so, I could stand
that. But the chasm in me went deeper. I could ape the conventional, even enjoyed that, for a genteel afternoon. After all, that,

too, was "tolerance." But I was never going to be able to live fully in the small cities of the categorized.

Yet even now I hold this one in affection. In its reverse way, it had broadened me. I had learned that in every state of our Union, there would be an "upstate." A region whose chill—not merely of climate—must be dealt with. Maybe even educated toward the exotic warm?

And, as it turned out, some there, some anywhere, do see that not all paths are straight. Bid to a ceremony up there, I was presented with a silver bowl, its rim incised: FRIENDS OF THE ROCHESTER PUBLIC LIBRARY ANNUAL LITERARY AWARD 1981, then my name. I feel the tremor of its maker, as the silversmith himself presents it to me, passing it on. He is nameless to me now, but in the end I will be so to him, to all the states up and down, and to all the continents. As with makers all.

The bowl itself is about five and a half inches in diameter. Suitable for caviar, or cereal. Its pedestal is first a circle of eight inch-high indented flanges, any one of which will fit thumb and forefinger, making it easy to hold. This set in turn on a circular base three inches in diameter, with a hole you can look through, if you turn the bowl upside down. There below, incised on the bowl's bottom, and inscription. First: a dark line, hammer-shaped. Below it the ritual STERLING. Below that, two initials, in caps. HC. Below that: HANDMADE.

A tribute that can remind one of the circles of reputation, of the tremor of its maker and of the honor of the handmade, is tribute indeed.

Now and then, I polish it.

We have not left the family behind. Father, mother, daughter, three of a family of four. Mine.

Nor those refugees, the father and son, a temporary family

of two. Whether the *Mutti* was rescued from Hitler, in time to come to *Amerika,* I cannot say. From that day on—a "day" unlike any our three were used to—they were never again to see *Onkel* or his son. A faint rumor has reached us, perhaps from the German side, that they were establishing a business of some sort, or would be doing so. *Onkel's* talent was in many ways "American." We were not surprised. Nor did we comment on their dropping into the void. This was our country, however spelled.

I have detoured only so as to inform you a trifle more intimately of the daughter.

She has "come up" from Wilmington, where the Experimental Station hasn't quite worked out for an engineer who, though tapped for the honorary Greek-letter science fraternity when a student, had earned a degree in mechanical, rather than the chemical, which a company devoted to potions and essences must alas prefer. (Though indicating this in the most kindly manner, via their Mr. Greenwalt, a very high higher-up who shares an interest in bird-watching with her spouse.)

If I now refer to her in the third person, this is because that young woman, seen now through the penumbra of the intervening years, is like a statuette one can turn this way and that, knowing what its composition had so far been, and how it had been made. Mr. Greenwalt's facts stick to me for quite other reasons. For one, because there are so few of them, yet enough in the end to combine.

Executives at Macy's had been scattered all over, as if from garden rows that had interpenetrated, but the pecking order, top-to-down, was generally kept according to business ethic; sexual connections could happen but were frowned upon, and as with social, except for the departmental occasion, were not the order of the day; the store itself was a city, each going home to his lot. Congeniality was not required; the executives were seen mainly as those with the power to be punitive.

In a small town, every aspect of a company is on view and chawed over. Down there, the company was the town, with the right to a job generational among the lower orders, and heirloom at the top, by reason of ownership. Social graces were required, and even if all the levels were absolute, a certain familiarity reigned, the whole town, for instance, referring to the owners by their first or first and middle names, and usually conversant with not only their genealogy but that of the secondary families who had married into them. Or not always secondary.

While I was still in hospital with the new baby, a veritable procession day passed its window; a Du Pont was marrying a Roosevelt. Though I would one day see the young queen of England pass in her coach on her way to be crowned, and would live in London later now and then, I would never feel as intimate with the very idea of royalty as when bedded down in my room in Maternity, with the nurses at the window chattering of the local one of the pair as neighbors might. While, turn and turn-about, I would years after have friends, man and wife, who owned a summer cottage at Windsor and employed one of the castle's retired gardeners. A widower. When the queen's garden party for staff came around, he requested the honor of escorting my friend's wife, feeling it only proper that his former and present employers should meet. It was a lovely snobbery—the kind you can depend on for style—which in my country is not always the case.

Corporate snobbery is just as distinct. Though it needs must seem hail-fellow, it insists on being hard to get, and feels most well met when among its own. While yet earning connection worldwide, and even various. Diplomats are worth acquiring. They know their country's ores, its biddable personnel, and how to mine both. Philanthropy is prime for public relations, and for the spirit there's nothing like being a known target; even giving makes you feel good if you are not too stingy—and look good, even while you wince. Agreed—if you're going to hang onto until you die you may be accused of necrophilia—or unwilling to see your goods disperse. On the counter side, you won't have to consult your relatives. Or tempt any to murder. Rather, they'll gather round in hopes that you might change your mind. In Wilmington I could see all that in microcosm—as not in New York.

Another route for the corporation man was to give up the paper-document route as much as possible in his spare time. All the clutter of instruction manuals, funding, conference notes and printouts, budget estimates and advertising mock-up—"All that gray eminence," a vice president groaned at my spouse and me, drunkenly hitting the bar—"And what's cardinal?" Then he sat up straight on the bar stool, which is not easy to do, and looked us both simultaneously in the face: You hold your own face still and shift eyes.

"Sorry," he says. "Mixing metaphors with booze is never advisable, but I'm making such good money, and education's been no help. Nor for my wife. She's studying modern dance, aleatoric composition—that's music, and voice production, intent on becoming a star (there's a bit of rivalry between us) and really is a knockout—you'll see her shortly—but she's forty-two. While I've already established trust funds for the three kids, endowed two good causes, and made my parents and siblings safe for life…" He drooped, then did the square-shoulder bit again, sliding on the stool but saving himself. "Only thing left for me is to start a collection. Met with an art expert last week, to decide what." Then he saluted, though nobody here was in uniform. War was talked of. Though it was on our minds, and like him we had consulted experts, we didn't yet know for sure with what enemy it would be.

Then he left. On the bar counter there were two drinks he'd

asked the barkeep to set up for him ahead of closing time, which was by state law—midnight? We never stayed that late because of the sitter, and our one drink was only half consumed. Yet it was a wild scene for such a strict place—as all these towns would in the future seem to me. And that was what scared me.

The barman removed the man's extra drinks. "Makes me do that every time." Then he shut his lip. He didn't recognize us. We weren't from here.

For a moment I felt myself sinking, down, fathoms down. The bar looked familiar, if only in the way such bars do. The barkeep—I seemed to recall an older man, not this know-it-all with the wavy hair like an ascot upside down. He could see we weren't drinkers, that maybe we had been here once, with an office crowd.

But where were we? All the towns we had been in for the last months since my husband here had been "relieved of his post"—as the phrase went in the letter from the Station—those towns where we were looking for work—we still said it that way. Those towns—are they eroding us? Or only me?

Because for a minute, maybe a minute and a half, I couldn't have named for sure this town where we now were?

My husband was toying with his shot glass. But not with the thumbs-up that meant: Another!—which we ought not to afford. But the long slender fingers were not fumbling anymore, as they might have done—no, had been likely to, during our tour. He had a job now, or in a month would have, procured for us by his father, also an engineer, but a VP as well, working in New York, but out of the main firm in—guess where? Another of the satellite cities, but in our own state. We would find it chill where this one was inclined to be warm—but with a shade more democratic version of the controlling powerhouse—cameras, and quite another, almost doubled social-commercial setup.

"Opticals" (Bausch & Lomb) has that dry, high-class scientific sound, and the noncolor of math. If you said Sibley—(not "Sibley's," which meant the department store), a smile would click in—from my pretty white-haired mother-in-law with the agate eyes, "We went to the same church," and even a mouth twitch from that ponderosity, my father-in-law, a Pennsylvanian Dutchman up from his farmland, who now spent four hours of a morning in the bathroom at his ablutions—maybe washing the dialect from his mouth, and shaving that Lutherite jaw, until it was suavely Episcopal.

During the week we were being scrutinized, up where we were going—(and warned that a wife could as surely sink a man or bride him up the ladder to the top brass) when the name Eastman was said, there would be a faint hush, quietly local-global, that could give the city cynic pause. The man himself (I had looked him up, George Eastman) had been "American inventor, industrialist, philanthropist, founder," a man who could drape his national interest on one shoulder, give a back kick to any money scourges, and duck in to his lab to dream up a dry cell. While on that estimate in my desk encyclopedia he would have placed "industrialist" last. Born in 1854, just a minim after my grandparents' marriage, he could have been their eldest son, was only a decade older than my own father—and had died the year I graduated from college.

I had been spoon-fed on mid-nineteenth-century ambition from pickle barrel to 339 Fifth Avenue "opposite the Waldorf"—as Oakley & Co. had been touted and would end up—though that was a decade away and would demand a war to do it in. If ever a twentieth-century child was equipped to understand the upstate preen and rock-hard gumption that had also had the debonair patience to build houses of cobblestone picked up on the vast shore of Ontario and set in rows like a game of tiddlywinks—wasn't it I?

My then husband had gone to high school there, during his father's employment up there before being sent on to a New York branch that was mere accessory. We were being offered as the generational tidbit—nepotism that society editors reach for and tired back pages sentimentalize. Up there we would have friends ready-made, a few of whom, when we were looking for a house, had already served me tea in a nest of those thin, light-as-air coin-silver teaspoons my aunts had but never bothered with (they adding, in the way our family sentiments are repeated *a cappella,* "Just tacky one-upmanship. Besides, everybody in Richmond who planned to be anybody used to get them four dollars a dozen, any good fair"). My father, teasing his sisters, excusing himself by saying to them, "Have to train my girl in chitchat." And then, treating himself to a bit of show-off. "What the French call *causerie.*" He doesn't often. Perhaps it has to do with Oakley's ups and downs. Or his youth talking, ever more distant from mine.

Though once in a while he will talk up a real ruckus. Usually about the opera, so vivid you could be in the box, and now imagine the voice you have only heard on the Victrola, my favorite—and his—being Geraldine Farrar.

Now my husband back there in Wilmington leans forward toward the barkeep. Perhaps wanting to be considered, yet too acceding to ask.

I should describe him here, as neglected so far. A tall, long-torsoed man with the well-shaped head and features that even as one looked at them testified to good, if archaic ancestors, like the steamboat captain on his mother's side. He had the quiet personality which somehow indicated "son-ship"—here of a Pennsylvanian "Dutchman," a real—and absolute—*Der Vater kommt.* Though the son had the long, tapering fingers that he would bequeath to our daughter, and later the son—hands so fine that those who make a study of such for anatomy might stare—he did not have the forceful accompanying habit that the possessors of such seemed to have. He did not put those fingertips together and fall into a protracted silence that points to a meditative power exceeding yours. Yet it was there.

"That man who just left," he said. "Does the wife ever really turn up—to meet him?"

Why, that's my question, I think—or did I say?—with a sudden spurt of love for him—the first-time love that I couldn't yet admit was dying. Not everyone marries the first-time love, but whole racks of us, taught sexual loyalty, have done so.

He smiled back at me, with that repressed intelligence I was never able to ferret out. We both know by now that in our two-party life, I am the questioner—though I would be years away from gathering all that odd, uncasual querying and fisting it together as my role-to-be in a life often misnamed "professional." The life that comes from the very valve of being.

"You may well ask." A barman's reply, tactfully putting such nosiness to rest. But after a pause, negotiating? Though not quite yet?

He is looking at me. Or rather, looking me over. Aside from whatever his own prejudices, marital, sexual maybe, what does he see? One more corporate wife? That engaging silhouette whose outlines, waltzing neatly within the ring of its life-belt, I evermore clearly see?

I don't know yet that I am resolved never to be her. Dancing neatly on in all the ladies' retiring rooms of this huge but yet ever gentlemanly complex that "the formulas"(the chemical ones, not the rose-leaf essences) have empired here. To huzzahs with which even I at times must comply?

There's such a sweet essence of locality here. To which the scribe still untapped in me must respond. For, in the dormant years, all of us are dictated to. The scribe as well. Someday, though that young woman in the bar can't yet credit herself as one of those, this too, may stop. And "city girl," as I will proudly remain, I'm entranced by what they have managed to keep here, behind even those huge tanks that stud a once-delicate river, the Brandywine. Sometimes here, the breath of the pastoral licks your cheek, or brushing a roadway in the open-windowed car, you are as if hugged by its leafy arm. Merely a ragamuffin form of its too-orderly gardens, in which every petal and its square of earth costs a ransom, as endowed by an heir. But still "ethical." That adjective which will haunt the American continent.

"She does and she doesn't. Turn up." A swish of the bar cloth, that punctuation always so scholarly. Drink is not my primary reason for bars. I'm addicted to bartenders. Their adages hold up. He was a beginning, though only, as with this husband, my first. The ultimate barman-owner would be a courtly man, audient to all of us if you said nothing, to whose majestic forbearance, this husband and I would apply, several moves on. (Russ Killoran of the Seventy-six House, a bar housed in the eighteenth-century building that had been the Revolutionary spy Major André's imprisonment quarters.) As we sat there, our own freedom exhaled—more than any patriotic ardor, or venom.

This bartender is Irish also, but from whatever other country supplies the dark ones, with the woodchucky mouths. Not that lion-blond teetotaler, to whom conversation fed girth.

Still, his eyelashes had that same fast geometry the best ones do. Has he decided whether or not we're residents? Or already knows who we are?

"She's one of *them*." He squints into a clean glass. Ratchets it into the line of those suspended above his head. "So she does as she pleases. He married into it."

No need telling what my then husband and royal employee might have said? Yes, there is: nothing.

"Born cousin to Henry Bielen, she was." There's only so much to do at a bar to which only two have applied, but he's doing it. No need to say the last name. It never leaves them. Certainly not when it was the maiden one. "She comes in here, yes. A regular. But at her own pace."

But we are shocked back into the couple we still are. Henry B—as he was known at the Station, and was known to me in the stingy annals awarded a wife at end of office day—is the Station's family-allotted boss. And the man washing the marble must know perfectly well who we are.

So, in the mouse gossip that must patter on even in the scrubbed basements of the royals here, even our little mishap is known? Or, more likely, there. For Henry B is one of the family's ameliorators—or as yet the only one, back then? Who not only schedules the monthly "amiability sessions" for his staff, but does this in his own house. Rumored to be unpretentious, as family houses go, and cannily are—but more so than most. Questioned, my husband had said with heavy approval, as of the boss his own father would expect him to have? "Ve-ry comfortable."

No wife of his appeared at those sessions. Nor at the stiff soiree Henry B had given during our time, the invitation issued personally, to each man exactly: "I look forward to meeting your wife."

And so he had, all of us, we in a kind of crescent formation but honestly attended to, our first names requested and repeated. We "sign the book" in which, cousinless, but "family"— as we were pleasantly hinted to be—we would, in the nature of chemistry, be adjoined to theirs. Even the butler, working in tandem with his own wife, was weightily informal, if with a bland air of having stayed on overtime for a crowd to be reported to his buddies later on as "not up to snatch."

I was finding such locutions crowding in on me, though

never on my tongue before. Meanwhile I myself had been more than cursorily noticed—the two house dogs, slavering, sniffing out that I was menstruating, could not be downed—then finally only by their master, who had borne them into another room. I could not afterward recall his face, having lowered my own. But I was grateful. At many of the houses where we had briefly "socialized"—along with median and upper employees who were clearly aping their betters—or in house-and-garden tours where we would have a glimpse of that high style, the dogs, often a brace or more, seemed the condescending hosts.

It was at the second soiree that I had met Mr. Greenwalt, the science boss supreme. He'd a manner I recognized, professorial but like the ones who had private money, and had been relieved to find I was "college"; in those days not all of the wives yet were. He had bemoaned the lack of literacy among scientists and had written an article to that effect. He had been an Eagle Scout like my husband—though not a member of a high school society whose aims I had never been able to fathom, called the DeMolay. "Perhaps its aim was that there be nothing to fathom," he'd said. Knowing him to be the passionate instigator of the bird group, I'd confessed that though I didn't care to sight our feathered friends (a phrase at which he winced "For shame"), I had never gotten over a Victor record that had detailed them by names whose syllables would forever imprint: "The rose-breasted grosbeak," which had hit me lyric, somewhere between chest and ear. But most of all—the "red-eyed verio"... "You seem to fancy rose color," he'd murmured, giving me the top-to-toe, yet only tutorally. I'd found him so unwontedly easy to talk to here, that I'd wanted to cry.

Yet, let it be a lesson to me: Ten days precisely after, my husband had not been asked, with the usual jolly note, to accompany Mr. G's bird group. The same period of time detailed in "our" contract as Notice of Termination—"we" had been given the ax . . .

Finishing my drink—a grape-juice "cooler" (that now moves to me out of the archives like a purple bruise discovered on a dead body by the embalmer)—I said, with a glare at him meant to elbow-jolt:

"We're moving on."

On the way out I go to the ladies' room. But it's okay, I'm alone. Who knows where the wives lineup is now scheduled, this lyric moon-night on the Brandywine? Who named it that? A river, surely, to sip from—but now in the chemical zone.

In the ladies', when no one else is there? What better place to be alone. Seriously alone.

Yoicks—and away.

And so we would. That is—we shall. In a wide circle of what I begin to think of as barnstorming—though we will stay in "upstate" five years, with brief periods in Elmira or Binghamton after Rochester, and I will get to know the actual state of New York: the marvelously vivid lake country, like Italian wine land that must every half year however undergo deep freeze—and how this perhaps can tighten the native lips to a suspicion of excess. A grudging sourness toward all not like them.

Then on to Grosse Pointe, Michigan, a suburb so flush, so consciously laidback in expensive ease, that a kind of newness exudes from its very pores, peopled as it is with those who only yesterday were not the elite.

And so at last the "the County," as Rockland called itself—then a special mix of New York in flight—if only so far. Actors and playwrights, ad men and political activists. All reveling in the price drop that at first so often occurred when farmland went fallow, and in the sensation, like a vibrato in the flesh, which can conjoin people new to house-living, or returning. Houses so cranky ripe for rescue. White clapboard like ours, flirty extravaganzas with carpenter lace. Or hovel-sized cots of that gloomy "early" home-cut stone, which resists addition as melancholics do medicine.

Barnstorming was a gawky word for a city girl to be thinking in. Where could I have picked it up?—other than in the vast agricultural fields that underlay the literature in which I had been schooled. From the early picka-pecka songs and characters of childhood, Chicken Little to Heigh-ho the Derio, the Farmer's in the Dell to Virgil's *Georgics*? Fields stalwart yet tremulous, ever under threat, even in Shakespeare, from the whiny-piney urban mind?

What I had discovered (at first commuting to Delaware from the Relief job until I was seven months along, then living there) I had kept to myself. Born as I had been, into city games like "points," in which one bounced a rubber ball in a high arc from the base of the apartment house to your hand, scoring if it did not hit the pavement in betwixt, and playing tag on pavement that offered no dells. When I was six, in the glossy garden of the house we had rented for the summer, I had had an uneasy relationship with its pea vines. Warned that if I kept picking the blossoms I would never eat the peas, I did watch. Then one day, the tiny pod, hung like an earring, with its companion lyric thrumming: Don't eat them, not yet.

When I was fifteen, our fortunes declining to summer boarding at the Catskill farmers who had in turn relapsed to such catering—I had seen my first barn. A second one, as a camp counselor overseeing my charges, who had been quartered there. That summer, just graduated not merely from college, from the student schedule whose rules had underwritten my reason to be, I had also been set a-wander as if in an emporium marked "Careers"—a choice which might define me forever, though I lacked the wherewithal for most.

Or so it was said; is always said, except for the lucky few who know from the first greedy appetites: if for food, what must be done to purchase it, if for song, how to practice it, if for the forum that any classroom is—how to lead. Only recently I heard a mother say of her middle child, "She's not self-directed." And was reminded, by an enlightened pedagogue's funding plea for a "movement" to which we both belonged, that to pluralize *forum,* you don't add the "s" that all the natural embowelments of speech would push—but write (with your little Latin pinkie finger crooked high?): *forii.*

All I would ever have was the implement of language. Not shaped, it was said, like a money bag. Indeed, not shaped. "Career," as language, had a dizzy likeness I could not erase—to "careen." For I had known, from when speech first came to me, that my instrument was double-ended, and usable at either end. Voiced language would always veer in my head toward a page. What was written there would amble, or fly—back and up—into voice.

In her progression through towns, smaller cities that at the time she thought she never would want to dwell on after, and was always happy to leave, this New Yorker was actually learning so much that in retrospect it's not easy to be topical.

For one thing, I was learning what it was to live in a house—all year-round—and how this could ramify, with each particular house.

In Delaware the house, my first for more than a summer, was a sternly competent stone bungalow so ugly, yet so sure of itself, that it made me laugh. It had been built by a sweet old man to satisfy his exact needs. Now that those had outstripped him, it sat on its acre like a smug survivor, waiting to see how we would grapple with its tight stipulations. But the acre, half in strawberries, half in mushrooms, watched him say good-bye to his plantings and turn a distracted eye on me when I later brought him a share of his crops. We had had to make it clear that we could not care for those. Nor could he. But I, country neophyte, would learn how the cultivated mushroom lives in the dark recesses, by nature a basement dweller. How the strawberries flame with something of the same indolence with which you carry a child. How, plagued with Japanese beetle, as all the coast was that summer, you police the rosebushes, tipping them from the blooms by the score, into a can of oil. I was in fact learning the little murders and politics that are part of "land"— the kind that is not a garden merely.

There may have been no tremors of the earth beneath the sturdy wood floor, but I was feeling those, in steady *rubato,* a sustained rhythm that neither pianists nor householders can wholly define. While land's ultimate is that it survives all households. Lastly, in this house, we were actually over the state line, in Pennsylvania. So the city girl, never a hitchhiker, was seeing how states meld without warning, on a continent that, except for its canyons and similar exhibits, seemed intent on downgrading its differences.

With time, I would stop counting up, intent each time only on fitting in the furniture, much of it the family's, and fitting myself—like a bivalve swept into new waters, into each new "community," where all too often the new one spoke the same interlocking Esperanto. Until I learned how the house could interpret them, as well as me, soothing my own ever-reflecting inner monologue.

There were amusements—like a telephone company's refusal to install unless we ourselves measured the distance "in feet" from us to the state road: a quarter mile. We had to threaten them with the Interstate Commerce Commission (on a hint from my father).

And here I would come to my own senses, seized by that brief spell of "city" insurgency. For it is not only the anonymity of cities that creates the impetus to stick one's neck out. Nor even that persons of such temperament find their way there. In a city you are not hostage to one brand of social conduct, or dress bondage, or aspiration. You are in a breeding ground. Which can dilute thought as well to an amiable shallowness, equally styled. Or to a fashionable attitude—in revolt. But you can have your acre, all the more steadying because, though it may have its particular, its "exposure," as the rental agent's term is—its common boundaries are ill-defined.

By the time we landed in Grosse Pointe, Michigan, on the day of the Belle Isle race riots, the war presaged by the arrival of our family share of refugees would be in flower. (When a country like ours goes to war far away from the battlefields, its riches can only increase—if for some most.) That was the sensation in 1918 when I was six, standing with my mother and her first cousin Millie, looking into the walk-in store closet, where all the boxed, store-bought food supplies were kept, later the two and others purring over their knitting, talking of the rental rises being imposed everywhere, but with a cocoa à la crème or *Kaffee mit Schlag* soon to come.

That is the sensation in World War II. The home front goes into heat, burgeoning. Society women grew lachrymose. Bundles for Britain ensue. The young men of course go to the front as usual, as the war memorials will in time record. There is a rich sense, even one profounder than normal, of having really enough of everything on hand in both materials and energy, nipped in smartly by the little lacks that show sacrifice, like having to give up butter for oleo. And gas rationing kind of uniting all in such a demo way, both with those Fords that tote the labor force to its factories and the sharp pleasure craft buzzing on the Lake Saint Clair, patriotically at half speed.

Not a cranny to rent, but the U.S. Rubber Co. heroically keeps us in a good hotel, and our stuff in storage until we turn up a five-bathroom mansion, whose owners, recently its heirs, want it occupied, for "the duration," for a nominal fee ($150 per month). Plus an acre of lawn this time, and fronting Jefferson Avenue, that when my husband is at sea now and then, for what he doesn't say, I mow without complaint, even exulting at dancer's muscles after childbirth returned. Wartime, we all have our loyalties.

My private one would be in part to my grandmother's furniture, which I have inherited.

For I am an orphan now, already thirty, and must think for myself.

My mother, perennially the young wife, no matter how long she would live, had telephoned me in Pittsford, the suburb of Rochester we were living in. "Come." I had always thought of her as breasting the tide of the family she'd married in to. Now there, at fifty-eight she would die of it.

My father's geniality had been shocked into silence. The household, long since shrunk from family epicenter, is now reduced to two—my father and my brother, then twenty-four. And the war is at hand.

My brother, Henry, born when I was six, had not displaced the elder child, contrary to the psychological convention our parents are warned of now. For one thing, as a family we did not have "psychology" yet, merely loud and forceful versions of our own. And, looking back, I see how on the question of love displayed, the Southern side did play a part. Not all Southerners,

I expect, are as warm and cuddly toward young children, or adorers of them when grown—but with displacement, as with ours to the North, ethnic norms often exaggerate. No food could be more Southern than the oysters and soups served at my aunt Flora's table. Or the New Orleans pralines (then featured also in Atlantic City) with which our father kept us stocked. (He brought us the boardwalk taffy also, but without tout.) Also scattered among us and our compatriots up here, there were the familiar "widow" personalities who, separated from the man whether naturally or mysteriously like my aunt Mamie, would keep their single daughters grappled to them for life. Later, reading in such Southern novels as Anne Parrish's *All Kneeling,* I would find such a household's slovenliness portrayed. In Mamie's case perhaps hinting at some deep-set collaboration between white mistress and maid. Between those who share the domestic, what sympathies build up?

The advent of a new baby hadn't been mentioned in my presence, but all the family were aware that the prospect had seeped to me, even before, when, hearing an exchange in German between my mother and her cousin and confidante, "Cousin Millie"—something like *"Wann der Kind kommt"*—I had triumphantly shouted out the translation into the depths of the store closet where we three were.

When my brother did arrive, I do recall a certain distaste at my first sight of him. So very pink, so very fat, and in the newly beribboned bassinet, until then referred to as mine. Physically he is indeed my mother's very Germanic baby, in no way resembling my father and me. This I believe was the burden of my distaste. Nor did it bother me that he was a boy. Rather, I felt proud for my father, who now has what gossip hinted had not been expected of a man his age. Not only a son, but as will be marveled among the visitors, the first male on the Calisher side since my grandmother's final child—that is, in more than half a century. What I may have felt also, again only a seeping from our gossip-dwelling atmosphere, was family pride, in how we seemed to bestride the centuries—almost at will?

If so, that's hubris, with which I would find myself dealing later; in American life particularly, you do have to keep that sort of thing down, but at the bassinet's side I really felt nothing more intense. Not wondering whether I was the little princess still. That status would be kept. More importantly, I was at school, and able to read well beforehand, was expanding there... As for how babies come, and from where, I felt no further curiosity, having in the process participated, as in a kind of vaudeville. Your belly swelled, as my mother's had. You came to breakfast in peignoirs, ever prettier ones. Sometimes with the addition of what you had never been seen wearing hitherto, a matching boudoir cap. Above all, it was promised that you not go to hospital—if you were us. The cap, a capaciously lacy puff with a broad pink satin band at the forehead, held my gaze each morning, seeming the most untoward yet significant clue. Had I been told, even instructed, that our baby, like all, would emerge from under there, I'd have answered as consolingly, and as mistakenly, as I would years later, at age eleven, when my mother choked over telling me how babies started: "Don't worry. I already know."

My father's delight in me was manifest and would remain so. Of this I was never in doubt. Each night, once I was in my pajamas, he would sing one of those songs to me, in his cracked voice, or read me a story—of which I recall none. Those were less important, now that at age six, I could read, and guzzled print where found.

The songs still sound in my ear. Giving me his childhood almost innocently, and his delight in mine:

Went to the river
Couldn't get across
Paid me a dollar
For an ole bline hoss
Hoss couldn't foller
So I swapped him for a coon
Coon began to holler
So I went back home.

He had given me the South as he had lived it, not edited. One day, I would remember that. Then he would "tuck me in." That, too, is a particular sensation. If at one's deathbed one is still conscious—the supreme sensation would be to be tucked in. My mother never came to these sessions. Once my aunt Mamie had, watching with a sniff at the point of her sharp little nose.

I have always admired those who, when asked to pinpoint the moment of babyhood when their sense of self emerged, can triumphantly do so, with a single episode. Mine came in gradation, each time with an added quality or element.

In the very first, we are in an open arena where the seats are boards, perhaps in the bleacher sector of that nearby Yankee Stadium. My face is enclosed in the white bonnet frill, my arms in the white corduroy coatee—in which that decade sported its little girls. A ridiculous picture of me survives, forever fixing that style: the bonnet so deep, the coatee's low waistband set under my bottom, mimicking what the next decade will call "the debutante slouch." The round, brown-eye gaze entombed in the bonnet appeals: so innocent, yet already bearing up. By the costume, I am past two, no more than four: settle for three. In the arena, someone has just set me down, on feet encased in high-laced booties, patent leather with white sueded uppers. I have just seen the gap in front of me, of us, dropping to the next row of seats, and say to the adult shoes stepping to join mine, "Watch out. We could fall."...From above, on high, someone says, "The child is right." It falls like a blessing. I am approved.

Second: Early evening. Our dining room. Table set. Standing there, already fed, about to be carted off, I find that my head has risen above the table rim, to the level of just above the plates. Children bargain for space. I am achieving it.

Finally: My fifth birthday party, the first and last my mother will give me. We'd pinned the tails to the donkey, have had the grab bag, and are now seated with our trove. The ice cream set before us is in shapes: apples, pears, roses, and other fantasies, the cream frozen beforehand in the pewter forms that will one day be entrancing antiques...The children vie: "I've gotta...*I've* gotta!"..."No bananas." The boy who would say that says it. From behind my chair my mother says, "The molds that make these are from Europe. We don't grow bananas there."

From across the table, my friend Justine's mother, standing behind her, having lingered, unasked, "to help," cries, "But, oh, Hattie, what a display."

I understand her status here very well. We live in a building called the Hampstead, she and her family in its sister building, the Letchworth. Constructed together, not too long ago, they occupy the Broadway side of the entire block, offering the musty, quiet neighborhood of upper Washington Heights (then more or less bounded by the Institute for the Deaf near the river and its crown jewel, Jumel Mansion), exactly the same modernities, social aspirations, and apartment layouts. Yet there was a rivalry between them, in which the Hampstead reigned supreme. Because it was built first? Or because its tenants stay longer, so appearing more solid, while those at the Letchworth are more come-and-go?

No one really knows why, though the rise and fall of neighborhoods, their advantages and detriments, are on every good
citizen's map. Though our families have the same amount of
rooms and bathrooms, undoubtedly at the same rental, it was
foregone that after my one ritual and nosy visit to Justine's
house, she would thereafter always come to ours. Our mothers
met "on the block," as it was said. My mother reporting, "She's
always making overtures." A maternal vocabulary has its own
distinctions, running much to the dip-and-sway of the social attitudes and obligations. Certain people could be "pushy" after
one had dined at a house—one did or did not wish to "recipro-
cate." While the "overtures," it seemed, were to be made by
us...A habit it would take me a lifetime to excuse as being
"shy." True. Those are the ones who expect "overtures."

Standing in the street, holding on to my mother's hand,
while the two converse above me, I hear what my mother's
phrase means. Justine's mother is comely, fair-skinned, native-
born, we hear, and has been to a city college, interrupted by
marriage, the father being "in business," if not one of his own.
But through the smooth, fair cheeks I see yet what at the time I
had no language for. Anxious bones.

She hadn't spoiled my party. Nothing could. How I had
basked as Mother bent to me, coaching the "party girl." How I
was to greet each small guest, some from "around the block,"
others from elder connections, with a politely extended hand
("And don't just stick it out!"): "So glad you could come," while
to the mothers I must curtsy. I was not the only child among
those I knew who had been taught how to curtsy, but none were
in our neighborhood. Our Southerners, though mainly elder,
had helped—by expecting that I would do so, and blinking to
one another that I had. And I was in turn acquiring my map. On
the Upper East Side, where one more likely did not go to the

public school my father had insisted on, to dip the knee was quite routine.

Nor do I scorn my mother's attempts. She made many such under the guise of "proper manners." But in my vocation perhaps nothing is of more worth than to have been made to see—alternatives.

Mrs. Schweitzer—for their name, ending like ours in "er" did indicate that they, too, had once emigrated, and likely from a European locality. Or her husband had. Which in those days constituted "they"...

Actually she had "helped," though not as she planned to do.

I had dwelt on the language for parties. A party was "given." A party was a gift. Ours was a household of gifts: one whole closet of perfumes to be ransacked by relatives, friends, and later my young cronies, and there was always my father's dumped valise. But it comes over me now and then that all gifts are not as unrestricted as those. Nor in the future would be.

Too shrewdly, I see that the elaborations on the table are not solely for me, but an exhibit of my mother's—like the dresses she embroiders for me with unnecessary zeal, that evoke amaze even from "the Germans." What she must have wanted was—as we say of the thwarted—"to express herself," no matter how. Those cool precise forms down the table are somehow what she would do with forms meant for sterner stuff, as my father had observed with a smile, "Meat jellies, dollin'. Pâté." Which word, smiling at me, he had spelled out.

Nor, in my short experience of her, does she melt easily—unlike that apple-tinted green with pistachio nuts, like that tutti-frutti-speckled strawberry.

But I have had—could you call it a vision? My father is not here to notice; he's had to be, as much apologized for, "on the road." But the loyalty he has taught me infuses the air. I look down at the boy. "I don't like bananas that much." Then at Mrs. Schweitzer.

"My mother's name is really Hedwig," I say. Giving it the softly breathing pronunciation, with the drawn-out "e," and the "ch" scarcely a coo in the throat. If Americans had not tended to pronounce it as spelled: a head and a wig, it was to have been mine. Instead, a name that was only suitable in France. "Isn't that pretty."

Behind my chair, I feel a tremor that means my mother is suppressing a giggle. We have our moments, when we are, if so briefly, "together." But this is not one. What I do feel is very odd. For one: There is a future then, though not a word I know. Merely a sense that the present will extend, will stretch on.

I am also no longer "the child," a word blending you in among the lowly, the ever inscrutable. I am able to send words rolling down the table, making that boy open his mouth and Justine's mother lower her eyes.

Even Justine, special friend, doesn't count the same as before. As before this scary but accepted unlocking.

I am separate. I am I.

"I" feel no pity for my mother, nor for any whom the selfhood leaves behind. Nor does the embryo? In life's successive stages, we must forge ahead.

But in due turn, at my mother's death, stages and stages on, I will feel such pity. Such whelming pity as will teach me at last—to express.

But my father, who appears only tangentially in those first stories—why?

(He was the giver. In the end that would whelm him. He would plead with me to give him what for once he wanted. But would be refused.)

Yet once, in my sixth year—well, let's not summarize. Let's have no insights. But put it out straight:

We are in the bedroom that is mine. The ivory-painted bed, dresser, and whatever are already girlhood-to-be, and will see me through my teens. As on every night, my father is putting me to bed. I am already in my pajamas but this night he will not sing. My aunt Mamie has for some reason come to watch these proceedings. What for? Maybe they will talk later about her own affairs. I am used to that, even at six. All the family affairs end up with us. Perhaps that has dowered me doubly. I see what is untrue yet state it with guile. "After the baby comes, your nose will sure be out of joint," Mamie says.

I say, "Oh. Guess there'll be enough love to go round!!!"

Where did that come from? We none of us were in the habit of saying "love."

I don't recall so, anytime. But for the moment, maybe, all the sweet talk I had been steeped in had triumphed?

Nearly. But we had snows up here, sturdy winds that knocked the nonsense out of you.

And in my father's triumphant look at his sharp-nosed sister, I saw that I had thanked him. As, alas, I never would again—until now.

"I sometimes think, Mamie," he is saying back there, "that you never really came North."

Nor had he? But so giving me—and weighing me?—with that almost military code of honor which can be peril to the civilian out of uniform?

"Maybe not," she says, the nose tip moving. "I never was too good at being sincere."

Did the North really make you so—with its weather hardships?

Down the years that reverberates—what's heard at age six still crying for solution.

I stomped on the bed, so hard that my pajama bottoms fell. Mouse-quick, Mamie darted to pull them up. Tying the waist string so hard against my navel, that my yell is ecstatic with all this attention. "I want to— I want to— I want to be in the waw!"

There ensues now an unhealthy bachelordom, between father and son. The young wife whose early winsomeness, oddly linked to a stern rectitude she could not fully wield, had long since deserted the charming image once exhorted to me. Except for a certain humorous irony, perhaps as peasant-based as her feet, she had become lost in her own bickering, bouts of which had set the family tone. Still elegant when she dressed for outside, this was when she could recover, if only to emphasize the tarnish within. Now she was breasting death's tide with a hollow-eyed foreknowledge, a wisdom I would never forget. In her last hours, she had been painfully received, gazing at us like death's acolyte.

My father, watching next to me the long susurrus of the dying, contracted as a bird does, when approached in a space too small for it to wing away. A black-feathered one, gone dumb. For long after, he was to be found alone, still standing as at a bedside, head bent.

My brother, ignoring her as he had from childhood, in a peculiarly adult version of how some males discount women, had scuttled away, my father acknowledging this with his customary headshake. He must feel to the bone what all in the family had: that Henry in private was nothing like Henry in company. Though they were unaware of its extent, their word for him being "inconsiderate."

My mother bore the domestic brunt of this, ranting constantly at his one obsessionary habit, presented us twice a day and more, like a dropped clue. The bathroom, steaming behind him as he emerged, was each time—and no matter how often during the day—a wreck, the mirror and shelves white with moisture, the heap of many Turkish towels always lying on the floor. Even my father weakly protesting, "Can you not hang them?" could not persuade.

There grew to be a ranting hatred in her for Henry, and a sneering response in him for her, even when at sword's point an unusual conduct between mother and son, from which my father shuddered away.

Once safely distant, from what at home I could only fend off, I took to ridiculing my brother, if only to myself, as "the ablutionary." I saw what he must do with the succession of towels, dropping each well apart from each part of him left cleansed. How, after shaking hands with anyone, he surreptitiously wiped his own with a handkerchief then stowed, or sneaked away, to rinse.

Ablution has a religious significance I didn't know much about: the priest preparing to hold the chalice? If so, my nonreligious brother must feel himself the chalice? Now I think it may have been that convention of scrubbing which "the Germans," some of them, needed to advertise. (My mother, exclaiming to me, almost a teenager, in a crowded bus, "You haven't washed behind your ears!")—that needed to be flaunted in him.

Certainly he resembled her: prominent hazel eyes, in him almost greenish, and the fairish complexion, her vaunted father's big bones and height, and later the Teutonic heaviness, not so much fat as bulk, clothed in a raft of custom-made suits.

His father had been a dandy. He would be the same. But the dapper man of the silk tie with stickpin under the twirled mustachio, from all of which the fin de siècle emerged slowly, had begot himself Hedwig's ponderous Bavarian. "The drummer," as salesmen were called, had become a "merchandiser," as he called himself. His son, smoothing it down, would became a "sales vice president."

Certainly from my birth, my father would be a main factor in my life. I had no sisters, and sometimes yearned for that tender side-by-side sisterdom I sometimes saw among friends. Of brothers who were tender to sisters I would catch envious glimpses only in my adulthood—or earlier, at home, between my paternal uncles Aaron and Nat and of course my father, and their two sisters, my aunts Flora and Miriam (Mamie). A solicitude, in various degrees, that had been ingrained. That my grandmother would have stipulated this was taken for granted. The family hive required this, as one of the givens that needed not be stated—and were thereby more powerful.

Not surprisingly, the minute I left our household, any latent or reactive antagonism to my brother had disappeared. We shared none of the intellectual interests my father had nurtured in me—books mainly, which interests college had increased. I simply forgot him. He no longer had significance in my life. He meanwhile, when he came of college age, had been offered that—if as part of a dual bargain. "I'll send you to college also," my father had told him—"though I'm not sure you want that. Or I'll help you get a job"—it being understood that the job would be not at Oakley's but in that general trade.

Whether or not "college" was too identified with me, my brother's choice was immediate. He wanted money, "success" at any cost—yet wanted above all to be like my father. This would be the image he would pursue all his life—though he would see only that gentlemanly, anecdotally Southern "man of business" who had once been a "man-about-town." Later he would pursue this image in all its ramifications.

Yet two of my father's characteristics, the half-stifled scholarly bent of the self-educated and the depth of honorableness that he had been heir to, the son never saw, or more likely never admitted to himself. What he wanted, and would pursue, was absolute—that he and his needs should be prime. Over and above anybody else's prospects or satisfactions—above all those of the father image he presumed to adore?

Who has examined how the limpet—and all human variations of—actually regards the rock it clings to? In a dependency half lurking to conquer, if not destroy?

As that now occurs to me, so do other possible lurkings, those that belong to the animal in us—that archive which my own century would so tiresomely cede to the psychologists. Where before, in the times we so pitifully call "immemorial," the documenting of how we humans balance enmity and love had belonged to all orders of the intelligence, and body of course.

As I revisit my family drama, long brooded on and left behind, I see, in the dramaturgy we so timorously call "Greek," the urges, simple and indeed animal, that may be observed in a litter—say, of puppies—though the biologists have long since advised that even the cells of all matter do vie, and nudge. How does hatred brew, except over possession of what is most wanted—food and safety. In which the "parental" figures most. One or the other parent being idolized. In humans, if we are lucky, sometimes both.

In our litter, were mother and son rivals over the possession of the father? The Hedwig, who had the guts to come to *Amerika,* had been downgraded to Hattie, retrieving herself by a marriage, in what was to her an ascent in money and American background, but clearly had sexual attraction too—if in time age-debased. While I, her firstborn—"coddled" being the family verdict there—would rival her as well. Not a son—but what would do an older man, and one steeped in the archives of inheritance, nearly as well?

All of it is in question. But what was clear—and quite plain to all, and sometimes comic, though never ridiculous—the "pater" did not see others as enemies, and as far as could be seen did not engender those, instead accumulating cronies everywhere, even "on the road," as he had widely done. After I had left the household, I could see clearer how hard the travel routine had become for him, both physically—which he never voiced—and as emotionally in his separation from home and us, which he loudly hawked, both at home and in the daily letters, penned in a black ink calligraphy, maybe nineteenth century, unique to him, on hotel stationery that taught me where our cities were better than geography class, and more profoundly.

What I was being fed was a viewing of what the mercantile life was: the small merchant's aims and its grasp. Listening rapturously, I wanted none of it—except the view. It would be my brother who would covet. He wanted customers, and to be personable (which he was) in and among just such crowds. Meanwhile my father's way of "doing business" was becoming very old-fashioned—or always had been? How too serene, to be satisfied, despite a slight financial irritation now and then, with one's niche—and with one's anecdotes, in which one kept handy the story of one's life. Unwritten, but that, too, is life. One day—after my graduation, when he was asking what I meant to do—he had hauled a notebook out of a drawer. "Poems," he had said, allowing me to see only that the binding was broken, the penmanship spidery gray; then shoved it back in the drawer.

So, now the drama is set.

Forgive me, if nearing life's end, I see a drama with a tinge, modest, all but ignorable, of the Shakespearean: i.e., those in which it can be seen, or should have been, that all the while the monologues meet and clash, the battles rage and disperse, the inheritors will continue to inherit, and the bequeathers, whether dukedom, or peasant-near trader, to bequeath and bequeath. All of them already locked in, by that *praeludium* once called Destiny. For which, ancient or modernly, there will always be private names. While the chronicler, as usual, draws from chronicles—before.

What happened to us four, by then three, was simple, though all escapees should watch carefully.

War has finally caught up with us.

A patch of daughter-at-home—in her marriage.

Ho-ho…and a ho, ho, ho. How safe, to be in the land of humdrum. We three, marriage still on, plus a little girl, now upstairs doing afternoon-nap duty. I am now in my late twenties, and am still as reported in a *Times* paragraph, perhaps owed to my father-in-law, *Bride of Engineer*. (With my first name initialed and the patronymic spelled out. Headlines, and the folk who inhabit them, have only so much space.) Lolling, I am smoking, after a frenzied search for the last cigarette in the house. An addiction that, like many must, comes when, planning to relax, you lie back, unwary, psyche suddenly clenched, finding that willy-nilly, at this hour, with husband away until nightfall, baby slumbering, is when you reflect.

What I am doing is accumulating anecdotes, in later years to be fairly repeatable, for a modest laugh. How, when I had my first haircut in town here, the dresser, a comfy sort, and adroit enough, noting eyebrows born black and arched, crowed, "Oh, are they wearing eyebrows like that? I didn't know they were wearing eyebrows like that—in New York."

"They," she says, speaking of my city with a reserve that in the five years we stay will ring from many a mouth there, patrician or plebe…Like, when, just last week, during this hour, the child wakeful but cooing, I dared a Flagstad record so worn it had to be played loud. Not the love-death, which is somehow not for afternoons or those routinely alone. The Valkyrie *Hoy-yo-to-ho*—the very bell and swell of the female voice—though of this, too, I was unaware. I play it often, this record I bought with a salesclerk's money. Which is why it is worn.

We are in the pretty greenery of Pittsford, an outskirt of Rochester, in a pleasant white clapboard house whose seven rooms we and our effects, only a few yet inherited, scarcely fill, except for the piano, scrounged in what is here called an alcove, rather than a dinette.

The rent having risen, along with us, to $125 per month, the site handsome, a median hill, with a view tumbling across others. An accommodating greenery, countryside still, in which every hilltop, able to stare at the others, has kept the illusion of expanse. So, by next week I shall have another anecdote. The semiretired banker who lives across the valley, where neighbors tend to be complaisant and locatable, says very pleasantly, meeting my husband at a company party, and intending only a compliment…"Your wife has the most bee-yutiful voice. We both so enjoy hearing it."

In my "town," those at a cocktail party can cut their city to bits in sardonic joke—and in half an hour feel it rise again in the fire of assorted eyes. But such anecdotes are not funny in the places where they are likely to happen. Nor would my mate, not a city native, ever be as easy there as I.

I had taken to writing poetry—some. Not that I would send it out. My poems are what you tell yourself, when tired of the daily anecdote, now concealed. In between, at other nap times, I shift the furniture around—a device I will find well known to other stay-at-home wives. Upstairs, the third and extra bedroom is now only an "ironing room," an absurdity for the meager linens we use. Though more than a few wives here aspire to the manorial. The piano, obtrusive here between the dining and sitting rooms, could have been sequestered there. Between the sectors of living which a day without streets imposes. I seldom play. Never did much, reading the scores for the Beethoven symphonies having been my personal delight.

No, it's the words now, that pile and pile. Having nowhere else to go? Yet often, buried as they must lie, in the sweet but mindless circle I'm locked into, they do as in that first line of a poem not mine, that now and then keeps recurring—over the trash barrel, say, or even taking my child to her nursery school. A marvelously musical school, run by Lottie Ellsworth Coit, a pioneer in what music could mean to the young. But when I'm there the words thump even louder, pulling that line of music consciousness altogether out of whack. Their context is quite otherwise. Yet the words crowding my head raise a syllable here and there, to undulate along with the cigarette smoke…So now and then, in nap time, I quote to myself, softly, "They flee from me, who sometime did me seek."

So, too, I lie of a nap time, in my early dawn beach chair floating myself along the lacy green tree tops just below our hill, while in my head the Scottish lays and Irish jigs I used to beat out on the piano keys now more appropriately thrum. Inside the house the infant daughter, for whom I gave up smoking, slumbers in fat babe-beauty, a preternaturally good child. Only a short time ago she crawled, that hilarious knockabout interim when I had to follow in pursuit most carefully, guarding her from the furniture's topless towers within, and from the verdant ledges without. What I can barely wait for is to hear her speak, giving her verdict on us. The ultimate cadence—and I hear it yet—is to hear reasonable speech from those whom one's own body has shaped.

Will she hold it against me that if I could perhaps chaw that green treetop lace into some sort of cud, or roll it dry between those papers once used to "roll my own"—that this holy green, however pleasing, will never replace the city's standoff tobac-cony chill. Or that, lapped as I am now in this cleansing, angelic light, what haunts me is the subway smell, that spittle-and-dust I would barter for?

Soon I must go in, boil the milk so that she may wake to smiles, those cheek-curves that to me are all the art for which I need ask. While she, with canny awareness of her own growth, has passed into that stage of connoisseurship in which one drinks from a cup.

Why is it then, that aureoled as I now am, in the pealing color that heralds the humdrum day alone with her, I each morning crowd the silence with a secret exercise.

I bring my "caseload" here.

Those I haven't forgotten, that is. The ones I expect to bear with me through life...

That arched tree limb, for instance, is crooked just the way the woman's great swaddled diabetic leg loomed at any who stood at her door, facing her bed. Or that webbed swathe where the caterpillars hang—that's for little mister *opoulos* who lost his coffee business, but trots his one room with a dozen make-work routines. Or Mrs. Throgg—the subnormal nitwit who exudes kids once a year, a brood pale as mushrooms, from being too often fed what is not food.

Why—the treetops could be lined with my former charges—who were never really mine.

Or is it that now, like that gangster whose family expected him to be counted in the budget—I, too, am "away."

"They apply as a cover-up, those Mafia," the supervisor had informed me. "It's a laugh." And indeed they had snickered throughout the interview—thinking me wise to them?

...Or that scrawny, black-haired powerful man, the writer not forty yet, with his unfortunate taste for the annealing, gassy cloud that would suicide him—his Adam's apple, swallowed incessantly, clocking him toward vomit, every time. A "biggie" at twenty-odd but now forgotten, his name was as familiar to me as my own, but one I will not tell...

Why am I so alone? I have daytime neighbors, until "the husband" (whom I would deny is now merely that) each dusk returns.

Nearest on our side of the road is the chirpy young woman whose smokestack even in summer puffs blue all the day. Who, when I appear outside during baby's nap time will turn up, neat as a doll in her homemade lawn "afternoon dress" for a chat over the fence. Her first name, said when first met but obscured by the chirp, is still unknown to me. "Too shy to ask again," my husband said. "I know you. Yet you look so bold." And sometimes act it, does he mean—and not quite suitably for up here? "I'm acting bold," I say. "Hoping it will take." Done that all my life. At first, it fascinated him, being so colorful—for which, in his list of girlfriends prior to me, he had had an alternating taste. One, an amateur actress twice as dramatic as me, and very handsome, in a demi-Russian style, then a neat-featured blond whose even, calm manners, glimpsed from a distance, might come from either abstraction or lack of wit.

Our neighbor, though rather the same type, "American girl," is not majestic. All her chat is so sweetly offered, "Yet I can't half understand her, that local accent. Anything she says is preceded by, 'As I sez to—.' And then a chirp. *Ert.*"

My husband guffaws—which is unusual. "I was only saved from that upstate accent by leaving town. Her husband's name is Art."

Listening daily, I become acclimated. There's a pause after

"sez to." So it is not a chirp. And—though she is breathy—not a hiccup. Also I begin to track other words, similarly bent, like "gairden," for which my town would say "gahden." Or: her mother-in-law is suffering from "the hairt." In fact, she adds, "We air on a sort of spell."

One afternoon, the husband is standing there too. I go over; I'm friendlier now. Only glimpsed from behind until now—as he dashes to the car mornings, and from it at nightfall, he is a tall, bony young man, who closer up shows scalp through the thinning hair. Is it that which so solemns him?

"He makes me a fireplace fire every day," she says worshipfully. "Only this morning he had to leave too early. I like to be up for it. Safer when tended. And it helps me breathe."

"Inventory time—," he breaks in. "Wouldn't think a bank needed. Or ought to." It's a joke said before. No doubt repeated each year.

"Oh, Mr. Bendick's?" I say looking across the valley. "Yes, we'd met." The "banker" who mistook Flagstad for me. But I won't say. I'm learning.

"The boss, yes," he says.

"Oh—you've met him," she says eagerly. "Me never." And I see I haven't yet learned enough. Not about the social sectors here.

The plume of smoke from the stack pours straight up. Late summer, not a stir of wind. The scent envelops us. "Pine," I say. "Smells wonderful. Hay fever or not."

The valley, dark and wet-grassed, contradicts me. No haystacks here.

For New Yorkers who can afford it, the real estate ads will tempt with domiciles that have a country feel—perhaps a maisonette with pine-plank floors instead of parquet, a kitchen "big enough for a rocking chair," mantels even in bedrooms.

Not me. "Country effects" in the city make me laugh, except in the kitchen, where a farmhouse expanse would allow pots of good size—and those copper, umber, and black-iron rows of them, mute sous-chefs that rouse empathy almost sexual in the cook.

But actual country, or summer island—in which "vacation" stands for a wild vacancy, a cessation? No. I want city rooms, tannic with mind. Bitter even, with consciousness.

And as I swing there, greensick from what is not native to me, that other timbre is fast speeding toward me. Though not in the version that simple longing asks.

Nothing to do with the tot, who sleeps upstairs in the house, rolled in the blue blanket each nap time and bedtime commanded as her signal of safety. Though when I find her again, the doll-like arm will have flung itself from the fold, the plump limb angled like a castaway, as if even that age knows safety must be fought for.

No, what is coming to me will arrive as in any one or other of those stagy plays still matinee-proof in the 1920s, in which the curtain rises on a "drawing room," whose very furnishings suggest the unity required of a drama that won't worry unduly. Whoever the star actors will be—Lunt and Fontanne?—they are still in the wings. But a housemaid, dotted back of the footlights as reassuringly as good punctuation, is just answering the telephone.

My father took me to the theater very early, as soon as I could be trusted to hold my water until intermission. When the stuff we were seeing was poor, he pronounced it so. Our first foray we witnessed "only a vehicle," entitled *A Woman of Bronze*. But I was to watch Margaret Anglin, the star. "When you see a fine actor in the sway of a part—you're seeing—the grip of life." When I quavered, "Actress," he smiled at my fifth-grade grammar. "In the beginning I came for those only. But to the professionals here, it's all one." What we were here for was theater. "Theater," I believe he said it three times hoping it would take. As it did. In the entr'acte, returned pridefully from going to the ladies' on my own, I found him with cigar case in hand— a shorter one for the cigarillos that were the quickies of that era. He fondled it but did not smoke. Instead offering the "house" itself, and all its floating cherubs, for my survey. "House is full," he said with baronial ease—and this time I did not quibble. He was saying that a theater is everybody's house.

That was the first time I saw him apart from the domestic and business worlds; it was not the last. Now and again, even when whelmed by family and a marriage he must have expected to be compliant rather than turbulent, he'd have moments when he seemed to be—not alone, but, in the old phrase, "collecting" himself.

But I choose that day in—was it the old Maxine Elliot, in which I saw him, without his anecdotal suggestion—as the inheritor of his own youth...No—manhood. Where once he had had a book of poetry, never shown even to me. Where, somehow, reared in that half-malleable, half-inflexible household of an antebellum South, itself emigrant from what educations unknown, he had those yearnings toward the empyrean of books, traces of which I can still track in the margins of those volumes left to me. And always cracker-barrel humorous.

When he took me to *A Woman of Bronze,* I was just emerging out of my own chrysalis, at that age no doubt visible to him. He had been giving me a taste for books, for theater, yes, in the "New York" way. But the theater keeps us in touch, yes. With what we cannot say.

———

"Values" is a touchstone word that, during my incarnation as a teacher, years ahead, I would come to avoid, thanks to the sleazy, too easy, well, *"values"* it was being made to serve. But there had never been any doubt that my father, both in his family role and his own conception, had been passing on to me those proper habits of conduct (derived maybe from Hebrew school and home, but not bound by religion), which he would have called "principles."

So now. So now comes the harrowing.

A harrow is a frame pulled across ploughed land to pulverize any remaining clods. That's what it would feel like. But now that the years have made me audience rather than participant, I see that we three—exemplary father, spoiled son, and priggish daughter—were a small version of those Greek dramas wherein the prongs of a family stressed in opposite directions pull the whole edifice down. Whether my mother's uneven but powerful role would have braked this, or been merely the lamenting chorus, cannot be known for sure. But we know her.

My guess is that her prejudices against her son, her fear of my father's "weaknesses" toward any family plea, as well as her constant, "Your father's not getting any younger," plus her own role as a German émigré in an American war, would have stopped the two in their tracks...As for me, untrustworthy though I was "in profile," since I had become a mother she had gone more female confessive. From amusement over certain neighbor women who'd sneered patriotically at her knitting German style, to worrying, once she knew she was dying, that Henry, emboldened by the beginner's job my father's company had got for him in that same perfume industry where he hoped to reflect his dad's image, would take over what was left of the family finances. Her own use of idiom again to the fore. "An ounce of money turns your brother into Big Ike. And he's always been able to wind your father around his little finger. Watch out."

Meanwhile, since her death, Henry, keeping his personal concerns outside the home site, and leaving his father to conduct his bachelor one, had been courting a girl not much approved. Not because she was Catholic; my uncle Aaron had married a Catholic and there had been other intermarriages since, including my own, at which time my father, taking me aside, had merely warned "Any marriage background may have differences. Religious background may add one more." But the parents of my brother's "intended" ran a "vulgar" bar-restaurant. She was handsome, but "not much for brain." Altogether no match for one of our family. "Ah, Daddy," I said. "Our family? Any girl marries Henry will have a handful. She has my sympathy." The harder truth being that now, several hundred miles away and into my own life and concerns, I saw my father, by then shorn of his business, his brothers, and returned from the job he had breezily taken on in his seventies, as still dependably head of himself.

As for the war—my husband would shortly be involved in it, though never as a conscript.

When the telephone calls me from my greenery, it is not a housemaid. Nor my brother. It is my father, tremulous: Henry fears he is going to be classified 1A for military service. He wants to claim non-eligibility, as my father's sole support. And wants me to promise to declare—in case the family situation is further probed, that I will not, or cannot, come to my father's support.

At my howl of rage, a drawn-out "Wha-at?" my father himself is speechless. Not just silent. My brother's not just asking me to deny the father I'm devoted to. He's asking me to ignore what no one of the family would ever deny another, even if the cousinship were obscure. We support.

Insofar as we were able—and even in rough times my father had somehow found himself able. He always had.

I speak into that silence. "Let Henry plead conscience. I have several objector friends who are. Activists for peace. Or against killing." I am sardonic.

"Have to have a prior record of that." How infinitely weary he sounds. Have they already tried that? Unlikely. My father has always had a sense of what my brother was not.

My brother has the most unremitting conscience. In service to his own ends. And knows well how to pursue. "Not to ask personally. How can he? Ask you. To ask me. To do that to you."

It comes to me now that to protect my brother at his own insistence is why my father, an eighty looking sixty, and in love with what he does, had suddenly retired. It comes to me that all his funds may well have been transferred to his son. Making him truly destitute. But I, the obstacle, am still here.

My father is a quoter. One of his favorites, "Oh what a tangled web we weave, when first we practice to deceive." Used on many occasions. When he excused defections he saw through. Or when my mother, not inviting to a dinner party the family leech, who would be asking for money, found him quietly instructing Josie that this cousin would be coming after all—and to set the extra plate.

To all of which, if posed now, the answer would be a heavy "Daughter—" addressed as so only in extremis, "I know."

We share an inability, he and I. Unable not to fill talk's gap. And silence likely makes us speak more.

"I know, I know," he says. "But he's making my life a misery. Nagging me to ask you. He's been at me night and day."

Then, in a voice as strangulated as if he's confessing his own sins: "Tantrums. Tears. To see to it that you—" It shakes. "You're to refuse."

In babyhood the son-and-heir's screams for more attention and more food than due were admired as lustihood, and rude health. Once he had grasped a rattle, even a grown man could not pry it from his fist. Once he was out of carriage, his brief spell of crawling empowered him to attach. People's ankles, clawed at, "what a fat little lobster," a guest said. Pulling a corner of the dining-table cloth toward him, what the table was laden with just barely saved. "Smart—" was the comment. "He'll know where the moola is, Joe. Look at that jaw." Fat and fine looking, yet as a toddler it was plain that he did not endear. Partly of course because he was given such rein.

We were still in the era when, in company, the good-mannered child tended not to speak until spoken to. And there were certain reports, of how our ever-hospitable dinner table could be disturbed by the small boy affixing his bottom to the polished floor, revolving on it, knees retreated, and screaming in three-quarter time. This was "a tantrum." The tears could be curiously large. The face turning purple and snotted. From all of which, if sweetmeat or toy demanded were proffered—or once even a woman's broad gold bracelet momentarily ceded—my "little brother," hiccuping with sobs but scrambling to his feet, would emerge. Gradually he was tamed enough for company and society, though the verdict of family and hangers-on remained: "Selfish to the core."

I kept my own verdict. Though I'd yearned some for siblings, he no longer interested me, as early on he would have done. Once or twice I did engage myself in teaching him words but found him sullen. After a while he was merely the younger-kid encumbrance common to many preteens like me. All along I had kept my own counsel. My father's idolatry of him did not disturb me. That fount of love was indeed endless, and if anything, my brother might justly resent that I had had it first. By my teens I saw that there was nothing much my brother and I would share, beyond the facts of birth. Barring that one moment at the bassinet's side, I was never to be jealous of him. But Mamie had made me well aware that this nobody would believe.

Grown, I could see that there yet had been reason to so prophesy. For from the day of baby's arrival, I was to be addressed as "sister." Miffed at first, I was to grow into the role of elder sister with some pride. Most of which had to do with the family image. Though when he was ill once with flu, I read him *Stalky & Company,* a favorite with him too—the name later by us awarded to a mutt he had brought home. Though my brother had intelligence—and even a way with language based on my father's pawky Southern anecdote—the fact that my superior school record and bookishness was taken for granted could not have pleased.

In later life he was not a reader. What he would imitate with all his heart was my father's role (long since historical and reduced to twinkly allusion), as a man-about-town, gourmet patron of notable restaurants. And of women. Though to my brother this would come post-marriage, when he, too, would be "on the road." For his second and equally-pursued role was that of the star salesman, at which, after my father's death, he would do well, if in the newer corporate executive style. In time, as the sales vice president of a perfume house, he would attain his own legend as an elaborately mannered imitation gentleman, rather like a blowup of his dapper parent, but effective with the lower orders of business, if faintly amusing to others—most importantly to those at the top of his French-owned firm.

In the years after my father's death, which I would ascribe to my brother's actions, I cut him off. As long as I remained the upstate housewife with nothing to offer, this suited him. He ignoring other family as well. But there are few, or perhaps by then, now none who spell our patronymic as we did, and when I made it into print, it had become embarrassing to him to admit that we were severed, and useful to him if he could flaunt a relationship. At the insistence of the very relative he had looked down upon (my mother's over here), a renewal of courtesies, not much more, was arranged. Token mutual house visits, after which, by his obvious wish he came to us alone. Now and again for dinner, or he would invite someone to meet us at one of his cocktail haunts, always fashionably Eastside.

By this time he could amuse us, as a ballooned imitation, though it was wise to be wary of the hard core of insatiable ego—he all the while oblivious that this was naked to most eyes.

As was his personal stinginess, though he was expense-account lavish. Though by the time he and his wife would live together in mutual hate, when asked why divorce wouldn't make life easier, he'd replied, "Not until I can *be* free and clear, with a million." Yet later, when even more must have been at stake, and she the offended party, unable to envision her receiving anything. While, when with his mistress, living in her house: "I can't tell you—," he would sigh with satisfaction, his custom-suit jacket swelling, "I even get my shirts ironed." My mother's same eyes, bulging but long-lashed, rolling upward...(Privately, we thought of him as hilarious, the way a self-enrobed character is in Molière.) Their one child, a Down syndrome young man, "adores" him, and though cared for since childhood by the state of New Jersey ("in the best circumstances," as was the case, but also virtually for free compared to private circumstance), was brought home at intervals for a home stay, when his father, to his credit, took him about, to the fancy restaurants...When he was brought to us—intelligence about age eight—which can be considerable, but packed in, unable to express. The mild sweetness, that many of that syndrome have. Dressed costly fashionable. But the teeth, the mouth of stumps, were a shock. "Couldn't you—a dentist?" I said, uncomfortably "social worker." "Oh, it's in the condition," he said. My brother was markedly evasive. But I was used to that. Only later did the social-worker guess come to the fore. Of course he couldn't admit ability to spend what might have been thousands. When the arrangement for the patient was permanent state care.

But the selfish inure you to their habits. Just as the generous do theirs. His father had earned so as to support others, except for his cigars. Any extra was saved by my mother, who was teased for her repeated plaint: "Little or nothing coming in. Everything going out."

My brother earned only for himself, in terms of the emotions as well. In the end, ego too crudely displayed would ruin him financially, and his reputation in his hallowed trade, as well. Leading him to ever-more fantastic "propositions," which rose grandiosely over the telephone, then unreportedly must have fizzled, being then replaced. He was always *too* in the high key of grandiosity. For sure, the best salesmen have to sell themselves first. With Mr. Oakley's heir, my father, the products themselves, dallying so lightly fin de siècle, had entranced—his lyric flights were by temperament an even more minor form of the poetry he had shelved. My brother's efforts were also parallel to his temperament, and curiously double. The product must remain superior, a prideful honesty there. But the selling game could be gleefully con—an endgame, with the results supreme.

All this, though only to devolve in full scale after my father's death, was already present in the son. Those many years later, when he wished to be friends with me again—and with my husband included—I would warn "There's danger in it. There always is, with Henry. In the end he'll always want something." And that would be true. Though by then we were impregnable...But I have run ahead. Out of wishing my father alive—and wishing my own guilt *away*.

Back then, still in his twenties, everything that he will be is already present. In action though, he is always the neophyte. Doing what comes naturally, each time, the only time. "Only do this for me." For "me," naturally. What is by every view of what "I" am threatened with, absolutely necessary.

Such egos give out a kind of smoke. My father, encased in that apartment, with that fierce, overbearing suppliant, will have been inhaling that smoke. Day after day. And what price that he pleads for an "order" not quite as honorable as of yore? He will save his son.

What's worse, in writing of this? Perhaps that in all tragedies built on a single display of hubris, all protest cannot but seem petty—in comparison. In fact—as the conqueror is sure to say afterward—only *"Krawall"*?

An old man's voice now, in my ear. He is eighty-one. But never before so old. Asking me not to repudiate him. With a word I hope never to catch. Was it: "Please."

I say, "I am coming down."

Which way have I answered?

Which way does he want me to?

My father loved a poker game. Weekend nights, away from the business gamble, a man's game, pointedly away from the women—and always the same players, with the same jokes, put out like stale candy from the week before. A sly atmosphere (genre pictures of card players are not for nothing) which the cigar-band girl, lingering until she was noticed, absorbed.

My father always lost. Since he was not a stupid man, this was perhaps related to his gentlemanly style at Oakley's? He was a sportsman, interested profoundly in the company he kept. Not in the stakes, which were neighborly, and small.

Watch carefully now. We are in at the death.

But what my father was never to display, even in extremis, was "a death wish." Losing money meant maybe too little to him, as my mother ceaselessly maintained.

But not—losing life. Are there those who, too aware of the world to believe in immortality, still hide a raging hope that life will go on?

While I am still shaken by that phone call, still brooding ir-resolute—What shall I do? What can I do?—my brother appears on our doorstep.

In that suburbia, his suit and tie brings the city in full force. My husband, at work as an engineer, is now head of "the foundry," and though still wearing suits, would not be so as for-mally. As Henry stands there, regarding with disdain the very pleasant white clapboard we live in, in its circle of high green, I feel his disdain. A city disdain, from those whom only city luxe would satisfy.

My little girl is up from her nap, and winningly so, but he literally brushes her aside. Perhaps she had connected him with our father, who had visited here. In whose laden pockets chil-dren were always invited to pry.

Out of my ever-present regret that she will be growing up without nearby family, is already doing so, I joke "This is my little brother, ducky. Your uncle Henry." But he comes at once to the point:

I see him standing on our front steps. To converse, not eager to come in, only to "put himself across"—the first proverb of salesmanship. My father had visited, but never he—it would not have occurred to either of us. In his eyes, bedazzled with the sight of the spoils now possible to him as a rising executive in a glamorous perfume-cosmetic firm—we were now miserably small-town, small-time.

"Fahthah's out of his mind," he says—in the lofty accent he would ever adopt for topics of importance—to him. "With worry."

We usually referred to my father as Daddy, though occasionally, in the way of business anecdote, Henry would name him lusciously, e.g., "Joe Calisher's known everywhere in the South." He's also prone to that other gambit—the repeat.

"Out of his mind. With worry."

"Over your going. That's natural. Nobody wants anybody to go to war." And we are pacifists. Though being female (in that wartime ahead in which the U.S. was an unlikely battleground and men would be "saving us") had made polemic for me impossible. So I, too, have my confusions. But those will wait, like so many of the imponderables.

"He can't live without what I bring in," he shouts. "He can't afford to."

"Please don't lift your voice," I say. "She's not used to it." As alas, at home we had been.

As his six-foot figure seems to loom, oddly thick and awkward on our horizon, I sense why. My husband is taller than he, rangier; I am almost five nine. But we, and others on our side of the family, have had other horizons. He has had only the one—the city boy—and shorn of any cultural interest or openness to others, its narrower version. Born too late to know our father's more than model love and reciprocal care for my uncles—and their joint if dutiful care for the aunts—Henry had not witnessed what a brother could be, and often was. I had regretted that once. When in the aura of girlfriends whose brothers, apart yet slangily available, swung with them in a kind of affectionate unity. Or in an even taken-for-granted difference, breezily mocked. He and I could not love each other; that I had acknowledged long since. But that I could not even like him did cause regret. College came most between us. Not because of education, rather, because it had equipped me with ideals I might be unable to handle, nevertheless there, dictating as well my choice of friends. Henry, as would become clearer, had no friends except in the way of business, and meanwhile, as his boasts exposed, all rated on a scale of worth.

Listening to his constant self-thrumming could be like watching an actor, amateur but still intrepidly Molièresque. Some of his poses were instantly recognizable, as belonging to the prototype he was bent on imitating. Where his father had in his youth been a patron of notable restaurants and still stipulated good food at home, but as one of the pleasures of the body that were our dower—he would have scoffed at the word "gourmet"—Henry was happy to be seen as one, often expatiating on dishes with which he wished to be identified.

After his father's death, Henry's imitation of his manners and speech became embarrassingly comic, even libelous. To any who had known both, it was like seeing the blurred later printing that had been pulled from the original. But not until my brother's death did I hear, chatting with the likable and smart woman who had been his last lover, that he had represented himself to her as having been born and reared in the South (and that all who did business with him had been told the same).

All of which could have been merely comic opera, as related by Sister Telltale. Except that, yes, he had come some hundred miles to make his demands—but will not step farther than my porch, it becomes clear—not until I ratify. After which, had I done so, we might have "closed the deal," with that collaborative air which admits to a third party being rooked. Though as far as I could tell, his hysteria was one of anticipation—and calculation. He had not yet been called up.

But when he was, he meant to be prepared. The army, the government—the world, if need be—were to be rooked, to meet the will of "the fat boy," as the family had dubbed him early on. He, born on the cusp of war, 1918, into that nest of my grandmother's brood, all of whom had borne only girls. He had lain in the bassinet like an heirloom egg, our family's only son-and-heir.

It was a heavy burden he bowed under. I could see that. Even I.

Standing there, a city boy, but enrobed in the strong-limbed physique of his Bavarian maternal forefathers, he was the first man—in how many generations on my father's side?—to be young enough to go to war.

He did give this ring of minor hills, in which he assumed I had chosen to live, one patronizing glance. He was wrong—in the way of married life then, it had chosen me. But now it comes to my rescue, that small green amphitheater. In its own way, that patient upstate greenery answers him. Before I have to.

"So—you won't give in," he says. "You let me come all this way for nothing."

That he had come absolutely unheralded is to be ignored. The self-pathos is endless. Copying even our father's sense of conversational drama—at high times in the family decisions. But neither he nor I see the mortal danger heritable to all. We were still too young for that.

"You asking me to say—to state—that I can't support Father? Or that I won't? On what grounds? That I'm either too poor? Or too mean?"

But the Henrys are never that kind of antagonist. Your logic is never theirs. So we spent the harsh words that always fill such gaps.

"Father's not out of his mind. You are." Me.

"If I have to leave, there'll be no money." He.

"Ah. You've seen to that, have you?" Me.

Silence. Whatever assets there remained—nothing from an Oakley long dissolved. Maybe the stocks my mother had painfully hoarded from her household allowance. Or the bank accounts, diminished certainly?

"Transferred?" I croak, horrified. Me.

"You gonna support him, you two? Down there?" He. That nasty voice knows we can't. Not at a New York rental, however modest for Riverside Drive. On an engineer's salary, however respectable.

My father might still have lived alone. In a sense he has been a bachelor all his life. Had there been money still—where had it gone?—I could have made the proper household arrangements, among the paid servitors—the black ones and the white younger Europeans, each of whom had over the years continued to visit the rental apartment they'd worked for and returned to, visiting again their own history.

"He can come here, Henry. He can always come here." My hand sweeps toward the house behind us. In fact, quite a pretty one, that white clapboard, on a small eminence. Not at all despisable.

I will never know the actual source of Henry's reply. On the day *Onkel* and his son, my mother's nephew, had fought, Henry must have been at the job my father had got for him at Bourjois, the subsidiary of Chanel. Though party to Oakley gossip as much as I, and like me shown off there throughout childhood, it was unlikely he had heard Ms. Eardley's account of my father and *Onkel's* confrontation. Or from family gossip, dripping through the family sieve.

My guess is that he had the account from my father himself. But in the peculiar trenches that so often divide what the body inherits, what the mind does—Henry was from the first flesh-bound to money-as-power. Revering his father, a merchant, though a lax one, for the very mannerisms that made him so?

Yet dead to the nineteenth-century sense of "honor," which occasionally made his father martinet. And bound to despise, as from the sneering power-world itself at the son's back, the droplet of bookish infection—defection?—bequeathed to me.

Or is what my brother is about to say common money talk on all the bourses, markets ancient and modern, that have ever been, and are likely to be?

An echo that is a statement, a statement that is an echo, its sources are not be analyzed. Yet are plain. Did it have little or no relevance to our situation—a father and his offspring? Or an embracing one?

"Why—I can buy you and sell you," my brother, Henry, said.

The call came soon, from New York. From "New York City," as "upstate" thinks of it.

Over the phone, an echo of an echo of an echo, though my father's voice is still strong. Indeed, though crumpling with hurt, sturdy enough to rebound from all the family walls, present and long gone.

Did my father want an ally, or a co-conspirator? He would not say.

"He's making my life a misery."

"Is he browbeating you? To make me give in. To do what I can't do, Daddy. I just can't." Yet over the distance, I can feel the torture on the other side. Each of my denials, refusals, a sharp fork in his side. That tailored pocket-side from which has come an immense largesse of love. Not only for me. For anyone, almost, who, swimming into his regard by whatever means, is owed a tithe.

Underneath that pocket, the paternal flesh a daughter rarely notes, except at the beach. To which, as I grew, my father had seldom accompanied us anymore. Though I could still summon, if I tried, a vision of a median man, well-muscled to a degree, the ripples of shoulder and arm flesh somehow matching his arcs of curly hair. A fan of prizefights, who yet took no exercise, nor ever had apparently, except in the bouts with the frizzies whose photos lay in our breakfront, lowest drawer. That legend he would have to his end. Like the curls. Or, as he sat, springy smart for an eighty-year-old, lifting the pant leg, two fingers at the knee, with that hitch one scarcely saw anymore except in his like, one glimpsed the ankle, sinewy, competent.

I understood now how one could fear Long-Distance—that easy coeval to my upbringing, by which he had kept ever present to us, ever caring, while "on the road." My own pride was now my burden. I have a housewife's image of it: powdered sugar, sprinkled on the military brass code of honor he had instilled on the first child, regardless of sex. As he would have done on any subsequent? Or had that long generational trail without male heirs irretrievably weakened the code?

Perhaps a son-and-heir, achieved after such history, and conceived of a father pushing sixty, must have his own apologia. For the father's sake, must I make such? Though the son is never known to apologize.

That call, not the first in the protracted sequence between my father and me, would it be the last? I have begun to fear so. The brusque "Miserable, he's making me miserable" seemed to alleviate. But he would not have me come down to New York.

"No, m'dear. And what would you do with the little dollin'?" There being by now a lack of the relatives who would have coped. In the natural order of things, we were not that kind of family anymore: large, dotted over a nearby landscape, standing to attention at the first bleat of need, and above all: alive.

After such a call, it had become a habit to sit awhile, clenched, interpreting over and over. No, it could not be. Or could it be? That the son was daring to make the father cower physically. I could not see it. Even with the memory of the small boy in his tantrums, I could not see the grown man raising his fists. Whatever he was, he would not do that. We had been too well raised. If in an absence of violence, then all to the good. "None of us," I whispered it to myself, alone now in the calm, provincial dark. For now my husband—employed by suppliers to the military, though his company, in the business of railway parts, would not bruit it—was often away.

Then came the call, after which I sat on, and sat, in the curious memory of an acquaintance, never much more than that, who for years hadn't come to mind. French by birth, a "substitute" teacher of that, she had a curiously instructive sigh. *"Enfin,"* she would breathe. *"Enfin."* Finally, I look up the word whose meaning I have known for most of my life...Yes, there it is, confirming. "Then." Few were surprised when she died young.

Certain memories, I ask myself, do they predict? My father and I had spoken last evening, with the same exchange. My brother is ever at him; yes, he is miserable, but, no, I should not come. We always spoke when my brother was at work. Or seeing "that girl." I no longer cautioned him on that, to advise, as I once had, that any such girl would have her hands full. If she would have him, a father should rejoice. I no longer cautioned this stalwart on anything, least of all on his son.

But saying *enfin, enfin* to myself as if turning a key, I go to the phone.

"Ah—at this hour?" my father says. As if expecting me. "But thank God, here you are."

There'd been a change. I know that—or heard it—at once.

"His number's come up?"

I hear the nod that I cannot see. And as if audient, that long French sigh from my own youth.

Suddenly, my father is counseling me. Humor always took him, under any clarion of adversity. Though later he might mumble grumble, as if to show himself distraught.

"We have thought of something," he says, almost gaily. "Or rather, I have...Your brother has your mother's feet, as you know. In fact, her father's whole physique. I never told you, the nephew, that Gerhard, had his picture once, from Switzerland. She would not look at it. But I saw."

I wait. There is such a pause then that I intervene. "And?"

"Ah. Sorry. We woolgather, you know. At my time of life." Customarily, he had never referred to his age. Leaving that to my mother, who did so constantly. "Ah, yes—the feet...I always thought your mother's were noble. Exactly resembling a drawing of a foot in a novel called *Trilby*. By one George Du Maurier."

"I know." If the long sigh I breathe is for the French for "And then," it will yet do. "You gave me it."

"Well, look at it again." He takes for granted that it will be on my shelf. Perhaps it is.

"Now?"

"No need," he says. "In any case, your mother's feet were what the army will no doubt find Henry's to be—and in its infinite wisdom will reject. As it has been doing, similarly."

"Ah."

Then at the same instant, we crow it.

"Flat."

Why that should cause hilarity, my mother could have advised.

Lighthearted, hoping for the same in him, I say, "Cheers," he ditto, and we hang up.

During the following days, cursing myself for not having asked when Henry was due at the draft board, I am unable to reach them, and hear nothing from them either. Finally, when I was about to search out a Mr. Caro—a younger "perfume man" once an avid admirer of my father, and other names slowly resuscitating, but for all I knew perhaps "gone ahead"—I heard.

"We were in Atlantic City," my father says. "Thought your brother could use a respite. Distance helps. Though not so far as he was at first inclined to go." That dry tone; it tells what it wants to.

"You mean—he wanted to flee?" I hear myself, skidding on that verb.

He sounds as he often had when returning from a trip that had had both its successes—the orders by the gross always touted, and other low spots never admitted. Tired, but jubilant, if only because the trip was over and done." I will sit," he sometimes said, "'and invite my soul.'" My mother liked to pun "And everyone else from the family."

"Called the manager of the Traymore," he says now. "Told him the circumstances." My father knew hotel managers all over the map. "Made me an offer we couldn't ignore. In fact—the Presidential Suite just the week before vacated." A chuckle. "By a quartet of Japanese wrestlers, they weigh six hundred or so? So we had it, while it underwent repair...Gave it to us for free. We didn't need that many chairs, you see." His voice was hoarse. The weariness has overtaken the jubilance.

"Invited that girl. Under my chaperonage. But the Farrells don't nearly trust us, I gather. She came down, but only for the day. In company with her brother. Nice-enough young chap. Not much Irish charm. But not too crude." Many of my father's long-term friends had been Irish. He knew whereof he spoke, I could hear it, in the "enough."

"Ah—," I said. "A brother." A proper one. This last not said. But we were always to hear what was in each other's voices, my dad and I. For that he has my gratitude. That knell, in all those filial poems, written or waiting to be, which "the pater," "le père," "Der Vater"—all those of every language, ashes, already scattered, bones, lying in the churchyard—are fated never to hear.

What's to be done.

Pay it out in filial philanthropy, if you've money enough: that hospital ward maybe, or feed-a-child social service; "Dedicated to," or "In loving memory of—"

...Or, patch, patch—you write this.

"Are you all right?" I say.

"Dunt esk," he says, quoting from a cartoon, read to me before I could read, which neither of us could now identify. "Or I might tell you."

"Tell me."

After a silence—is that him breathing, that susurrus?—he does. "Had a little accident at the Traymore. Must have fallen over a nonexistent chair. Came all over queer. And broke my glasses."

My father still wore that pince-nez. Clipped so tightly that the places where the nosepieces indented the high-bridged nose were ever inflamed. In all the time I knew him, those two lenses never dropped. Never broke. People in his day maybe wore the same lenses for thirty years—the eyes somehow managing.

"And Henry?"

"Asleep now." (He often slept late on his days off, nothing new in that.) Then came the sigh. One of the many that push aside the ruckus at the breakfast table, the slammed doors at dinner, quickly, into a family's past, but cannot forever hide. "But at least I got him back to town," my father said.

Takes me a minute. "Draft dodger" was a serious phrase then, not the apolitical hassle of later wars. Even the objectors of conscience teetered on a shaky platform, ceded them by a reluctant democracy. But saving your skin merely, at the expense of the rest, was a military offense. You went to jail.

How? I didn't want to hear. But again, he heard me.

"Told him I'd turn him in."

So this is to be a Southern story after all. If my father has his say? I saw my grandmother, giving birth while the town is under siege, gathering the others to her knees, sneaking the older two, Aaron and Nat, to Hebrew school as she could (in the old Bible there was Nat's certificate). Keeping the girls home for fear of what soldiers could do, braving the neighbors who knew or suspected her pro-Union sentiment? For in a war you answered, "Present," keeping your own conviction hard in the breast. Sliding the heavy portieres together against the cannonade, Awnt Nell at your side. Later the portieres came North, with a whole hegira of furnishings. And all the sentiments.

"When's his health exam?"

"It's been. When I got him home. Been in a pickle, if he hadn't gone to it. Had a hard time convincing him."

He's never had to do anything he didn't want to. But this I couldn't voice.

And what is the verdict. I wait.

"He's 1A."

So, the feet weren't flat enough. I have the feeling that my mother could have been glad.

"Heff's getting a furlough," I say. My then husband is known by the first syllable of his long Pennsylvania Dutch surname, just as his own father is. "Officers get these, too, I gather." All the engineers have been given officer status, though not so titled, or addressed. A raise in salary, however, and the title no doubt emerging for when or if, on board ship, on short local naval voyages not to be disclosed even to me, but obviously still local, an engineer were to be killed.

"I'll come down, then," I say. "I'll come alone."

Though my father cossets his "little dollin'," this time he does not protest.

From behind him, as it happens, I hear the angry shriek neither of us needs to identify. My mother's longtime cleaning woman, Frances, elegantly retired except for a weekly morning "to take care of Mr. Joe," has expressed her opinion, as she was often wont to. Henry, up from bed and in the bathroom showering, has found on the towel bar that is his, only one of bath size. My mother had never commanded her to do otherwise.

"He'll know I've been talking to you…Ah, here he is… Good God, boy. Put some clothes on." And this, too, was nothing new. His son never goes to the bathhouse—as too low-class for a young man cut out to someday patronize the best hotels. Meanwhile he strides the home halls in the buff, whether dripping or sated dry.

"'Lo," he says, adding my name. When he does that, so negligently familiar, it does induce a twinge of sisterhood. Aware though I am where he has got this ability. From the master namer, who could make the very syllables of yours a flattery.

Did he think I was reneging? Ready to agree? My mouth wanted to form: No. Not a shout. Slithered out between gritted teeth. But I could see the humbled figure standing behind him, as clear as if phone-sight, ever predicted, had been dropped on me—a technology of the heart.

Home had contracted twice since I was born. First, from that long-halled, indolently attached set of rooms in the Hampstead, to five rooms in a smaller building, wedged on the curving south side of 116th Street, just off the Drive. In a somewhat alarming but distinctive symmetry, the central window of its living room, opening in two crescents, had been almost circular, and though quickly curtained with some ingenuity on my mother's part, allowing us a glimpse of the river, and during my college years inspiring some of my Columbia boyfriends—the more musical ones—to stand below and whistle up.

A few years before my mother's last illness, we had moved around the corner, to the red-and-white brick building fronting the river, known as "Four Twenty-five." In those post-1929 days, and so mid-Depression, yet even before and after, one moved pretty much at one's wont within the terms of what one could afford, or else wanted to pay, for whatever ambitions accrued. Parents were closer-mouthed than now—or ours were. And in the "modern" way of offspring eternally, we were really not that much interested. The more so when one's bread-and-butter is never really threatened. Oakley & Co. had gone bust some years back, but quietly, a balloon losing air.

The keepers of the house are almost always instrumental in these moves. What fascinates me still is how a mother's ambition would have run in almost exact tandem with her fears. The new building, a stylish effort of Paterno Bros., who were known also for another one on Cabrini Boulevard, is impressive on its corner still. A revolving door allowed one the entrance and egress much needed during the Drive's severe winter winds. Behind it, a thick, large Oriental rug rippled toward the lifts. Often the more professorial tenants did use that word instead of "elevators." But though one had a sense of being cozened toward modernity combined with just enough luxe for a university neighborhood—that might not have been our case. It did occur to me that my mother had been apprehending not only the "moment"—as when grown children leave—but also her own widowhood.

For the new apartment, the last to be, was only a "three-and-a-half." So does the apartment dweller express what those who "roll over" their houses do—a signal to oneself, above all. That we know there's no permanent "going to Florida." Or to any of those flushed, hot-cheeked Rivieras for old bones. But by moving on, we will avoid the drag at the heels of what life itself extracts. That, by moving, eluding death the faster, we will leave it behind.

In both of the cities I will in time be resident, I would see this most of all in the rich. A clan house, too lordly in taste to bear, would go into trust, some worthy social cause for it being found—if solo, the money to museums, gardens preferred. Or in the corporate line, status picked up the house that lay ahead, scoffing off what it had lived in to those behind. Often in either case to find the same quart of cream you hadn't ordered before already on the front steps.

Strange, though. These three rooms—each the "size of a postage stamp," as my father had initially grumbled—should have fiercely humbled us. The clan, gone not just to death and taxes, but siphoned off from closeness in the way that *Amerika* had fast taught immigrants less stable than we, should have robbed us of all amplitude. All the finery of the city, from business vanity to the proper little gambles, theater, the racetrack, wardrobes shifted seasonally, eating well. And hospitality offered, if as duty, with a pleasurable largesse. Which lent what would never be paid back, or gave, and turning its private penny, evaded debt, almost to the end.

That clan, and all its fringe friends, those token aunts and uncles of my youth, could never be accommodated here. After the first few, there'd have been an impossible squeeze. I could see them, arriving unwarned, welcomed just as we had, those droppers-in from all over whom my father had seeded from his travels: "Be sure to—anytime you're in New York," and duly recalled, "Why, of course, you'd just been married, last time I was in Kokomo," and to our mother's ritual backstage squeal, "Dinner be about eight, but come early"—after which, hanging up the phone, he'd say, "They'll expect it, Hattie, people out there have a front porch. No sense to keep them dawdling over drinks, wondering." As she bestirred herself to comply—which they both knew she would do well—he would say, "Potluck.

Tackiest word in the English language. Going to do it—do it up right."

While from the kitchen door, still swinging, would come "Your father's Southern hospitality. Stretches from coast to coast." She always spoke of him to me as "your father." I wanting to counter, "Why not—your husband," but not daring. Not wanting to face her regrets. For these conventionally fake squabbles seemed now their warmest intimacy.

Meanwhile he, whose spirit soared with the prospect of company, would be pulling out a good bottle from its cold. Wine chests experimented with had been scrapped for a corner of the spare room, kept heatless, and facing north. Opposite, a hoard of Nick Carter paperbacks (among the first American detective stories, I would be told years later) spilled recklessly on the floor. He never referred to them, nor had I ever caught him reading them, though I had an inkling he must. Perhaps when prowling, in the dead of the night.

For if I knew anything for sure about him, I knew that somewhere in his core, and despite all his savagely embraced joys, my father was a homesick man. Once—that time he took me to see the old wooden hotel—I'd had the temerity to ask him that, carefully phrased, though he was a man of whom you could ask anything. "If you were ever homesick, what would it be for?"

He had reflected, much the same as he had paused in our nursery years, when choosing one last song to sing me to sleep with. Usually settling for one of the other of his two staples, "My Old Kentucky Home" or "Old (uh) Black (uh) Joe!" *Kaintucky* tripped lightly—that not being his real home. But that other one came out hoarse, with the high, talky wail of a man who couldn't sing a note.

Back at the hotel, or forward all the years later, he'd shaken his head over the question, brows raised. "Wa-al, suppose I'm homesick for all I've ever had, God bless it." Then a slapped knee. "And for all I h'ain't."

He'd never been one to use black dialect, except to our maid Mayry, over what they both obviously felt to be some common experience. In this high-ceilinged Northern hostelry it sounds homespun. We had left it at that.

Until that same night at the hotel, he taking me to the bar for the adult drink I by then rated—but ordering for me from the barkeep, Lorimer, from the old days. "Lorimer, this is my daughter—let's have a Dubonnet for both of us."

At home, his liquor protocol is stricter. One after-the-business-day Scotch, proffered also to any males, customers, or cronies who might have come home with him, after weathering the same storm. Sherry was stocked for the timid, his more general verdict being, "One before food, if you must; I don't favor fortified wine. More than that, it's for women drunks."

We'd no drunks in the family; until college and thereafter I had never seen a drunk. Now I was admiring both the tact that had ordered the same for both of us. As well as serving to introduce me—as he would my brother—to the art of the aperitif. While I am sipping, awed by the vast woodenness of this period American hotel, complete with a bartender named Lorimer, he says, musing, "Homesickness. We called it 'hankering.' Standing right in the middle of what we still had, you hankered after it. Account of we always knew we'd be leaving it."

I would never hear a better diagnosis of them all. Of what fretted at me and my brother, his inheritors, like one of those slight, fraudulent fevers that, lucky for me, a powerful intake of Northern air would always dispel.

In the "new" flat, the last one—any of the aunts, cousins, or even steady visitors, if crammed there, would have noticed at once that the view here was only a slant, from windows that if awnings had been proposed would not have known what to do with them. What is most missing in these three tight squares—the one-half obviously the bathroom—are the extras, that blithe aura of those, which we have touted all our lives. Here there is no extra anything.

Then how was it that the minute I walked in I felt at once the cobweb of family? Whistle-clean though Frances might be keeping it, I smelled at once the old cobwebs of habit and mood, clinging as devotionally as she.

When I was a child, and perhaps because for so long I was an only one, I had almost always been allowed "up," for the predinner family gatherings. Though relegated to early supper in the kitchen with Josie, I understand quite comfortably that dinner with the elders was not to be awarded until a young person had learned not only the sequences of cutlery, but also the polite usage of the tongue. Once or twice, sneaking into the hall from the kitchen as the serving went on—at a formal dinner party, say, when my mother proudly rated two in help, as one of those extras I myself overheard that conversational chamber music—the sallying, and the reining in. After which, coffee being brought to the other room, the guests following, I would be found there, already ensconced.

Thanks to an indulgent father, as my mother never failed to inform, I sat obediently quiet, in the to-and-fro of the tall personages overhead. Seeing how, as they bumped, they talked. Or exchanged seats, with a flourish, from sofa to love seat, armchair to mere chair—the piano bench being the lowest rung. Sooner or later, their host, seized perhaps by a newfound cousin, or that nervous brother-in-law who had been borrowing, would see their isolation and rescue them, extending her a courtly arm with a "Come out of the woods, m'dear," or equalizing him with an "Arnold, I want you to meet—"

I learned a lot, watching. Though I couldn't have phrased what I saw prime, in my head. How people in society are monologues, really. Bumping, they start up, like wind-up dolls. Or else stalk each other, strides intent. I liked the clumps of people particularly. Such a pretty sight, as the haircuts and the hairdos revolve. While the acoustic rains down, in syllables carefully not too much more than that. Though there's always the chance—or worry, in the best company, isn't there? That out of the patter, some too-forceful cogency will erupt.

My mother watched too. "How the Calishers do carry on," she'd say. Only the aunts referred to us so, both to themselves and all the paternal crew. My father never did; she had caught it from them. Once adding, to me, "How you Calishers do." A sign that she had given me up, if ruefully? I was too proud to hope.

The ride down to the city on the New York Central train was my Rhineland. Should the stranger sitting next to me start up at the tumbledown castle looming, I could whisper, "Bannerman's Castle—they say he never finished it," or nod when a patriot, waiting for a glint on the other side of the river, cried, "West Point?" Stops that were my private ones, bringing me home. A hankerer. No wonder there were so many names for it—*Heimweh. Nostalgie.*

This ride, I missed my little daughter, wishing her by my side in the natty gray plaid coatee, knickers, and poke hat I had scrimped to buy at Saks Fifth, after my mother had deplored the sloshy upstate snowsuit. In coatee and bonnet, she could vie with any of the Eastside nurslings around the Central Park carousel. Upstate it singled her out as already too distinct for her own comfort, which had been my case also; I worried that her peripatetic life was not knitting her in. Even among those provincials, soon to be met in first grade, whose mothers had already made clear to me "We are where we always have been."

She and I and her father are such a small triplicate in the industrial surge, not only of the war, but forever to be magnified by what wars do. Eventually its feverish metallic swell would uproot and scatter the old localities, whether of city or small town. Most "Americans" would have had no nativity except that. A virtue that could still preen itself, back then.

Reentering Four Twenty-five I must always feel the grip of my mother, almost as if I am the one vanished, and she retrieving me. We were said to resemble, as anyone new to our circle at once remarked of me, "A brunette version." If so, owed to city lights in family salons, and to how, under the pressure of the generations, focused on a good supper, the irregular may be mistaken for the composed. "In the face?" she would parry, in mock demur. "Not in the temperament," my father would joke. Under the riposte versus monologue, which was our salon conversation, the sly suggestion that my father, rumored to be part Spanish-Portuguese Sephardic, had the dark good looks that might be Sephardic, my mother, like her maternal cousin and closest friend, Millie, née Rosenberg, looked as if somewhere, in the dim kiosks of a Palatinate that antedated even ghettos, a Christian had raped.

My father was exceptionally proud of being a Jew—an "Israelite"; our whole tribe was, rather inordinately, if you considered the race's history. They had, that is, no sense of having been repressed or made to suffer for what they were. Rather, it was to be taken for granted that we were among the superior—in morals, intellect, and charm. This not out of arrogance—nor was one to act so. Rather, out of a humility that found the truth unavoidable. The word "among" was the important one, since he numbered so many friends among those not of the race—as befitted a traveler.

One is reminded that the literature a self-educated man reads is maybe spottily wide, not from curricula preconceived. In the classic alembic that fed the eighteenth- and nineteenth-century authors he seemed to have had access to, the role of the wise traveler, sometimes himself the narrator, was a hallowed one.

As for the blacks, for any white reared "down home" and in the severity of biblical ethic as well, their role could not help but be a double one. They were biddable entities to the extreme. Long thought of as (and kept) childlike, even the kindly might then accept their adult-bodied toil. Freed, they may still live in the Underground Railroad of themselves. Yet adoring your white children as royal—as he was adored. Beyond that, best to romanticize, in your turn. My father claimed to have once known an Abyssinian Jew "black as they come," who was a rabbi. Perhaps he had. Dr. Johnson's *Rasselas, Prince of Abyssinia* being one of his favorite books.

While all of life could be resolved with that humor which can both endear and salve? One of the anecdotes he loved was of the steady customer, who looked forward to being "called on" as to a celebration, buying and buying, so that the merry companionship might be prolonged, a mutual satisfaction that went on for years. One day, this man, speaking of another customer they both knew, called him "a goddamned Jew."

Everybody at our table would wait, knowing my father's reply. "Why, sir, I am a Jew." This was not credited, or accepted in that well-worn trail from bluster to fluster which those at table seemed to know all too well. "No, Joe, simply don't believe, can't believe…" I would think of that in Grosse Pointe, where our next-door neighbor, who went on wartime grocery-shopping forays with me like two birds of prey, both of us laughing over our civic responsibility to feed our children better than any of the lax richer folk around us. An older woman whose counsel would be keen as I listened big-eyed, she stopped once, midstream, to compliment me on my "lack of vulgarity." I was puzzled, until she elaborated. "You are an example to your race."

Dumbfounded, I found an anecdote to hand...So what had my father's customer said, Mrs. Bugbee, when finally convinced? "Okay, Joe. Okay. You may be a Jew. But you're not a goddamned one."

It's in the provinces, I find, that one had best be seen to worship formally. There will be social divisions, depending on which God is worshipped. Most Americans have swallowed democratic tolerance, if still disinclined to hobnob with those of "broader" views, much less in those days to marry them. But what will most condemn a newcomer is not to worship at all. There, too, the city can mask. But the devout may still have their necessary confusions. Perhaps I'll dare to tell my father—that once gay blade with whom a daughter wouldn't likely share such a joke, but who must so crave one—how an older neighbor, a strong Catholic, had confessed to me that if I "happened to go off to the kitchen" with her husband, she would trust me the more if I were known to go to a synagogue. It being sadly evident—if not quite to her—why she chose the kitchen. For there was where few of her female friends, agnostic or not, were likely to trust themselves with her jolly if light-fingered spouse.

But in the dusty train, whose sinuous path was like a narrative between my two lives (as a brash, self-concerned metropolitan grad gone to ground via what a shrewd friend had called "the three M's: marriage, maternity, and not much money"), I would have said that I had no time alone—though I was not yet self-valuing enough to complain of it. What I sensed but didn't phrase, and wouldn't until I had long since bootstrapped myself out of that well, was that many young women of my generation (like me schooled to the nth, then thrust into that home-all-day, which was the nether side of the "homemaker" the newspapers petted and patronized) would become monologuists. Who grew to recognize each other—and sometimes dared to shoulder-weep on each other. Which I could not bring myself to do.

Some of us would ultimately be served by this situation. We would search for jobs that would pay for home care, once the children were old enough (wondering how old is that?). Or would bury into the syndrome—if we'd gained perspective enough, to write speeches for politicos, say—as a friend had. Or if you were weird enough to keep thinking of trains as narrators, to lock oneself to the typewriter, and be a train. Or divorce the husband, either blamelessly by either one of you, as merely according to the impulses that flesh was heir to—or blaming him for standing by too idly complaisant to what was happening to you. As, trapped by circumstance, a husband to whom home-makers were synonymous with wives—he may well have been. Divorce came out of the blue for both.

But our little triplicate still had one more suburb to go through. In Rockland County, which called itself "the County," the social company would be much more sophisticate. Indeed, thanks to the nearby Rockland Hospital for mental patients, al-most any gathering would have its encapsulated psychiatrist, whether standing aloof in the pose that so often advertised what he was, or else that other type, chatting us up for free. Those like me, for instance. Women already done with being the best cook and bottle washer, and wandering (maybe with a talent still wrapped in its napkin) the wastes of too much unused in-tellectual time. Possibly this man's wife was one of those?

They had just had a little girl.

"Fathers make daughters," he'd said with pride still pardon-able. And almost too worn to be fashionable.

A woman in the crowd called out, not quite respectfully, "And who makes the sons?" Our own doctor said sourly "And who makes the psychiatrists?"

We all savored the rivalry. For that was also the generation of the psychiatrist, psychologist, explaining all except death away (you were not supposed to notice that). And some were perhaps working on that. But forgive them. They were not to know—in the second half of that century—that very soon the public, smacking its lips over the "psych" prefix, in the ever-yearning quest, would soon shift to the "phys–icist."

So I come now to write—what I cannot bear to. What—after dervish spinning subtly meant to delay:

What I must bear.

Joe Calisher was an early morning kitchen prowler, rising while everyone else was still abed, including the housemaid. There he would make coffee for himself...When still a toddler, I have begun to get up and follow him, as soon as heard. Silently, he would give me my orange juice. As a bachelor for so long, he knew how to provide for himself to a degree, but what he gave off those mornings was a strong and indeed traditional sense of the *pater familias,* there for us and the new day. My mother, actually responsible for the household, would, when she arrived later, bring domestic bustle with her, and its clucking concerns. But it was he who, meditating, but affectionate, say-ing little or nothing until the newspaper came, held us in the cup of his supportive hand. A kind of lesson, or message, that was absorbed, lasting until I was of an age for school. After that, one became the product of his household, sent forth in worry and pride, more or less fulfilled.

Now, though he is a spry eighty who could be taken to be in his sixties, he is beset. A monkey is on his back. Only it is my brother. Whose weight is not merely physical. One hundred seventy-five pounds, and, yes, of fraternity. Of calculation and hysteria, I wasn't under any delusion that I could "handle" it. I could only be what I was.

Nowadays, as I pass that building and its corner, I give thanks, never sardonically, that it survives. Two blocks on, 116th Street curves to the river, enclosing at its Broadway arc the college I went to, and with its terminus on the east side of the river, those university-owned buildings in which many acquaintances have lived, and beloved friends still at this time do. Should I be passing on north, to a meeting, say, not at all congruous with my youth, it will be also to the Heights, the neighborhood where I was born, and lived until I was fifteen. I have the nerve to thank the river as well, sending it my fond regrets that I no longer live on the banks of its hag-gray waters, under winter sunsets that flamed.

Farther north, at the Tappan Zee, say, it may at times be almost blue. Even at Schuylerville, New York, where it passes through, it is never cerulean. This I can swear to, having lived on or near each. Up there, the Hudson is barely a bay, a hoarded trickle one greets with the same smile one allots to the baby pictures of children now grown.

We pass that baby Hudson, on the way to and from what the real-estate sections like to call the "second" home, whose up-country innocence, posed against the baroque city, grows on one like the cap, purchased carelessly, that supercedes hats. White clapboard again, that siding which for so long has wrapped the East Coast in summer dreams of a cotton-wool past. Once it was the tidy but draftier substitute of those who couldn't afford brick—or hadn't inherited the ultimate ancestor—a house of old stone. Older than the Pittsford house by a hundred years, its four "eyebrow" windows, spaced at the top, tell you so; four fierce eyes, impossible to curtain, which never close. Which tell you that the hill above, its acreage, may still have bears. Seen not ten years ago—a mother and cubs. While the deer, once an amazing grace daring only to nibble the hedgerow, today stand in the yard, scatterable only by a shout from the front door. Yet up there, 180 miles from Manhattan, reminiscence is only as sharp as the tricorne pen point, wedged in its pen holder, that lies half hidden, in its painted-over slot, behind any keyboard brought to that old desk. The pen point would write as my father did, in high-angled swoops that sat like Victorian cornices on the square letters running below. But I no longer stock the ink for it.

Down home is my Manhattan, any of whose streets I could parse back then, listing by city zoology what breed might live or work where, and on what funds. Down there is Manhattan's river, ever sinuous in the heads of those born to it. An image ever craved, ever acceptable, windy, cloudy, rain-screened, or at the Seventy-ninth Street boat basin idling under a spritz of launches and sail. Once, battleships were to be seen on it. It still had a voice, though not much of one by day. At night, as I leaned on my windowsill, reading in my college Darwin of other animals, the foghorns yearned, from the docks farther downriver. Falling asleep, one heard them, cruise ships and cargo liners, their hoots clambering the night.

On that train, do I find myself looking forward to all that—in spite of my errand? This fills me with shame. So does the errand itself. To rescue a father from a son? That so generous a father could nurture so greedy a son; we had been warned of it. We had never been too haughty a family; the doors had always been wide. But at its center, some there for the handouts, we might have been thought so. I could hear the aunts, dead or alive, still chattering over the brother Joe, who had married too late a woman too young. Making themselves into parents who could not wield authority as a pair. Leaving neither in control. Look at the daughter: high marks in school right enough, but nothing's come of that—and now lost to the provinces. But hoity-toity still; she takes after Joe. Underneath, she's almost all Joe.

That was not true—though back then I might have joined them in thinking so. For can so unsuitably young a wife as my mother ever leave behind a respect earned? For her what could have been the commonality? For him what equilibrium? And she a foreigner as well, to meld here with a family—who said that? Must be a visitor. Whatever we were, we were not xeno-phobes. Which in *Amerika,* spelled whatever way, was or should be ridiculous.

...Yes, it's the "visitor"—a demi-cousin, German but reared in Britain, whom we were to see only once. England has some-how muddied her. Her khaki jacket and skirt smack of the mili-tary, but whether this indicates actual service, past or present, or mere allegiance, she doesn't define. Black hair, square-cut to those points at cheek which will forever mean 1920, and for her a coming of age about then, so, about forty? She was a most pe-culiar emissary. (Afterward, few could recall her name.)

Yet though half German, presumably on the mother's side, she was British born, and related to us. I, then in college, had de-tected "university" more in what she said than in speech. A relic of my great-grandfather, the first Calisher in England, she never said exactly how. But we already had a few such, long since res-idents—my father's first cousin Julius Curtis, his wife 'Rica, and their daughter Adelaide, at whose wedding I had been an eight-year-old flower girl. A jeweler, he had long taken care of the fam-ily's needs in that direction. 'Rica cooked fish in a profoundly sympathetic and tasty way that must come from an Albion surrounded by sea. Adelaide, a talented designer in her father's trade, still concerns me: what could have been her destiny? For, all through the wedding of this soft, pretty, but rather quenched girl, the tears ran down her face. "Why was she crying?" I'd whispered, when returned to my mother's side, but wasn't told.

The "visitor" had had the same flat-cheeked irony of discourse as our cousin Julius. He, tall, immensely dignified, always, even at home, in dark suits overweeningly respectable to me even then, and with a manner sidelong, had (I heard whispered) sometimes been challenged on the quality of what jewelry had been supplied. But, being a cousin, was not pursued. I have a ring that purports to be a canary diamond, a brown one and a white—that I shall never have valued, preferring the teasing doubt—and my own solution. For we had another British émigré in our midst about the same time.

A Mrs. Campbell, widow of one Bertie Campbell, she had become chummy with my mother, who seemed to admire her elegant wit. According to her, Bertie himself had once been in prison for forgery, but had later been pardoned (a case of mistaken identity) by the then governor of New York State.

No one ever mentioned that these Curtises and Campbells might once have been Calishers. Nor was I ever to hear, laid out and dissected, as with our Southerners, the very text and timbre of their relationship. Nor, like my father, would I ever pursue, thanks to the thrill of suspicion, wary but cherished, akin to the Nick Carters on the spare-room floor.

I think they were related, yes. Had they flitted toward us, as bees to the American honeypot? And flown off again, finding it less than half full? Even the Curtises, he a resident first cousin, never came to the house, much less became its habitués. Had all of them had a flighty, pragmatic approach to what one might name oneself? Almost in response, I detect now, to the in-grained respectable?

How bourgeois we must have seemed to them, with our constant bloodlettings of principle, ever fearful of dishonesty's illicit joys. They disappeared quickly and competently. Criminals do so. I could not wish my brother to be that.

But, fearing the heavy scene to come, I could wish that he (in his dodging, his hope to cheat the world, and willingness to deny his father comfort) could have been merely what they had been, debonair and sly, hoping to take their cut of *Amerika* without fanfare. Cons?

And this "cousin" has us in perspective. "How you do manage, Hetti," she said, addressing my mother as if they two are alone. That was the way the Germans said my mother's name "in *Englisch*," but now the vowel has swerved to "British." "Admirable." She levels a khaki squint at the rest of us. "In such a crowd of—syllables."

I know now that our family hours, when we had been merely "in syllable," had been among our tenderest—being in a crowd. While in the plea that came often from either parent: "Don't make a scene"—one could have considered them as joined.

In the train, that plea keeps sounding in my ear. In a staged drama, the "scene" is always shorter than the long preamble leading up to it. As in the last act.

I found my father alone. As I had planned. But this afternoon Henry is not at work. Even in the "misery" my father's embrace has just now conveyed, his cheek has that amused twist common to all on the paternal side. "He's gone to give his girl the ring."

"But—he's been dragging his feet on that. For years."

"Mmm."

My father hadn't fostered that delay. Rather, he'd done just as he had on my own marriage plans. Stating his views once, he had from then on "stayed out of it." Though to me saying now, "Too cheap to? I did lecture him."

"My brother finds it hard to spend money. Except on himself."

I seldom had expressed myself that sororally. Or not to him.

"I gave him the ring," he said. "Your mother's."

"His wife-to-be should be pleased." As my mother had been. A Tiffany stone of good but not overwhelming size, set high on its recognizable gold prongs. "Your father has good taste," she would say of it.

"Helen deserves it." I like Helen. Not much of a brain, but "black Irish" good looks. And strong will. Maybe would surprise but perhaps balance him? Though outsiders could be too psychological about other peoples' marriages. I could hazard what some would think of mine—especially so since I was in part becoming an outsider here.

While my father and I make a meal together, I regret for him that his two children are such outsiders to each other. By then I had seen some of the happy founts of spirit that could bubble between "insider" family members, even at a funeral of one totally loved. If the gathered mourners were insiders all?

"Maybe we should have gone to a restaurant?" I say.

What a lifelong patron he had been. For him, the habit of eating at table, in strange but observed company, under the solicitous etiquette of waiters neither toady nor smarmy, but who recognized an expertise the minute the menu was offered—all that could cheer.

"No, Henry and I go to restaurants a lot. It's the one thing we share."

That was an admission. Grudged.

—And who pays?—

Once, I could have said that.

A joke—between family clowns.

As for what my father has said to me at countless partings in the past, "You all right for money?"…Impossible as the gesture that had followed: embodied in the envelope, not waiting for answer, slipped like tact into wherever it could slide.

"No, m'dear. Thought I'd wait in for him."

At the small size of what he now depended on, my heart twinges, but doesn't break. There being worse ahead for which to hold firm.

In the silence he says, "Any more things of your mother's here you could want?"

A head shake from me.

One from him. "Cleaned us out, didn't they."

That had been the shock. The greed with which the women: aunts, cousins, even Millie, had hung over my mother's sacrosanct mahogany dresser drawers, to whose elegantly neat secrets even I had been a latecomer, if a finally invited one. "Not much here," a sister-in-law had grunted—giving me the stare.

Or how they had pawed at her garments, pretending to fondle. Annoyed even, "Her style was beyond ours," one said, lifting the nose. Though one—not even related—did bury the nose in a pile of lawn handkerchiefs and raising her head, wet-eyed, used one.

"I was shocked. Suppose it showed. But I couldn't believe."

"Happens," he grunted. "Saw it when your grandmother died. Came like blackbirds. One of my own sisters. Picked at that sunburst given Maw years back. Said, 'Nah, Joe, admired that ever since. Was it for her eightieth, you?…Eight old-fashioned single-cuts in a circle; Maw wore it like a badge…You wouldn't begrudge a woman that, would you now?'" He chuckled. "'Not at all, sister,'" I said. "'Only I've got the woman picked…' Not that your mother ever wore it."

Nor would I. It's for a fichu. But I will treasure it.

My father and I are at the "side table," once in the living room of the old apartment, where it had been his habit to pilot a crony for a private drink, when a gathering was at its height. "Arnold and I have something to hash over," he'd say. Though the family might well suspect what it was. Or on the midday of a dinner party to come, when the dining room was off-limits, and passed with a head shake. "Set for a banquet, Hattie, m'dear," he would whisper. Then to me, "Let's you and I have a bite alfresco," and sneaking into the kitchen, he would bring snacks back there. I knew early what that phrase meant: Dining in the open air. And a tease, since we had no balcony, nor "terrace" as those oddly useless eruptions on the newer apartment houses were now being called. Nor should we want one. "Fancy a rocking chair on one of those. Or wash hung."

A secret had long ago filtered to me, the way such does to children "with big ears." Early on, in my grandmother's day, he, or he and his brothers, had bought a brownstone, itself apartments, and had bought wrong. Eastside, but "too far up" and the neighborhood "getting run-down," it had never been occupied by us. Whispered of down the years until it must have been disposed of, it and its tenants—how to treat them decently but firmly?—had weighed on him; he was no landlord. What he must have wanted was to give Berthe Bendan the backyard she merited.

So are we again in an imagined outdoors? I have brought specialities he favors, and urged him to bring out a bottle of wine from the one or two I know he will have stashed. Somehow.

It's not Mouquin's for sure, legendary to me. Nor even that much later—Longchamp's was it?—to which he had taken my mother and me, sending back a dish—to her hushed, protesting, "Joe. Joe," and his later apologizing, "Couldn't help it, Hattie. The place was a farce."

I, too, had been learning what the land of Somehow meant. Felt good to share. Felt good—to love.

Now that he has at last mentioned my mother, I can too. The dead did not disappear for him. But death itself was a topic he would not—could not?—face. Any obit that emerged during family gossip—they had all known so many people in common—he would drop one bowing snort, and move fast away. Was it because to my mother he had been "not getting any younger?" Or that he had for so long been, except for "poor Beppie"—the youngest son?

Now, rather, I think of him as a charitable wizard, eager to keep everybody dear to him alive—who grew out of temper at any mention of a miracle he could not perform.

"I have things of hers that mean her when you first knew her," I say. "About four pair, it must be, of long white-kid opera gloves, and the opera glasses. And her wedding handkerchief. She had it tucked in with Granma's—can you believe it?"

What endeared was how much those wedding trifles resembled each other. Sheer lawn, microscopically embroidered, surely by those nuns that went blind in the service of brides, net-bordered to the same width; were they a testimony? To "the inheritance of acquired characteristic." We'd had no swords, dirks, or daggers to show, as far as I knew. Yet the one had sailed alone to a strange country, in time nursing me to femininity maybe, with nine months of mother's milk. That other, owning an opinion counter to, even traitor to the state in which she lived, and to its War, had got by because she was a woman. I could see her standing by her convictions as she had stood by her trunks. What she had brought me was the salt-and-pepper-haired gentleman across the table, who was being bullied to ask me the one thing I could not give.

"Your grandmother came to think the world of your mother," he said. "Expect she gave her a token of it." But I could see he was uneasy. "What's taking your brother so long," he said, pulling out the watch on the chain. Deriding often those who hung too many mementos on those chains, "Did it myself when I got my first watch," he would add. "But don't look for me ever to wear time on a wrist."

So we wait. For the scene that will be unconscionably short. Which is why I have described us—and him—in such painful detail. The torsions of this family of four have a hard simplicity, too easily recognizable, also as what the Greeks had words for. A family group whose destiny is inevitable? The pity, if it is to come, must arch toward the spectators as the single, sad unity come of all the small actions, tender to brutal, that presage a— destiny.

My father loved kippers. Not the kind with tomato sauce, which according to him was a travesty on what a good kipper should be. This repeated like an adage. Idly I knew—maybe from novels?—that the British had a taste for them. These were the moments when I might well have asked more about old muttonchops, from why he had come, when emigrated, to how far along the road to New York, the actual residence here, he had survived. Perhaps because he remained such a blank in the welter of all the Southern detail I was always eager for (only an occasional "Paw" linked him to the general picture), I never thought to press. Nor as to whether they (who and which exactly?) had left because of lack of money? Or in order to escape from that beaten-down postwar city, left draped in its old prides and the fine manners I had a scatty glimpse of. Or more likely, from the energy they'd shown here: that they—we—had often had to move on, so knew best how. What I had taken in, more or less instinctually, was that, though certainly not wealthy, there had never been any mention of poverty or severe stress. We always had seemed to settle in.

If I assumed, though never told, that my father had brought them up here, delivered them, it was because, an elder statesman now, in all the family memorabilia verbal and pictorial, he had so clearly been the young prince. With an addendum? As scions of an old-young marriage, though he had been the next-to-last child, and I the first, I came to see that we, my father and I, shared a quality I did not phrase but sensed. It was a kind of obligation. To be special goods as marked? In persons like us there was certainly more "old" (in one) than usually. Not wisdom of itself, but a more than ordinary witness of it? As instilled in a physique that by contrast could seem, even to its owner, intemperately, even viciously: young. In my own blasts of temper I sometimes felt that. Or of tears. Or—in the curious way that caused a prescient "kissing cousin" to call me "you little old lady," a mantle-over-mantle of a benevolence, certainly not mine.

My brother had the physique. Intelligence that had—perhaps shrewdly?—refused "higher education." A roar of selfhood that one ounce of objectivity could have made admirable. A politesse that charms as *bal masque* does, and as suddenly drops, almost juvenilely, unaware that onlookers cannot help but spot the shift.

All this was merely what could remind even me of Molière? With one exception. A lack that did not appear to cripple its possessor. When my mother had her operation, he did not even visit her in hospital, alleging work, then queasily admitting, "I neglect." But when she came home, still bedridden, he refused to enter her bedroom. She understood why sooner than we.

"It's the idea of the breast cut off. It repels. He's washing his hands of me." Later, my father, vainly urging him in, says, gritting his teeth, "He admits it. Faugh. He admits so easily."

When she was dying she said to me, "Watch out for your father. Henry will do him in, if he feels the need. He'll abandon him."

During the years when I was already safely away, and still open to pop psychology, I thought I'd diagnose my brother, those scenes where he'd kept our parents alternately at bay, in thrall. A psychopathic personality—unable to connect?—only not in toto? Of course I was wrong. Smooth in business, sugary in society or unwittingly boastful, he reacted as intensely to people as an actor to an audience. Tailoring his responses ever to his own needs. Curiously, whether he saw others' needs and ignored or did not see was moot. Whatever it was, even in his rages, it can make him seem oddly automaton.

The absence of pity is of all human conduct the hardest to diagnose. Especially when so absolute.

Our father was eating kipper from the tin I had brought, one of our mother's large linen napkins meanwhile on his lap. Some dating back to her trousseau, thin and monogrammed with ghostly initials, others sturdier, acquired later, they hung on, tokens of that era to which he had most belonged. Now and then he had teased our mother by tying one round his neck, saying, when she forbade us to imitate "Only acceptable for lobster, in this puny time." Describing how once you could see whole tables of men bibbed for a banquet, the napkins not always hiding the paunch. With now and then "that Chauncey Depew" turning up for every public dinner on the calendar, "slips my mind what else he did"—or even a Teddy Roosevelt, rising to speechify.

While I clear away I wish for one or any of the anecdotes that flowed through our days like the advises on a hymnal, and at mealtimes particularly. A rhythm counseling us that a meal was not to be snatched but taken in loving memory of those meals past, and with a lively shiver for the expected, whatever it would be. We never said grace beforehand. He was saying it, we were, while we ate.

But now, that anxious swallowing in the wizened throat the stiff collars no longer fit. The annotation is up to me.

"That banquet menu you saved, still in the silver drawer." In the six-foot-long sideboard, mottled marble top and brass handles clanking, that my mother had wedged in even here, as she had all the gloomy, imperial pieces in any place we had ever lived. A talent mandated at marriage when all such had been turned over to them. That I was acquiring too well? *I shall have to fight for my own all my life—but I'm not sorry.*

"What courses you had…Six or eight. A fish entrée, then meat. Ices in between. A savory. To say nothing of the Frenchy bit at the start. And the desserts—with names like songs. Gondoliers' songs. Maraschino…Or Pêche Melba."

Now he will sigh—as once, when I had discovered a libretto saved as well: "Nellie Melba." But he does not.

Try again. "I always wondered, did you eat it all? Or choose? How did you manage it all?"

The mustache is not the double-flourish, as pictured then. Or the slimmed one, still pointy-ended, that I first knew. But it can still lift. "The wine list was as extensive."

I smile back. Then we fall silent. Nothing's been said about what we are waiting for. Nor do I dare. We don't know—quite. Only for whom.

After a while he takes out his watch from the vest pocket that houses it. From waiting out hide-and-seek, breathless in the clothes closet, I know those. "I used to count up all the pockets in your suit jackets. I still suffer from pocket envy."

I've made him laugh. The eyes water. But he stares at the watch. Far back in the annals is the one time I saw him cry.

"Funny how this place— It's still the old place."

"It's your grandmother's furniture does it. Every time."

Together we number it: the three-piece suite: love seat, armless side chair, and a barrel-framed freak that except for its central carved shield holds only air. All our objects always give us the once-over, as if they are the onlookers. I'm used to it...May they give me strength. Who knows from where?

"Henry know I was coming?"

He does.

"Heard your call. After that last session I had with him. Wasn't long after, he asked for the ring." He gets up slowly. "Looked high, wide, and handsome as he left. Maybe that'll take care of it."

"What do you mean?"

"Wants to marry her within the month." His nostrils flare. "No doubt with your mother's wedding ring." The handkerchief, drawn from somewhere, is like the napkins, larger than most—one of the birthday gift half-dozens that aunts and others give to the benefactor who—what else can we give?—has everything.

"Of course, of course—," I say, but don't finish. The war isn't taking married men. Or not yet. So she's the ace in the hole.

"Excuse me dollin'." On the way to the bathroom, he blows his nose. Or so it seems, until he blots his eyes.

He leaves a modest scent behind; where does he get it these days? Pinaud's Lilac Vegetal. Plus a jaunty hint of Baume Ben-Gay, for the rheumatiz.

No, it isn't just the furniture.

Twenty minutes or so later, when he's just coming out of the bathroom, there are loud knocks, hoarse yells at the door. "Forgot his key I expect. Does it all the time."

He's holding on to the doorknob, the other hand at his chest. "Have these little episodes. Happens when I'm on the throne." He blinks a joke to me. "God didn't make the right connections?...Went to that doctor round the corner yesterday. Not much of a one, seemed like. But he's near...Go let Henry in."

"Daddy, sit down."

"No, feels better standing up."

When my brother bursts in, red-faced, inarticulate, my father has braced himself against the wall to meet the rage we know so well.

"You—," my brother snarls, brushing past me. "Come to see the works?"

Confronting my father, he stands tall. Long, heavy Germanic bones, not easily knocked down. Above, my mother's smooth, fair cheeks, her large-eyed almost-green glance. Since last we met he has brush-cut his hair. A noble figure, one might well think—if passed on the street. No buttons or insignia on that navy pullover and slacks, but with that knapsack he hoists (this former wallet-and-gloves man) the effect is indeed military. With those high-colored cheeks especially so.

For a fleeting moment I do see my brother as noble, if in reverse. A petty officer, bred to standards he cannot bring himself to serve. That he will make enormous effort to evade...The view from here will be aslant, yes. But anytime one enters now, a crowd is at the riverbank. Gawking at the Hudson and at what is proudly riding the waves there. Small waves that slop at what's anchored, but not likely to linger. A navy battleship.

Henry slams into a chair at the side table. Mooning there, half slumped. During the six years between us, by when he was born an era had slipped on. I am from its fraying border, where it was the elders who sat, the young men who stood, holding their newly initialed barber's mugs—in each new shaver that mix of love-and-fear which the dainty-tongued had labeled "respect."

While their women, old and young, sat or stood, crouched or kneeled, without much thought except for the task at hand. Maybe Western with misgiving, some, yet somnolent. Under the great, arching, still Oriental shield that protected them. In exchange for their remaining what they were.

Three talkers, waiting now. The father of all anecdotes, his story-infested girl and equally adored son—whose fingers will be too glib to hold his treasure. All of us silent. Two of us wishing my mother were here. To say something sharp or silly enough to break a triangle. Though she cannot always be trusted to, even from the grave.

"She won't have me," my brother says at last. "Not on my terms."

"Ahhh?" A hopeful breath. Terms. Orders. A businessman knows that route. "And yours, son? Still as was?"

"To announce now, yeah. To marry in a month, two at the outside. Wars don't wait."

Ah no, Henry. I was a 1911 baby. You were a 1918 one. It's the wars that wait for us, every time.

"Should think she'd see that," our father says. Reaching for the umbrella stand, closer for comfort than it used to be now that there's no hallway, he takes out his briar-head. Once it was a dandy's cane; now if "the rheumatiz" gongs too hard, he'll use it to stomp with, if only in the house. "She's a gal looks ahead, I'll say that for her."

He'd done better than that. Said more, and very politely. I teased him once, remarking on how former rakes when mellowed do take the woman's part. I getting a twinkle for it.

"Her family's got to her. They say I'm a—an opportunist."

"Ah. Purt fancy language. For the owners an Irish bar."

"Heff was in there once," I say. "When his ship docked here. Though he didn't tell me where the ship had been until weeks afterward; he's that gung ho." Stupid of me, that last. I get off it, quick. "He says the bar's very nice. Not all that much Mother Machree. Horsey, some. But no Irish Sweeps tickets ever at your elbow."

My father guffaws. "Here the Irish don't buy them. I do." He stares at the head of the craggly briar as if it's duty is to tell fortunes. "Mebbe, Henry—can you work on the family?"

"Not a chance. They insist she wait for a year. Ten months at the outset. So their stinking constituency won't think there was anything wrong."

The cane is stomped. "Hold your tongue—I won't have that. Your aunt Jo, your uncle Aaron's wife, is Catholic. Your mother's bosom friend in the old apartment, Mrs. McManus. And a goodly portion of those who used to come there." His voice falters on that, then hardens. "Not to say that potentate—and one of the finest, most loyal friends ever—Geoghan, who in the midst of dying wasn't too busy to help me get you a job."

"She's solid with them, Dad. Her family. And there was nothing wrong." A shrug then, a half smile. "She's never let me come near."

"Glad to hear it," he grunts. "Way it should be. Way it was with your mother and me. And, yes, should be." He cocks a grin at me, a party long since to the frizzy beauties in the breakfront's bottom drawer. "At least when you're going to marry the lady."

...How sure he was of me. That—woman though I was—we both knew what to revere and yet when to joke. I marvel at that surety between us—even yet...

"Pity, son. 'Spect you'll have to oblige. Never that safe to bargain with the frail sex." He seems amused.

"And take my licks? What do you mean: 'oblige'?"

"Licks?" He has stiffened. It's one of his words. *So take your licks, hon*—when a teacher misreading eagerness for sass had marked a paper, "Deserves an A. But a B will maybe teach you not to go beyond."...Or, "Hattie. Have to take our licks on that," on the relatives' borrowing.

"When you nagged for that ring, Henry. Thought I kind of knew what you were up to. But only so far. Didn't like it. But I overlooked. Never occurred to me you meant to go bargaining."

"She wasn't too hot for the damn ring. Maybe even queered the deal. 'Oh pretty,' she said. But kind of giving me the razz. Wanting me to put cash down for one of those knockers she can show the other girls, I wouldn't wonder." He takes out the Gucci wallet bought along with a jacket from there, when he was sure of the job. Removes from it a small tan drawstringed pouch I recognize—when she went to the beach, say, it used to house the ring, safe in the sacred drawer. My brother flings it on the table Frances keeps very shiny, from which it slides to the floor.

I bend to pick it up. My father intercedes, his foot against mine. "Lout. Lucky your mother's not here to see." Bending, he scoops up the pouch reverently. Using the cane to hoist himself, he rests on it, chin near its seamed head, breathing heavily.

"Ha—" comes from the table's other side. "She'd throw me to the dogs like the rest of you. Was a sucker for a uniform. Like Missus Gung-Ho here."

"Heff doesn't wear a uniform—if that's what you mean. Though he's in as much danger as men who do." For a sec I feel like those women who gave slackers the white feather—but push on to what has enraged me. "And don't you dare include Daddy, who'd give his life—" I leave that quick...For you, if he could.

"Who says?" comes sullenly. "Had to be at him for days, before he would agree to call to ask you."

I could see it. I had. "At him. Like a dog— No, not like a dog. They have a clue as to what people are."

My father has bowed his head. At the sight, my big mouth opens wide. "Buy the ring for her, Henry, why don't you? Have a second try. As you say—you can buy and sell."

The head lifts. "He said that to you? Well, watch out. My case, it was shutting the barn door." *After the horses are gone*—an old idiom of his.

"He have the bankbooks?" Always a couple of them, visible in the chifforobe, top left-hand drawer. Bank branch not far on Broadway. And the pleaders held out for cash. He even had a story about one of them saying to him, "Checks are so depressing, Joe." Cash or check, there'd be no chance my mother wouldn't catch on.

My father gave me the business glance. On the question of money, women—family women—never catch on. Not to the business game. Or not in our family?

(Not so. Only that they had no place, couldn't take part in the game. So did it behind the men's backs.)

I think I know what's coming. "You mean—there's little or no money left in them?"

"I still do the shopping," my father says. "Your brother pays the rent; it's only fair and square. And so he'll have the checks to show. Just in case."

And the dwindled bankbooks as well. I'd bet on it. But I cannot say. That humiliated salt-and-pepper, curly crop drooping now, trusts me not to.

After my mother died, my father gave me the key to the safe-deposit, "Here's the key to the vault. Your mother always took care of it. Things in it, jewelry stuff—belong to you." He grins. "And the Confederate money." He was giving my brother power of attorney in exchange. "Nothing much left, but it's a son's right. He'p Henry out in his firm, 'case they hear of it. Can't do otherwise." He means the Oakley name.

He was "giving in" to his own nature, as we both knew. In his, there was such a shrunken safety net, between giving—and giving in. But when you are shopping for others? "What else can you do?" was his favorite phrase.

I see him on our Saturday afternoons, coming in loaded down from a grocery deli spree. Upgrading us on all the luxuries—and oddities my mother might not buy. But always in a mix of wing-collar taste and plebe, all the way to the out-of-season vegetables. "Celeriac, Hattie, Hawaiian pineapple, Georgia peach. Case of French Vichy—last they had." Hearts of celery, plump white-and-yellow, that the crude Texas stalks of inedible green string would one day supplant. Maybe a crock of whatever, for which he would pronounce the French name.

After which, placing a tin of kippers on a radiator if it was winter, he would wait guilefully for the fishy fume, and my mother's customary shriek.

We've had humor. No smoking-car jokes, though well into his first third of the century of Lindbergh and Amelia Earhart, most traveling men still went by train. Even Henry here has his merchant-style josh, carefully traded.

Reminding me of the one taste father and son truly share— hovering over us three there, in invisible blue puff.

Henry will have been also bequeathed the "about-town" habits as to women, which his generation will dilute to a "yen." Also the clothes, though only briefly near-dandy, and quickly subdued to corporate. He doesn't really invest, either in people or in the bright wild of "the salad days," as that other era had worded it. Even as a married man, financially he will cautiously risk only what's close to the nose. He does have the impeccable aura owed to not seeing the rest.

"He keeps me in cigars," my father says.

"Havanas"—Henry's chin lifts to the cigar box on its meager shelf. Two individual cases of bomb-shaped silver metal. Perfectos. The Garcia Vegas I had been sent for on occasion were sold at the stationery store. "And what do you do for him, my own sister?"

I am confused. I can't say. I know I do something. But what?

"Except dig in," he now adds, with the lofty mien—and tone—that our father here used to dub "high coachman," as usual not defining where that came from. "Except to keep house. On that wee-wee-size salary Heff must get...And crab."

"Here, here. Don't talk to your sister like that."

"Well, what's she gonna do for me?"

"I'll go to the draft board," I say. "I'll tell them he needs your—your care. That he shouldn't live alone." Not that he couldn't, even now. I know his resilience—and his shopper's faith in the good things of life. He still has friends, to whom his son is abjectly deferent if they are powerful, rudely off-putting if they are not... "I'll testify that I—we—can't afford to keep him down here. What I won't say—" Here I choke, because I have to speak of my father as "he" in front of him. "What I won't say is that I can't take him in, if it comes to that. He'd not have a bad time up there with us. He's a cracker-barrel guy; they'll love him up there. And so will we."

That's not the point, and I know it. Sunk—as we say. When you hear yourself—floundering.

"Love, yah. What he's asking you to do is to save my life."

I look my father in the eye, or try to. What I can't ask is— "Are you? Asking that? That I'm to say, 'I won't take you.'" He won't look at me. Which must mean that he is asking.

His son speaks for him. "Family feeling. You haven't an ounce of it."

Here's where I begin to play the prig—that will in the end damage as much as he. "Shouldn't plead that, I were you. Knowing what their feeling is."

My father half covers his face with one hand. Leaning on the cane with the other.

"Does fahthah have to go down on his knees to you?" the brotherly voice is holy. The acolyte, invoking God the father. To save a son.

No. Nor you. To whom on your knees to save your neck would mean nothing. "I don't mind lying to the government," I falter. "It's not that. But you're asking me to deny that I can feed my father." Who would manage to feed us, were he near destitute. Who has kept his whole brood going, ne'er-do-wells included, when often himself on the edge. "I can't stomach that."

My brother starts a low keening. The most peculiar sound from a grown man. As if the child who began its tantrums that way is harbored inside, ready to swell.

My father, cane clutched, is staring into a distance, where maybe my brother and I merge? Is he seeing how the family feeling he has taught me has finally come to roost? Mourning that this fine allegiance to "honor"—which he will now cede— cannot be persuaded to his other dollin'?

A guttural blurts from him. His free hand presses against his chest. "Call that doctor."

We do, we do. One of us hacking out the number, but frozen. One of us to the phone.

He comes on the double. My father, head sawing, has refused to sit. The doctor's ear is at his chest. "Make coffee—," the doctor says. He is truly the doctor around the corner, having forgotten his "bag." In those days brought to a house call.

And there is no coffee in the house. This pair goes out for it.

My father solves all our dilemmas, the cane slipping to the floor.

We are at the death.

Sixty and more years on, I wonder still whether my acquiescence in what he asked would have saved him, for what I know full well would have been his choice. Hurly-burly or no—to live out his time.

Fathers make daughters.

A safe-deposit vault can be such a consoling place to come to, whenever you are a bit *ein bisschen* broody, over what you may have done with your life. Especially if you were once the sixteen-year-old girl immigrant who came to this city alone, driven by the stepmother wind blowing from owning nothing of value except your dead mother's snake ring—a worn circlet of gold with a turquoise dot of eye that never stops looking at you; she died at your birth.

On the voyage across the ocean, in what you will forever after deny was "steerage," a few of the old biddies aboard did clap their hands in awe at the sight of the long braided rope of chestnut-colored hair that hung down your back, they advising squinty-eyed that such a marvel of natural growth would be in high demand for the manufacture of false fronts; she could market it. But though that girl would come to crave ornament her own purse would not supply, nor the good *Tante* would think to provide, she has never parted with the braid. Now and then she has a look at it, lying as it does next to some of the glittery ornament marriage has brought her for free. Or in the way that needed romance had?

It's at such times, perhaps, that you go "to the safe-deposit," not to take anything out. To look at what more you have. Guarded there in one of the two long metal boxes provided are those husbandly gifts, some dating from the wedding day, some from when you yourself gave birth, that are too valuable to be merely kept at home.

The visit, however, is cherished for itself. Your home is chockablock with visitors, daily ones, ever crowding in, and, by the way, ever estimating you in your role there. Suave glances, elbowing each other, or greedily negligent, so as to concentrate on the meal a visit will impel. Yet your performance has won them over to the degree that their affections, once-and-forever fiercely localized, can permit. What they do appreciate is your "style"—which is not limited to dress, though there you do well. A kind of modest, tight-jawed assurance, hard to define? Better so. But now and then they agree, even aloud: "Hattie has backbone."

At age fifteen—a banner year for me as alertness goes—I listen scornfully, half willing to go along. In the articulation of our skeletons—this not entirely known to me—where would such a bone be? Where is it, in mine?

Meanwhile, for me, today is what people call "a very special day," a phrase that, when pointed at me in token of what I am to be newly allowed, I have begun to loathe. All days are special for me. I may never forgive the word itself, for constantly demanding emphasis.

Yet this day—whose position in the week, whether out of school or holiday, is lost to me—will be ever blazoned otherwise. For we are standing in front of the building that houses our hoard. I am at her side, for my introductory visit there. We are not boastfully dressed for it. Shoppers merely, stopping by. Yet as she stands there, looking taller than she is, thanks to the leftover slim waistline and the long jacket and ankle-length skirt. In this year of the above-the-knee flapper skirt, and the ever-tan stockings, in which women's legs old or young look like chicken legs cooling in broth, she's what she likely always will be: appropriate. To her station as matron and mother, and to our mission. Topped by a matching hat that, however proper, brings out the great, wary eyes.

The building has its name lettered on it, flat and discreet as the facade.

"Here it is," she says. "The Morgan Guaranty." On her lips a brief song. Though a limp one to me, uneasy at what we are approaching. Inside there are the worldly things, guaranteed. While inside me, growing slowly, stiff and vertical as a sword might be if carried internally, is the fearful but sometimes brash push toward a vocation. Which I intend to be as unworldly as possible.

When about to finish high school I had confessed as much to my father—to me the apostle of words. "I think I might want to do poems someday. Like you once let on you did. Or else maybe just words—in a line straight out." I could see those henchmen, marching rough-and-tumble, waiting to be curbed in. But I already know this would mean being unworldly. And that could be dangerous. I was being apologetic. I knew how worldly he had had to be.

"That's all right," he'd said, patting my cheek. "So long as people still invite you to lunch."

My mother's motives in taking me there were blent from impulses so long harbored as to become a single one. But children learn early to decode contradictions that lie like knives scattered on a deceptively warm hearth. Countered by the unity that glows over all? Yes, that too.

When she and I were ushered in, I under her duennaship, I hadn't had to sign in. But as the two men in charge here rose from behind the reception desk and extended her—as if to an honored patron on their roster—the book where one did so, I began to understand how the roots of all possession were here. And the risks. Even to there being two men in charge. When ushered in we stood with them before the bank's wall of boxes, I watched how the set of keys was produced and handled in a kind of back-and forth double dance, then for a second held high before being plunged into the identified lock, as if to demonstrate that what might be inside had no connection to them, nor ever had. There were two long metal boxes in their cell. She indicated only one. Then, as the two held this trove high, trundling it and us toward one of a line of small cubicles, then laid it on the small table before which rested two chairs, and left us to our secrets, noiselessly closing the door, I first felt how, in such a bank, one's self is also deposited.

Though the impress might be for life, a single visit doesn't take long. When, years on, I took up the duty of examining the second box, I would do it in installments, grief weighing heavier than the contents alone. So not discovering—or even passing over?—the secret that lay there?

That first time, what the Morgan Guaranty had offered—or seemed to offer a snotty trainee—lay right on top. At fifteen, I was too young to much envy the glittery tributes as each jewel was displayed, and the occasion disclosed. The dainty wedding-day lavalier, that to me lay on its white satin like a butterfly embalmed. The square ring awarded at my birth, a diamonded square whose central stone had maybe imposed on me both a love of deep blue beyond any other color and a distaste for the word "sapphire." Or the brilliant bar pin that had so appositely heralded my brother's advent in 1918, the first male since "poor Beppie" in perhaps 1865. Was it even possible that their designer, that Adelaide who had wept at her own wedding, had had each piece layered to suit her personal bias, for the journeyman jeweler to pincer in and seal? To the end that for me diamonds would never express love, merely attitudes. Though as I watch that high-pronged solitaire engagement ring hover over each, hearing meanwhile the litany of what was in store for me, I fore-saw that her pattern would not be mine. For, watching the ringed hand at the end brushing that frilly bill for the lobster-and-champagne reception, held "at the house of Mr. & Mrs. Sig-mund Adler, on August ninth, 1910," I was old enough to see what else had been rendered her. All her satisfactions lay here, to be visited. Plus all her regrets, neatly boxed.

The second long metal box would prove to be an excava-tion. Dutiful, it felt more like an interment, at my elbow those commentators who wished to have say. I am going through my father's life in reverse. Almost all of it on paper? No surprise. So much of him has been, even to the crushed hotel stationery that tumbled routinely from a suitcase whenever it and he came back—he having used such to wrap his shoes (and the gifts).

In the top layer of this metal box, Oakley's demise...Below this, notable correspondence from its history, some directed to him, or on him personally...A file from the Hundred Years Club confirming the date that the business had been founded, and a neighborly letter from a Mr. Fenno (possibly a co-member) attesting to that date.

Nothing on my mother; she was documented elsewhere. As were my brother and me, all our data, schools, and other achievements being already in brown folders in the chifforobe. Nothing on my grandmother, who had been at home for long. Just the death notices of his brothers, my uncles. No trinkets. Those, a hodgepodge, also in that upper-left-hand cubby, that I had been allowed to finger and hear about, had disappeared: the portrait of Aaron Burr, slightly larger than locket size, and once part of a collection. Various small *objets* not considered good enough for "the curio cabinet," this a Verny-Martin, wedding present from his real bachelor roommate, that long-ago Louis Housselle. In the cabinet, the conventional preciosities of a belle epoque circa 1900 taste: Japanese ivories, little Meissen statuettes. There, too, lies the solo memento that I can attach to Richmond, and the only one he ever remarked on as valuable: that snuffbox, "Very early, made from a black walnut," pewter lined, with a retractable lid that a fingernail can lift. The curved nut fitting so comfortably in the palm has another name, identified but not these days printable—though I will vow to do so, before this account ends.

Nothing from that New Orleans youth once indited in books as J. Henri or later verbalized to me, in pidgin French. I want not to see any of it, really. Viewing my mother's box had been more natural—so much of the femininity that women pass on, or enjoy with their pals. She and I were never to be that. Though I had once been told (never by her, but by a college friend who sat next to her in the audience at a college play I had a star role in) that she was proud of my achievements there, it had long been plain that she was jealous of the books that absorbed me, that aligned me with my father—and in her German convention might keep me from being properly marriageable? Yet I was introduced to her box at her behest.

Now, opening the second box, I face a mood that whelms me. I know I am looking at a life that must have had an inner self-consciousness well past hers. He had expected his business life-to-be, and had enjoyed it to the full. One never had the sense that he felt he'd failed himself. But there was a half-intellectual life that he himself had not probed—and she did not share. Of which I was the symbol? If so, what would remain most remarkable to me was his mild but obvious assumption that women's capacities were equal to men's.

He has not, for instance, ever shown disappointment that I, both the elder child and sympathetic to interests he had quelled, had not been a son. He seemed to take it for granted that women were as powerfully endowed. Son himself of a matriarch, as he had been, with elder sisters who were "pretty sharp" and like so many Southern women of their time could have been more when the times caught up with them—well, I thought I saw why. Even why he could seem to a degree "bossed" by them. But even his passionate statement as we left my grandmother's deathbed hadn't yet sunk in...

What I was doing, whether mayhem or mere sneakery, must be incumbent on all legatees.

So, when it was due for my brother and me to meet with a lawyer and "get it over with"—well, that was a sentiment for once joint. The lawyer, Herbert Zelenko, though young, seemed unduly aware of how the two of us might vie, and relieved that I did not. No, I didn't want to trail the bank deposits, or other funds. I would be happy to take the furniture, though some would have to be stored—even though my brother had long since got rid of the ancestral sideboard, an eight-foot marble-topped affair whose many drawer handles still clanked in childhood's ear—along with a vision of my father, bent for the evening sherry, that has lasted. "Gave it to the superintendent," Henry said. I saw that Zelenko was not surprised at what might be a usual division between such siblings. But over one item he did disapprove. My father had apparently lent my half uncle and his son a sum toward their starting a business. Not much—a few thousand, for which there was a proper IOU. Any payment thereof would go to my brother. "Let it go?" Zelenko suggested, to him.

When Henry turned red in the face, it would often be because some attitude he had just expressed was being scorned. This he apparently knew and seemed to enjoy. "No—," he said. "Damn well not. We'll go after them."

Whether they did or not was between him and Zelenko.

But might have explained why "we" never heard again from the debtors. Or why I had not. They would take it that pursuit came from us both.

The papers were easily and swiftly divided. My brother wanted the Oakley ones, as pertinent to the trade he was now up-and-coming in, and fascinated by. Even at the famous firm he was now with, it must bring him some reclame.

I took the personals—not much. As tokens and some letters to him showed, this life had celebrated talk. Had heard Mark Twain speak, yes, gone to brass-knuckled prizefights, had stage-doored and opera-ed—sometimes all in a week. A few small fat envelopes of clippings showing family anniversaries and a few interviews with him at 18 East Seventeenth, a small hoard to investigate later. One larger envelope, half opened, spilling out that oddly pastel currency—Confederate. A few of those bills had been in the chifforobe and we had been allowed to handle it, but had been forbidden to call it "play money," as once overheard. "Your grandfather bought a lot of it."

"Play money," my brother said.

When I asked about "the Aaron Burr," as we had called it: "I think Father sold it." I had no reason to disbelieve. He might want value, but not that kind.

There had been a silver case once, cigarette size, had a girl painted on the front, leaning forward, chin in hand, her tutu upflung, the kicked-up back leg showing above. Turn it over it showed the pretty bare behind. My father had had a fit when, early on, asking to see the fascinating Burr (we had a book about Burr's duel), I'd accidentally seen the other.

Once later, I pried, but it had disappeared. It had never seemed to me in any way lewd, but rather a delightful token—not a symbol—of the lighthearted era where a theater had been named "The Gaiety," where a woman's backside, prettily framed

as in a valentine, had been worthy enough to be painted on silver, as a fond joke without thought of insult—while her head
might be paid its own tribute. An era in which, suspended by affection, I had lived for a time.

In a mute epilogue to that death, I cut my brother off entirely.
Not hard to do; we had never been close. In the welcome absence of protest or word from him, I took it that he was more
than willing to comply. Post-1948, however, when stories by
me began to be published—in the *New Yorker*—family stories
among those, I was told, oddly enough by *Tante* and Cousin
Millie, the very "goodies" whose distaste for him had been re-
ciprocated, that he wished for rapprochement.

   "People in the business ask him, is he related to that Calisher
who writes," *Tante* says. "It embarrasses him, to have to let on
you two don't meet." Millie, an innocent, whom I occasionally
saw now and then as family, meanwhile nodding sagely. Such
publication, never mentioned by either of us, had recently been
welcomed by her with more than open arms: "Why did you
never say you were on television?"—a greeting that I wished I
could have laughed over with my mother in her own vocabulary, saying to her perhaps, "It did tickle me. Getting from Millie what's really the public pulse."

   And where had they picked up this gossip? "The Germans."

   My great-aunt still lived in Yorkville, but many of those had
removed to the Westside, including Riverside Drive, where my
brother and Helen, married, with whatever wedding band, now
resided. "She brings the little boy to play," *Tante* said. "He's not
quite right."

   I recall expostulating, "Oh, come on. Gossip can be really
mean." But nodding deep, she had described what must be a
Down syndrome child. She has confirmed, as only "family" can,

what I could not allow myself to feel singly—that life had caught up with Henry in its own way. "Same age your vunderful boy," *Tante* said. Yet she remains in my sight as the calm angel of goodness she truly was, pulled from behind by convention's strings. My mother comments further: "They see what they see, people like *Tante*. They can't help driving it in."

My brother's visit to us turned out hilarious. We lived now in Rockland County, in a riverfront house, at core an eighteenth-century inn, whose added-on Victorian wings backed on an acre of hill. Bought from the writer Edmund Fuller, who had first recognized my work, and had approached us when he and his wife wanted to move on, it hadn't cost us much—merely what it had cost them.

Henry arrived with a bland air of having "paved the way"— a phrase suddenly shot at me from the business talk overheard at my father's poker games. Further, as he estimates the house, its site, and its neighbors, I see we have risen enough to be worthy of his esteem. For he is now sales vice president of Chanel, and what he wants—ah, here it comes—is to take advantage of my "ability with words." Shortly he is to deliver his first speech to the gathered sales force and company officials. Would I listen— and critique? All of us welcome, in fact. It was a Sunday, "everybody," including the two children, then nearing teenage, and their father, were home.

As the "uncle" new to them took up his stance center living room, their eyes widened. Many of our neighbors on the river were in the word trades: actors, writers, ad men, plus painters and others in "the arts" who were slaphappy with speech *au naturel*. At our cocktail parties the kids, quietly helping to serve, were hangers-on to a sophistication more dégagé than they might get at their very good schools.

The speech is a beaut. Larded with every cliché known to

the corporate, delivered with slow, lordly gesture, in a kind of elevated croon. As it progresses, the speaker raising his right hand each time he declares, "...And I say-ay to-oo you-ou, gentlemen—," the kids, sitting on the floor, slowly edge under the piano, hands clapped to belly and mouth, convulsed.

When it is over their father rescues us. "A classic, Henry. A classic of its kind."

At dinner Henry says, "I wish Daddy could have heard." I keep quiet. I will be sad forever that he hadn't survived to know his grandson, my son—and that my son (unlike my daughter briefly) wouldn't know him. But this I couldn't say. For my brother's attitude toward his flawed heir is impressively open, accepting—as, he has informed me, Helen's is not. In fact Douglas has been sent away. Henry's report of Helen generally now patronizes her limitations. I felt a need to interpolate: "Of course—at home, she'd bear the brunt of it."

In any case the boy was in a New Jersey facility—where he had proper surveillance with others of his kind. "Public?" The answer isn't quite forthcoming. "Quasi. I was lucky. Otherwise the costs would have drained."

I knew of those costs, and could not blame—even a man who, having achieved his "million," preferred to suffer an end-lessly complained-of relationship because divorce would force him to share. But his description of Douglas remained tenderly idyllic. "I bring him to New York, buy him the best clothes, we go to restaurants. He loves his daddy to phone." And tinctured with the old Henry: "He adores me." Yet I have to admire the evident affection, even if tinctured with the old line. Suddenly blurred when I see "the boy," long invited, brought for a visit to his auntie. "Say hello to your auntie, Douglas."

A young man about the age of my college-instructor son, he is of limited intelligence, yes—but wildly eager to express what at every point is instead expressed for him, he addressed persistently as a child. I know of some like him who were these days given jobs they could perform, and stretched to them. This "boy," permanently juvenile, was yet, in a weird resemblance to his father's status with our father—also the apple of his father's eye. Yet, elegantly clothed as he was—one horrifying departure. His teeth were still a jagged, pitiful line in his mouth. As they left I couldn't help asking again why no dental repair, the answer the same magniloquent: "It's the condition."

"But how does he eat?" The answer: "He manages. Don't you, Douglas?"

I will always retain a conviction, not medically feasible, yet hovering, though I am not ever to see this "boy" again. Surely not average for his age, nor ever to be so, he has more intelligence than is credited him. But lacks the very bodily cells, the somatic ones clustering at normal palate and brain—that would allow him to express?

As he and his daddy leave, he turns. Are the weak shoulders almost squaring to military? The jagged pumpkin mouth attempting a smile? "I . . . a . . . age." Manage.

I know then, that in the pity whelming me, my brother is at last included.

"We'll keep in touch."

We do. Mostly by phone. At intervals longer than with most so related. At least so for those elders among whom we two were reared. For whom "siblings" would have been a word either unknown, or repellently chill—or mirthfully anthropological.

Long since, with a new marriage, I had become a city person again. The one I was born to be. He was the same. That much we could share, though little else. Perhaps a taste for notable buildings? He and Helen come a couple of times to our eccentric one. We go once to theirs—both our spouses less nervous than we. Was it a kind of "high tea," Broadway style, as proper to the Drive, a block or so north of its end at Seventy-second Street?

Again I admire his wife, not only for her looks, but for her apparent immunity to the way he keeps muttering instruction on the serving to her: a running accompaniment he cannot possibly think we don't hear? We do hear as well that he addresses her, or refers to her—in her presence, exactly as he does in her absences—as: "my bride." Her face does not change.

After this they come to us once or twice, then no more. Lack of mutual interest we could sustain. But not the spectacle of how each is keeping up a curious front. All considered, an oddly similar one. For in company, my brother and his wife are clearly moved to demonstrate that they are imperturbable to one another. Each absolutely unmoved, despite little hints and flicks, by anything the other might say.

A "front" often becomes the person. But here it's a tango. Hands clasped on the coming "million or so," as they slide and dip.

When next, and for the last time, my brother comes to ask my help—and my husband's as well—he is reluctant. The savvy man with him—a friend, a lawyer—has been trying to convince him of a horrible truth. That "to all intents and purposes," Henry's company, using the nudges it hopes he will recognize, is trying to force him out. Unable to convince Henry, this man has suggested a second opinion, at last agreed upon. So who would he trust, on such a confidential matter?

It's us. Saddest, that it should be only us who are available. But he will have admitted, even to himself—which doesn't often occur—that we know him well. This time, though, he's not here merely to consult an elder sister. My husband has earned his respect because he earns everybody's. But also because, though in the arts, or worse, an academic, he also heads a corporation, if a nonprofit one.

I am resolved to hold my tongue, whatever. Not because it's sharp. Because Henry's endlessly immaculate command of cliché makes me respond, on the double, in kind. Except in my mind, which will comment more austerely throughout?

Henry, entering, is "the picture of health." And well-being. His business suit fits too well not to be noticed, but is as usual so subtly a darkish gray compromise that one can at once excuse. Only his mouth has a foolish, trembly smile, his voice, as he greets, almost a giggle. He has had a look at the monster, and almost believes.

This—company. For which, since he was eighteen—he is now near sixty—he has been its proudest musketeer. A French company, down to its founders' very gaiters, those still perhaps in storage. Yet though much urged by me and others, he has never learned French. His reply—with right middle finger crossed over forefinger so raised and shaken between him and urger: "Pierre Veal and I"—the current company owner, and demigod, Weil—"are like this." They even meet and talk and presumably lunch, every time "Veal" comes from France. "Every time."

Why the two men are here is now put forward. The lawyer-friend is convinced that Henry is being eased out. His office suddenly downgraded, secretaries not always available. "The classic routine," the other man says. It always surprises me that American business, or any, has "classic" anything—but when our opinion is solicited—yes, he's being eased out.

That naïveté, which must come of power too fatally limited, or long enjoyed—in recent years it's come on so strong. It can be winsome—as the only charm he doesn't consciously exert, I can never forgive him for instigating the miserable death of a good man whose portion should have been to die encircled by love returned. But I know as well that as a brother he has been the vehicle—and in this instance the cause—of self-criticism an elder sister might not otherwise embark on, openly or privately. Or consciously see? For over the years I had tucked away in my secret arsenal of failed obligations, or worse—hidden crimes— the fling-hard fact that by refusing to collaborate with his hoked-up story, I had collaborated—helped to cause—my father's death. My father had schooled me in honor and in principles— both of which he in fact, during Prohibition, must have had temptations not to satisfy.

In fact I knew of one. During Prohibition, gangsters had approached him, he having a large license for alcohol for perfume use. Sneak it to them and they would pay a fine price, meanwhile helping him to cook his books. He refused—this medium-sized man, describing with glee the way the big hunks had oozed in, gawking with awe at the frilly merchandise.

Far as I knew, he had always acted so. But never with the outward rigor—or vanity?—that I now saw myself to have displayed. It was even likely that as audient to a cock-and-bull fancy, I had been the booby, the outside naïf—obsessed with her position in the front row. For it was more than likely any decent draft board might have seen through my brother's airily stupid concoction at once—or gone on to verify. All the way to my bower of clapboard and green. Plus an "ironing room" functioning now and again as a spare, and pleasantly vacant enough for a grandfatherly dream.

My father had schooled me on "truth" in the simplest way, by exemplifying it. But his male manners, briskly dismissive of the little social prevarications of his nest of womenfolk, had confused me—though he, forever generous, would have found a lighter word for that state.

I see him even yet, his right fist on a cane, his left palm on his heart. He is about to fall.

I say to him: "The best testimony of my love would have been—to lie for you."

"Ah, dollin'—," he has time to gasp, "the sight of death does rattle one, yes...Call to mind how the sight of your grandmother's rattled me?"

Ah yes. But that was "before."

Closing that family account book once again, I think of how many times it has served me, fed me. The festival old South, drawn and demi-quartered by the smart-aleck North, with the usual excuse for such accounts: "It's mine." Suitable only for sofa conversation? Or, if the *auteur* (college French for "anybody") insists: sufficiently layered, scabbed, and congealed—to be History.

So it is. I do so declare. But why "so pale (and fondly) loitering"? We all know the process. "Laundered" will maybe do. Family accounts, evasively tender, telling "all" in jerky overrun. Skittish on the agonized detail.

There, it's done. For *what* people. (that is a statement, not a question).

Yet there's an image I would add. A doubled one. That black disc, rimmed effulgent. The fiery one, risked when we stare straight into our sun.

What lack we here?

A waw.

Not just any war would do. Nor should one have to go looking. Best is a war endemic to what you've started with. "You people."

In the War Between the States, our family had slipped through generationally. Had our grandfather, himself too old, had sons of draft or volunteer age, he might have indicated commitment by buying a substitute—for a son, either unwilling or commanded not to serve. Or excusably embroiled in some industrial activity that took precedence. There were no formal clues to my grandfather's sentiments. But in that listed business address: "S. 17th, between Main & Franklin," his situation—in the capital of a Confederacy that had declared for slavery—was clear enough for any descendant to see.

A merchant must keep his sentiments to himself. In the memorializing chatter of my aunts and their allied company of visitors, I heard none of the traitorous "Union" opinion I had hoped to find. Rather, come of a high school that had required four years of Latin pursued through the sixth book of Virgil, I fancied I could hear in their fond reiteration Virgil's first line purring low: *Arma virumque cano.* I sing of war. Indeed Virginian and Virgilian came to float in my ear equivocally: evincing opinions of such serene self-importance that they seem to issue in their own grammar.

Yet hadn't I heard somewhere that quite a lot of Virginians had been Unionists? When I'd dared query this in that company, such heresy had been, as the cliché swings, "roundly denied." My father, turned from that circle to offer neutrality in an *harrumph,* if with a funny smile. "Never try to argue with your aunts," he had once said in some other context. "Israelites we might be, but they were finished off at that Academy of Saint Joseph, where the nuns could high-tone like Jesuits."

So I could only hope—or trust—that as a self-educated man, he had spied out what they had not.

The Morgan Guaranty suddenly contributed. As if per my mother's adage, "Money speaks," I received a notice that the rental time for the box would shortly be up and continuance would not be renewed. Contents to be evicted after a certain date, the bank not thereafter responsible.

Had we done something wrong? Libelous, or worse: innocently harbored there, but traced by the FBI? Or could old paper thickly confined turn combustible?

On my way to the bank, I half expected to see that honorable receptacle in shambles, birth certificates in particle, the single stock certificate my mother had left us—one share of U.S. Steel Preferred (for which the company had been years nagging us to cash in) now streaming with watery ink. It had amused me not to cash. Tempted to reply: "No. A matter of sentiment." So far, they had not compelled.

Stand at the eastern end of the Rockefeller Center skating rink, gaze west and slightly north. The bank's modestly flat facade was an anomaly. Were there faintly carved letters above? If so, they were what a branch was permitting itself. Otherwise, a bank for persons who would conceal their august social standing, whatever the financial one, rather than flaunt an elegance not really "Midtown." "In" from Oyster Bay perhaps, "up" from Aiken, or from Scottish or Canadian golf?...Or perhaps here was where all the quieter portfolios were enfisted, by managers who knew one's name. Such was the mien. One knew better of course.

Inside, the lift, escorting all incomers for the boxes one flight down, had for years been run by a pleasant Irish woman, her throat and mouth so gashed by surgery that she could smile only with her eyes. In this valiant silence one descended, as if to a sequestered corner of the bowels of the earth, discreetly carpeted. Plus a ladies' room whose very air was ladylike. Emerged post your stop there, the same two men bounded toward you, smiling. One visit and you were known here. Short men, of a same size; they had no doubt been chosen so that you were spared telling them apart. Everything was spared you, in deference to the contemplation ahead. Every milling stranger upstairs might be merely cats come to look at the queen of cities. Here you were perhaps some royal indolent, stepping in to visit your stable of cats. Customers bred to a certain kind of acquisition met here, chumming wordlessly over what was mutually precious to them—while quite sure of never being introduced.

My mother must have relished coming here. So had I, once reassured by the two courteous flunkies—always the same two—that my manners had qualified. Both quietly implying that signing the book was for us secondary.

But this time the young woman who interceded us—upstairs no less, eyes like keys and a lockjaw chin—was too much enjoying her clout. Safety boxes were now at a premium citywide; we could not be further accommodated. "My mother had an account here for some thirty years," I said. "Closed at her death. Perhaps reopening one would accord us box privileges?" Her smile was cool, inoperable. "Only if the balance one brought never fell below one hundred thousand dollars at all times. But I'm sure you can find some commercial bank still open to you."

Why is it that dozens of repartees swarm to the throat only when useless? Sample: "Ah, I see. The Morgan deals only in kid gloves?" But more than wasted on this poor repeater, likely just ascended from a pencil-behind-the-ear job.

But what I saw in that bank was the era deeded me and filially acquiesced in—at least until I had enough clout myself to be revolutionary. A state of mind (and of pocket, of course) but uniquely lollygagging even to the heights of art. As well as a trove of careless fun, alas now melting from all its elaborate cornices. An era exiting like one of its not-quite-nudes in chiffon, scurrying out from behind what was no longer a bead curtain, but a hard-and-fast new-age door.

Another bank was to be found: there always are. Now that, more than half a century later, "the Morgan" is hiccuping its troubles, I fancy old J.P., its founder, laying a forefinger alongside that hugely carbuncled nose to warn that a household

name, unlike an era, cannot as openly shift character. Meanwhile their young lady would unwittingly serve to turn up a
crack in our own. For in the interim, all the family's papers came
home...So tempting to paw over, for letter gossip, or even lost
peerages. According to my father, a British cousin, one Diana
Belais, former head of its Anti-Vivisection Society and possible
candidate, had unfortunately been female.

Finally, tucked appropriately in the envelope stuffed with
Confederate money—we found Henry Jacob Calisher, all that
was left of him. First, in a kind of pouch stuffed with Confederate money I did not stop to scrutinize, only noting that the denominations were larger than those we'd had at home, I was
about to cast the pouch aside when, tucking the bills back in, I
touched something else within and drew it out. A thin old envelope of stationery size, yellowed, flattened by the years.

What I drew from it first—a tiny envelope, too small to be
mailed, addressed to a Mrs. Fitzwilson by a spidery pen and no
doubt delivered by hand, proved to be the invitation to my
grandparents' wedding: Printed on paper bordered all round
with a pressed-in design, and so folded in three that the inscription was centered in elegantly curved modest run-on style, as if
handwritten also: "The Pleasure of your company is respectfully
solicited on Tuesday next, the 13th inst. at 7 o'clock P.M. at the
residence of Mr. Ellis Morris, to celebrate the Marriage of Mr.
Henry J. Calisher, to Miſs Betty Benden." Beneath, to the left, in
tiny ordinary print: "Richmond, January 6th, 1852."...Yet even
such formality can display the personal. The seven has been
inked over a printed 6: we shall never know why. The third letter
of "Miſs" is indeed an elongated "ſ," as in that old style which dif-
ferentiated the first "s" from the second. The name of the groom
precedes that of the bride—which is misspelled. Otherwise, all is
in order. On the tiny envelope, beneath the invitee's name, is a

flourished handwritten "Present," and the tip of the back flap torn, from a faint blob of pink sealing wax. But above all, on the invitation itself, "Marriage" has been capitalized.

The second enclosure, thinner even than what encloses it, is a marvel of the stationer's art, its left-hand border, top to bottom, inch wide, scrolled intricately in pale brown, surrounding three white medallions inserted lengthwise—all of this of course engraved. Each medallion contains a tiny picture inserted sidewise, so that to identify one would turn the whole left-hand side of this slip of paper upright. The top two tiny engravings are beehives. The center is an eagle's head, beak down. The whole thing is a form for a note of hand—what we would call an IOU. At the top, in Old English print, "Richmond, Va." Then in handwriting, "Dec. 5th, 1850" (the 5 being only partial, so not certain). Inside the border top left, a slanted engravure with a dollar sign, this inked in to the sum of 1888\frac{64}{100}$. The whole reading (as inked on the provided categories): "Two Years (after date), I promise to pay to...Henry J. Calisher...on Order without offset Eighteen and Eighty-eight...Dollars, Negotiable and Payable at _____ Bank of Virginia." Below that, on another line: "Value received," and again in handwriting: "With interest from the 22nd January, 1845." Below that, right, the handwritten signature: "Jacob Ezekiel."

What do all these dates mean? Presumably, that the money lent in 1845 had not been paid as of 1850—or that the debtors note was dated ahead by the bank. What is pertinent is that as noted in the book also written by an Ezekiel, that family and ours had been among those arrived in Virginia together, so there would have been a certain fealty. Secondly, the IOU, never destroyed, i.e., not paid, had been kept. Not by a Shylock, dealer in such; there was no whiff of that. Rather, it likely meant that my grandfather had been able to lend.

A second enclosure was a square of modernly thick paper, dated Oct. 1, all of it in my father's strong half-inch-high writing, but in pencil: "Dear Henry: Mother requested me to give Hortense Grandmother's pin—her watch and her lavalier, so I have permitted her to take them." Signed, "Daddy," and beneath that "Jos. H. Calisher."

But it is the envelope enclosing both their wedding announcement and this paternally savvy note to his son that rivets me. Both the latter as having been enclosed by my father in a thin yellowed envelope addressed to H. J. Calisher, and in this same flourished penmanship on two lines below:

2 Insurance policies on Servants
expires January 8th, 1856.

On the envelope's upper left hand, printed versatilely in seven different styles not replicable here, so reported consecutively but on the envelope actually forming a great square: "For INSURANCE ON LIFE, HERRING'S FIRE AND BURGLAR PROOF SAFE, MARBLEIZED IRON MANTLES and for Letter presses, Paper, Ink, Pens, etc. CALL AT STATIONERS HALL, No. 21 Pearl Street, Richmond, Va: KNOWLES & WALFORD, Stationers."

And what stationers they were.

It's the one word on the property insured that immobilizes me. "Servants." As insured in 1856.

I go to the encyclopedia, to look up the Emancipation Proclamation, copy the following:

Lincoln wrote these words to Horace Greeley on August 22, 1862.

"If I could save the Union without freeing *any* slave, I would do it; and if I could save it by freeing *all* the slaves, I would do it; and if I could do it by freeing *some* and leaving others alone, I would also do that."

Yes, Abe was honest according to his lights. And the date, 1862, seals our private history. At the date my grandfather purchased his insurance—and why otherwise would he have done so?—years and years before the proclamation, his servants would have been slaves.

And they would have been servants to him, in and about his properties—as would befit a man steel-engraved after death, but not further described. Not by his objecting—and to her surroundings objectionable—wife. That "ramrod" who declared, "Not in my house." As asserted to me by her adoring son. When I was twelve.

So it veers on—the personal history forever in the vise of the public one. Citizens: Ask which chaos is yours?

At whatever latitude?

But back in our living room, in and among those sweet-talkers, the visitors I think of as our "parlor relatives"—you haven't to be bothered with any of what is called "That." Hosts have to be polite to visitors. While if ever there's an unhostly reference—like maybe a pushed-down snicker at the phrase "the War Between"—I come to note that most of our visitors, whether "kissing cousins" or real ones, have a secondary lid like a bird's that drops conveniently. Like it is "manners" to do that— and as they themselves joke, all our parlor people are first-class handicappers there.

Yet sometimes there can be a flicker of venom, like a snake's tongue darting out. I sit in my corner, disregarded. One of their favorite words, whispered: "Don't disregard the child."

After a spell of that once, I went to my father for enlightenment. "What's an abolitionist look like? . . . I mean—we got told about them at school. Sixth grade, they begin teaching you a lot more." It was the turning point, where ideas were being rassled up. No pictures.

"Why what did you imagine?" he says. "Gorgons?"

"Ah no. Just maybe a bit stiff, and ramroddy. Like from New England maybe. And preacherly."

He looks at me long. Always careful of me, and of my future. "Well—I'll tell you." His drawl comes out more. Enough to notice. "There's two kinds, abolitionists. Up here—they look like us. Could be anybody. Bit more talky, maybe...But down home—you'd know one right away. By the pointy ears. Cloven hooves, 'stead of feet. And a tail." He's enjoying himself. "And likely carry a pitchfork to jab you with."

"Ah, you."

"No, I'm serious," he says. "Had one around our house once, when I was a boy. Or so neighbors said. Though they never cotched her at her tricks. Mostly sneaked while we were at school, I fancy. And your grandfather at the dry-goods store. But there was an awful stew when he found out what she'd been and done. A dry-goods store is kind of a meeting place. Where maybe the lawyer, dropped in from the courthouse, and the owner the wood yard that also sold us coal, could both be buying socks. And gossip running like kerosene from a punched can."

He'd stopped the litany. It always set me back on my heels—how this man of the town, of the cologne and the stickpin in the tie, can cite at will the homely specifics he'd been born to.

"Could have ruined that clubby meetinghouse—and a good part of his custom as well. For a dropper-in had to buy now and then, to save his face...Could have set things going—any rumor that your grandfather harbored such a traitor—though more than a couple the menfolk might sympathize down deep. And then there was that part of the back floor he'd sectioned off for black people, where they could buy from our Percy, one of their own. Not much cash going. But Paw let them buy on tick—and took it out in service. Couldn't use it all, he brokered it. Dry goods?" Father slapped his knee. "Covers the waterfront. Once we got swapped a block-and-tackle job on our sewage line, in exchange for three Sunday shirts. Some labor time left over, so swapped with the liquor dealer. Bourbon. Two fifths."

He rubbed the knee. Reminiscence brought back the rheumatiz. And I am lost. "But what's all that to do with the abolitionist?"

Now I waited for the coup de grâce—a phrase he'd made common to us all. Having played my part well. Vaudeville had its "straight man"—a routine I'd learned at that knee.

"Well, silly. Black people wouldn't have dared come near the place, not with any freedom talk going round. Wouldn't a been safe."

He lets that sink in, then adds his little shocker—in that rhythm familiar also. "And me no more than a six-year-old at the time, I'd almost been the one responsible. Me—and my new brown boots."

It was almost bedtime. I was too old for pajama songs now. But once snug in my youth bed, yawning over one of the stories that replaced those, I would fall into dreamland with the satisfaction of those who'd been traveling.

"New boots," he'd said. "Rubber soles, stamped Goodyear. A fine word for a first grader who already had his letters. And a leather strap with schoolbooks I could swing. So, one night, I noticed the strap had been loosened. And the next night, the person who still put me to bed was rubbing a finger over that cut in the rubber, lips moving, same time."

I knew who that was. Would be. So fell still.

"So, in a state that half considers Abe Lincoln has been plenty honest enough. Where it's held that house servants, if pushed beyond their station, either start dropping your wedding-band china, or go uppity enough to try on their employers' hats. Where to tout emancipation is just not—neighborly."

My father suffers usefully from "catarrh." Blowing the nose under a pince-nez can be graceful, if the pocket handkerchief is large. "I was only a tyke but I knew something was up. When this person who usually gives you a cuff, saying, 'Scrub behind the ears, Joe. Both ears,' and shuts the door on your manliness, instead stands there trembling, staring at your copybooks as if they're floating the Milky Way...

"Can you guess what had happened?" he asks.

I give him a princessy kick; this is routine.

"Summers we were put to bed at six o'clock. There were eight of us, mind—at that time most still home."

This was a story I had never heard before. He had been a theatergoer during his unmarried years. Melodrama, then much in vogue, had left its faintly gilded residue.

"Ran down the stair. Neighbors on the veranda. We hadn't that big a house or yard, but those days everybody had big names for what might only be a yard and a porch."

It was summertime, too, when he told me this one. Maybe heat brings the riddles out?

"Can't you guess what had happened?"

No, I couldn't. He wasn't usually a tease. Maybe we were both showing our age—a half century between?

"I had a dawg then, needed no encouragement to run in circles. We ran round and round what was generally called 'the vista'—me shouting my news."

When I did not react he said: "Of course you can have no conception of how unmannerly that was. None. Or of what I was letting out, or how it would ring round the vicinity. The stores were off Main Street. Ours between Main and Franklin. None of us lived far."

He and I at the moment are in what was to be the last of the summerhouse rentals we were going to be able to afford. An amiable house of a size to accommodate the stream of family, but except under duress, only "for the day." One of those houses that often snuggle next to the estates. He is thinking of that small mercantile Richmond, Virginia—a city that always seemed to have its state name alongside. Where we had been beginners, if never interlopers. Where we would most certainly have known a circle of neighbors, maybe at times "too close for comfort." At other times—weddings and cemeteries—as close as needed. Here we do not know the people next door. No, I had no conception.

Whether we two are alone, at this moment, I can't say. When he is on anecdote, we always seem to be. No storyteller can do much better than that.

"Sit up!" he says. "I'm going to tell you something important. Don't for the—." Voice failed him. Had he been going to say, "For the love of God—" or protest similarly mild? He swore from time to time. A ripple of "goddamn's," sounding rather dashing.

Now the pince-nez glitters, an eyepiece that always seems to have the past behind it. "Don't slouch," he says, in utter tenderness. What he says next has the same.

"Our house abolitionist, those days. You can make a guess who that was?"

I think I can. I so signify.

When he tells me, our four hands are clasped, on that always slappable knee. To speak takes him a swallow.

"She had taught Awnt Nell how to read."

What's a memoir? Ask the living. Hear the dead reply. Not all of them yours, but some—and that's what history is.

I cannot begin to answer for all the people in that envelope. Or to them. But it will begin to seem to me—that I should. Not because I was, as dubbed early, "a holy reader." Meaning one of those for whom anything in print—baseball scores, to the *Areopagitica*, to street porn—was treasure. No, every reader in the same instance is a recorder, no matter in which kitchen we learn.

So—to that envelope. My first reaction is political. It will be my duty to excoriate. That passes quickly; I am used to all that. Early on one may see that politics might not be a seeking of solutions. It could be the art of being blind to alternate paths, and of assuming that blindness as hereditary. No more richly practiced than on my home base?

For a while I might use that envelope as the repository of all the hush money a businesslike country will pay in order to keep its uncivil liberties in health?

No, I must take it personal. My first American ancestor is there. And his son's life...Of which, finally this: I hate the word "ambivalent." It gets you out of anything. Yet his Unionist strain was not unconscious. He knew it well.

We're standing, for instance, in front of the curio cabinet—in which each object—the Japanese ivory that men there wear at the waist, the "hundred-year cup" that is all European curlicue—on and on. Down to the dark brown snuffbox, like a finger joint some carver had popped that meaning into...snuff.

Almost any child who came to the house, either by reason of family or visit, reared its gaze toward that nest of—"toys?"—three sides of which were curved glass, and would likely be given a tour. Some of the curio cabinet's contents must be relics of the Richmond household, others collected by my father in his "New Awlins" days. Which would have given Housselle, the French-descended roommate, the idea for his wedding present? No such source book was ever rendered. These "objects of virtue," as I would learn antiquarians so term them, are what those of us rising in the middle class buy to assert our taste, or those already there display to confirm their longevity. The display could have been either, and probably was.

The small, knuckly dark-brown object had intrigued me ever since, in that schooling on the American Revolution which comes early to our citizens, I had learned about the eighteenth century. There, right behind our glass, lay a pinch of it.

Once before, my father and I were standing alone in front of the cabinet; he always happy to give the tour. In the course of which an object, an ivory deer, or a Meissen statuette, might be delivered into my own hand. Once or twice, this one had been. Incised on it, a crisscross pattern of almost invisible lines must have been pierced by the sharpest and smallest instrument imaginable—as aided perhaps by a pair of tiny oval spectacles similar to the pair on the shelf above. For our snuffbox had once been a nut; this long known.

"What nut could it be?" I said, this time putting it back carefully on its shelf place. This is not the first time I've asked. Answered "Oh, dunno. Not a Brazil. Nor a pecan, that's for sure."

This time we were by ourselves again, after a claque of our Richmond and Lynchburg guests had departed early for "the train." The air seemed still curly with their soft talk. "We used to pick 'em up same time we poached the melons," he said, the words reverent, the way these clues to a childhood always were—and as if preserved for me. We are sharing the unforgettable.

"Black walnuts, maybe," I say. Though next to me, I feel him stiffen. Nothing like his mild disapproval when my mother, talking behind a maid's back, of what she should not hear, warns: *Die Schwartze!* Nor yet a kind of held-in tolerance, veiled, when the aunts cooed, "The nigras." And once in a while, "Those darkies!"

There is a word never to be said in our house. One time a local delivery boy had used it, casually referring to our back-elevator man. My mother's eyebrows rose high, recalling: "Such a dressing-down your father gave him; I never heard the like. I said, 'Joe, the boy—what did he know? He was only some poor immigrant.'" And what had my father said? She shrugged. Explosions held her fascinated, but she had little instinct for an anecdote's ending. My father, a man drawn to kitchens in order to overhear—even sneak the lower half of his dailiness—completed it for her. "Well, Hattie, at eighteen, so was I."

He was having a hard time now, saying whatever he was going to, what he felt bound to say. In the arm around me, I could feel that.

In a new century now, and in the foolish way we count off our lives in that outmoded decimal, I feel it yet.

"We called them 'nigger-toes,'" he said.

The self-regard of a family as conscious of the world as his—ours—is like a palimpsest. A word I discovered on my own, using it first in a high school senior paper, and again—natch!—in the freshman English exam required of us if we hoped to skip the beginner's English course altogether.

A palimpsest is a parchment that can be written on, rubbed out, and the inscription written again, maybe several times over. Or, any kind of paper on which one can do the same. My use of it back then had earned me some of the teasing ridicule of those pals with whom one swapped "papers," but of the college faculty most severely. Why?

Easy. To hunger as I did for the syllables that shrouded the complex? As a student, that can earn you calumny, though not from those who instruct best. As a part-time academic later, I would see the syndrome working in colleagues as well, exempting myself, I hoped, by my allegiance to, blind identification with, the young. This would be why I would never stay in academia too long, though I will forever savor it as the supreme arena where ideas can be tossed like dice, and playing that game of craps is properly revered. But invidiousness haunts any packed group. Fear crawls between any two groups isolated each by age...If one does not see youth as holy, one should not teach.

A vocation? A word nuns use, dooming themselves to the sect. Or to the God in themselves. Though I would once hear a nurse say how she came to hers, the word itself a prayer. While her hands were for once folded in her lap.

What I'm after seems more like a sect of one. In which the words have marched me there...The long Latinate words of my language, dangling like swords too heavy to lift. Able though to stumble me forward with a prod from behind. Then the blessed monosyllable that thrums in from the bottomlands, a flail to flog the wheat. While a foreign word may suddenly sound in like a stray chorister.

I am meanwhile always a trifle purse-proud about how I came to my trade. Education, yes, a soaking in many waters. But the first stories, like the last—and the next after that—lie somewhere deep in "family," or the codes taught me—or the lack. And there I was surely like a member of one of the old industrial guilds, clasping my truths to me—like a member of the ancient order of bona fides, an hereditary legatee of one of the medieval industrial guilds maybe—those leather makers, furriers—architects of material translated into marketable goods, rag and wood made into the finest paper—and I, too, here and "before," holding up my sop of truth.

But an envelope can change all that. Even though one can no longer, through someone's careless disposal long ago, ever be sure of the amount the receipt was for.

Yet I am saving it here, somehow—this sop of truth awarded me.

The envelope is always with me now, not in a vault. In one of those small metal boxes where one keeps the certificates, birth, passports, and the like, that one must show to all border guards.

At first, holding the envelope like one of those trinkets given to a medium at a seance, which, like the armature of a piece of sculpture may counterpart the very self—or the spirit you are looking for—I tried to imagine the person of the insured.

It would not be a woman. Those, serving in that house, had walked the world carrying their heads untaxed.

Was my grandfather a dealer in such merchandise? Gambling on a rise in the value of the inventory? No, he had dealt in "dry" goods only, far as we knew. The smell of flesh traded would have permeated our annals, somehow.

Couldn't the one insured have been Percy, the man in the store, about whose quirks there had been a trace of jokery overheard, whose meaning had to be weaseled out privately?

"Sell you anything, smart as a whip. But no head for figures," Flora had said, looking down her nose at my father; whenever Oakley's slowed, this restricted her borrowing. "Liked his slap-and-tickle, too, but Paw finally married him off."

My father had said "Flora!" for the language presumably—which I already knew the meaning of.

Was that the groom in a wedding picture, in among the family ones? A high-collared man and kind of buskined-tight woman, both stiff as the thick cardboard the photo was on. But not the same as in our board photographs. "Which cousins are they?" Shocking the parlor visitors tallying up the cousinly score.

"We-ell, Joe," one had said. "Sure got yourself a lil ole Northerner."

To which he'd answered, "Percy was light-colored, dollin'. Came from the Bayou." Mamie, tying things up as always, adding: "More bad blood than was good for him, I reckon. Gave him that extra gumption. Paw knew he took from the till. But worth it to the store."

In school that year I was twelve, in the new course called biology, we had been learning about the venous and arterial systems of our bodies, although I am ever to forget which system brings blood to the heart, which sends it forth. But the blood question draws me topically, as it must all women, and I had recently had my first brush with that. Yet what intrigues me is how the word "bloodshed" differs from that, and when talking of "the waw" is sacrosanct.

Asking my sharper-nosed aunt, Miriam/Mamie, will sometimes get you somewhere. In the family judgment, she "lets things out."

"What's 'bad blood'?"

That will be the last time I ask questions in visitors' company. For the living room is this day full of our regulars, including three of my favorites, the Pyles, Aunt Beck Pyle and daughter Katie, off whose Long Island dock I had been allowed to fish, and old Mrs. Edel's daughter-in-law Lee, wife of "the Commander" Albert. A pastel lovely and naval wife whose low-voiced greeting: "Hay-lo Cudden Hoh-tay-uns," clinging forever in the ear, has been the first to elevate me to adulthood.

I see by the stirrings among them all that they don't know how to answer me. No—I see more... With that bottom-of-the-well sinking when it dawns on you that the grown don't always know how to answer themselves.

"You go too faw, Mamie." Flora, whose serene white pompadour usually floats her through the family waters like a sail, isn't really angry. She's elder-sistering, if too early for me to recognize.

Mamie says under her breath, "Well, Joe should curb his darling."

Family savior though he is, I see how their spatting reduces him.

Clarence Winstock, my uncle, who substitutes for him on my Sunday walks—how he emerges now from his brother-in-law quiet. "I'll tell our niece." He flashes me a smile. A strong face, and a handsome one—why did people ignore? But this time they wait. "Bad blood? It's when white people have the least smooch of black blood in them." If you can hear a pin drop, he's ignoring. "Not the case of anyone here. But worse still—it's when black people have more than a drop of white."

No one said a word to me of it ever after. Though of course they now do, constantly. As the early interlocutors will insist on doing. But as they recede further and further, mustn't I apologize for any strictures I may have made here, on my Southern communality?... Or rather, offer my regrets?

Meanwhile, my admiration to you—dear sly, intemperate, hot-blooded folks—for the example set me, though in my era it can be puzzling to comply...

You always spoke in character.

Leaving me behind, with the envelope. Which, at first sight, I knew I must fill. With the identity of the insured.

For if Southerners tended to be complacent about their background, hadn't I, with that secondhand locality rich in my mouth, done much the same? Now, with that discovery, I am hangdog, ebullience gone. Complicitous. Over a secret blot on the old escutcheon that few would give a hoot in hell to hear about. That would be pompous to tell. Like some fake noblewoman bemoaning her lack of the full eight—or is it sixteen?—"quarterings" required for a mention in the *Almanach de Gotha*?

But that year of my father's death I can put it aside—clutching my fealty to him. He had been middle-aged at my birth; I was now thirty, having had the grace of his companionship for

longer than my mother—the young wife who would prede-
cease him—would ever have credited. Yet in living with a parent
through the years, one learns with exactitude their limitations as
well as their scope. Just as one's own children will do, should
one live as long. Though it would take me more years to voice
what I must have begun to sift and absorb. "Southern paternalism"—what an outsider's phrase for the world of tender evasion
I had known so well.

Years on, an editor would call me about the first line of a
story he was publishing: "My father was a Southerner, but a
very kind man." Wasn't the "but" a typo for an "and"?—No, it
was the story of a man who would never in this world say "nigras" as his sisters had, but would refuse to grant our maid an
adult confession she very much wanted to make—his grounds
being, "They're all children, y'know."

But I still held back on that envelope—to which he was one
generation closer than me. For by then, I had been dissident in
what had seemed to me, and to most of us, a far broader war—
Vietnam.

What we were all undergoing was the gradual withering of
America's vision of its unsullied patriotism. Back in grade
school, during World War I, we'd had flags thrust in our fists
and were led into assembly shouting that fiery song ending—
"The Red—unh, Cross, unh Nurse!"

After World War II, when living "in the County," I was asked
to teach English to three of the Hiroshima girls, victims of that
blast, who had been brought to the U.S.A. by Norman Cousins, a
resident near me. I did give such home lessons, all four of us
bowing in a polite postwar swoon of self-abnegation—while
Hideko, most injured of the three, slowly faded, absented herself—and died. In Vietnam days, one took to the streets in

nonviolent demonstration, or signified by taking one's turn at Riverside Church's pulpit, reading out the names of that week's military dead—while the flow of conscientious objectors widened toward Washington, D.C.

By then, our Confederate sins would seem so parochial—and partially atoned for?—that one might weep for the days (not when patriotism had been unclouded, this was likely never to come again), but for the time when national fervor still had a firm native niche—and our confidence. Even for the blasé.

Halt. Am I discovering that the conceded difference between autobiography and biography is even more curious?

In the former, the process is at once horizontal—as if you paw at a corpse intermittently alive and vertical—like at an archaeological dig. Is it that you know everything—or merely have forgotten nothing? Meanwhile pursuing an intense process that is out to define, yet is unable to ignore all rubble not admissible as "fact." You must blame yourself ahead of time for any added gloss, yet outwit any smarmy tendency toward guilt, and carefully test the niggling area between self-consciousness and conscience. Meanwhile, the fountain of your youth, reconsidered, rains paradoxes, in an atmosphere shot with sun that strikes the naked eyeball, only clouded because you have long since sneaked on your shades. Are you being too hard on yourself, or too kind? You would have to jump out of your skin to be sure.

To the reader—of whom you must always be aware however negligently—these discriminations may yet count. Nor is honesty, however passionately avowed, the same as accuracy. What's really the challenge—if you use that heroic word—is that unlike the biographer, you have not been free to choose the "life." Nor the calm of ultimate hindsight, in which it is to be surveyed. Particularly so since the "autobio" more often occurs when all the eras of a "life" are present at once.

Both accounts, of course, share the same pretension that they are "art." But in the former, the talents of a Sartre or a Mishima, or even such a founder of self-revelation as Rousseau, are not quite in the same class as a call girl or a Lord Admiral—even if both the latter have written the book themselves.

But, ah, the biographer per se. Choose the "life" at will, according to private interest or the availability of research. Choose the attitude—as whether to embrace or disgrace your subject. Make it a period piece—always less dour than history, and commanding a tolerant, even broader audience. Sometimes the very facts of a life are so poignant, or the life itself so unknown or neglected, that one or more of those circumstances will be enough? Enough for an effort that however worthy can at best rate that adjective "masterly." For at best biography is examination, not invention. However sensitive or clever or wily as to thesis, it's by nature secondary, and too orderly a candidate for art's plume. While in the case of biography about the literary, the purling analysis from a mind not equal to the original can keep one at a mortal distance from, say, the loping poems of a Whitman, the wise ingenuousness of George Eliot's prose.

Meanwhile—how will I get my freedom—from that envelope? What frees the obsessionist?

In the world of ideas, it is much the same as in the affairs of love; if you are lucky, you go on to the next. No longer transfixed—merely preoccupied? A philosopher may not find the shift that easy, most being hooked to one path. The physicists prefer that—although the danger of the random may lurk. But ply an art and it can nurse you out of your corner. To find that you are robustly singing another song. Or have shifted from oil to pastel.

I stop mulling over the identity of my grandfather's "servants." It's a mug's game, for, should I discover, won't that weigh me, not release? Better to mull on what it is to be such a "servant." How is it to be one? How would that weigh on one, from day to ponderous day?

To do that, I shall have to creep into that envelope. I try.

A hard fit. To do the trick, first shrink yourself to the minimal, as a slave must. Then spread yourself, obedient, along the five inches or so, under that tight epitaph. Don't close the flap.

Since the receipt is missing, I can't tell how much I am worth. As auctioned for a sum heard long ago: "A healthy specimen, teeth counted, parts examined, as with any stock." Maybe the value has risen since purchase, maybe not. Same deal there as for any mortals—outside. What's that called? Doesn't have a name? Sure does. Freed? No'm. Means those who never had to be freed—that other. No name for those.

But we inside here have our distinctions. Field hands. House servant. Those are the aristocrats. Close to the jollity of the kitchen. But the field service has its song: heel-and-toe, buck-and-wing.

How I am fed and clothed will depend on the marster. Note my boots, which have the gratitude to shine. (Everything is noted, of course.) *Those niggers down to the hill farm, their toes coming out...* Inside here, that's a word is ever on our tongue, like salt and pepper. But all that's just the handling.

Otherwise... Well, in the main I feel, well—dateless. There are no regular time-spots. Even the days of the week shrink from this permanent calendar. We don't need one or are not conceded to. But our datelessness is not vacation. It's serving a stretch.

Except for Sundays. We share the outside's Bible—at least some of it. With moral habits attached. But to live at all in this space well atones for the underneath datelessness.

Weddings. Yes, there are those. Or matings. You make your

own space—or almost it's yours—almost...I open the flap, gasping some. Air. For what will the child of this servant be— except to serve? One more—a "value added."

Yes, the Bible—shared. Nine times out of ten it will donate one of the mighty names given to the child. "The owned of the owned"—will that be what is written of them in the register?

"Suffer the little children to come unto me." But it does not add—did not say—how the transportation was to be arranged.

Finally—I thought to stop this practice. It has been a mockery. With no certainty as to which of us had been most mocked. And what I had done—or imagined I was doing—was only a smidgen of what went on in the world. Not all of us envelopes being for the black-and-white situation. For surely their sum might be seen as measureless? Consider all those who hang by the topknot—or the scruff of the neck, from an unseen grasp.

So, I lock the envelope away in its good metal box, one of those dark-enameled with thin official stripe. Boxes like this hold documents by the thousands, in a trillion vaults. Including pieces of anti-property like mine.

So, by fouling the clean lines of what is rightful, or whatever that envelope is, I spend a nice, normal, crass week away. Except why should my normal routine—which usually has a fair bit of anti in it—suddenly seem crass? Is it that I act—against the rape of human rights, say—only in committee?...Instead of inhabiting that more personal envelope. Testing it.

So now, I make a game of it. Of the test.

The deadly game—half public gamble, half private hysteria—that any croupier watching the tables can spot at once. The person who has a system. That suave man in the ascot, say—a Cambridge expert on higher mathematica, who has worked things out logarithmically...That woman with a wealth of beatifically imprecise curls—not a wig—and one tiny scarab of the true Egyptian purple, affixed just above the base of her nose. Both very becoming, until she claims to have been up all night drinking potassium water, which, jump-starting her pulse count, will instruct her what numbers to play.

My "system" is topical—as befits my trade? I have no hope of knowing who my grandfather's "servants" were. Their identity is flotsam, in a long-ago sea. Perhaps it was never much.

I have put the envelope on a little rack that came out of the family ragbag—yes, we were that sort. The ragbag came with the furniture. Or rather, I saw that it did, that it must. Not everything a family collects should be valuable. Rather, bits of lace— meant for trimmings?—that nobody will ever sew on. The rack from a mah-jongg set, a gift scorned, except for one solitary afternoon, day after my college graduation, when I lined the rack with as many tiles on it as the rules allotted a single player, and sat looking at them. Yearning for them to tell me what next to do. Knowing they would not say... My children, cynic scavengers, did away with the tiles.

The rack has held pencils, then pens; it returns, disappears. That it and the ragbag have survived gives me a joy without measure. In which the throat tightens, but only the mind weeps. Hankering. In the midst of all you have. I place the envelope on it.

Closing my eyes, I force myself in. What will it tell me today?

That these days the world lives in dread of losing its localities? Even such locality as this? Despite which we all must think globally now. Is that why I seek even this discredited envelope?

Each time I do better, thanks to my trade. Swap my twisty talent for "the story hour" (not all of those for children), for a family record with some holes in it—and I find me in a dry-goods store... I want to see particularly what "notions" are offered the good citizens of Virginia, as distinct from merely their needs. But so-called "imagination" always outwits.

For there is the grandfather, down from his picture. No one else is in the store. Or in the street outside. It is after hours for both of us. His wife is at home, with however many she has so far birthed. The roster perhaps already up to Joseph? So named out of the need for at least one infant destined to wear a coat of many colors? A midnight craving excusable in Henry Jacob, a man arrived here in the land of Canaan-to-be, in '27, who finds himself, after industrious toil that has amassed well, in a conflict where the color scale has slipped down to two at times almost the same: a bloody Gray and a bloody Blue. While skin—over here that's not, as in Europe, color alone. Over here it's not color per se. Not in a land whose imports, unlike the animals, pro-create even in a closed zoo.

A hundred years on, in a New York soda parlor, a woman over-hearing two college grads, cousins, first time met, bad-mouthing their common ancestry (one of them me), will rise from her table, her chest held high as—her grandfather? No doubt a Gray. "Y'all don't understand, you noth-nuhs. No more than a tick knows what it sups." An adage, not ours, that still bewilders. What's that got to do with the price of tea—or a vanilla sundae? Leaning forward, she whispers it: "They-y out-numbuh us."

…Enter the man my grandfather is waiting for. He is furtive, quick. No time for a "Nice place, you've got here." A bit miserly on the "sir's." Early carpetbagger, home style? His bag is his inner breast pocket, from which he pulls an envelope. "Here's your receipt, all ready. Policy's to follow. Head count of two, right? There you are."

My grandfather opens the drawer behind the till. Counts

out that pink stuff to the proper amount. Plus a couple of bills extra, placed to one side.

"Ah, no," the man says, with the sigh that implies a problem met constantly. "Home office is in Hartford, Connecticut, suh. Only government currency acceptable."

And so it is done. More drawers than one to a proper-size till.

"Ah, that's dellycut of you," the man adds. For the new money exchange has extended to the tip. Stowing it away, he spreads. A vest encourages certain wearers, rather than restricts? "Done a pretty business among you Israelites here. Perfect gentlemen. An' like you never seen that ghetto. Shake the hand."

Since the picture of my grandfather vanished with Berthe Bendan's death, I cannot refer to it for hints of what he would have replied.

The insurance man? He's well within character. In those days of the door-to-door book salesman, many a household had its Shakespeare, as respectability obliged. In a home sullied with further ambition—toward Hartford, say—the books might even be read.

The handclasp I can perhaps vouch for. There'd be no blood on either hand.

For, I'm finding out, as many are, that "global" thinking dilutes. Too much prompting from those in the news—where being in the swim is so often confused with depth. Maybe one's better off moseying at one's stick-in-the-mud desk—where the single thinkers from other desks can congregate without warning, saying gently, "Not to impose..."

The envelope has become my oracle. To which I apply.

In Delphi once I was shown the wall with the sibyl's hole, and though newly married was brave enough to apply my ear. What I heard, I swear, was the silence of the planet, riddle enough.

My envelope is of a lower order. Do I really seek to know, feel, even be—what a "servant" knew, felt, was? Or merely add to my genealogy with a final spasm of misbegotten pride. "Ah, yay-uss. We were never plantation class. Nor were we 'colonial' enough to come under the scrutiny of, say, Lafayette. But we did have a passel of—well, you know—those."

At times in search of one or other of the documents—leases, passports, contracts, all that jumble for which one goes to a little black box—I continue to take out the envelope, if merely to remind myself that it's there, rather than in the "safe-deposit"—a nomenclature now used exclusively. A box so named is for what you want to keep, but not be confronted by from day to day. Or for what the tightfisted must check or gloat over, sinking back on the "portfolio" that is good or better than swansdown. But a vault—that's for what ought not to be found.

When I was very young, my father brought home games which were small and elaborate, parlor size, chockablock with cardboard and styluses or even compasses, as if left over from Victorian nurseries where a nanny might oblige. Or games trembling on the educative edge of the sciences. Or mimicking the kind of art that you go to a palace to see. Or your elders once did.

Often one played such games with the elders. For whom, as with the bisque dancing doll in her swirl of ruching, these gifts had perhaps been designed. One did not wind up such toys oneself; it was always done for one. As if otherwise the illusion might be destroyed.

So, it was with this not-quite clue that my father may have intendedly left for me. If only to explain—or honor—that fiery little woman in whose eyes, though glistening oddly when light hit them askance on what must have been cataracts, had all her life only the one lid to them. From beneath which an imperial principle still gazed?…This daughter of Dan. Which in the old Hebrew means—a judge.

Brought to bed of eight children by Henry Jacob—what had she thought of him?…My guess is that she would not have deemed the question relevant. In her "day" (that word which can be a kaleidoscope in a single piece of glass), the women—and the men too—had many more closed envelopes than we. And kept them so.

My father enjoyed keen eyesight to the end, adopting the pince-nez, its lenses very nearly plain glass, as a protection from the "bills-of-lading" dust that business brought, as well as "the society of fools even greater than me."

I think he left the insurance premium for me to find.

So now I have surveyed me—and from the apex of that "champagne" time of life when all eras do indeed convene. But is the perspective that much more definitive? I think of Stephen Spender, much mocked by his compatriots for writing his autobiography in his forties. Leaving him to spend the rest of that already-audienced existence in attending literary conferences, at which, given the podium, he would intone to the anxious faces ready for wisdom "Why are we not all at home, writing poetry?" Or prose?

Why not, indeed? In autobiography one practices doublethink, blowing hot and cold, tincturing the very common milk of most people's existence with a little hemlock that happened to be on hand. In what the Teachers College crowd calls a "Lesson in Learning"? Meaning a kind of lunchtime in which you study meat sandwiches without getting to eat them, but earn your citation—a profoundly empty brown bag? In the same hope, am I cracking open, just a wee, that six feet of mortality in which we are all enclosed? History is a patch of patches. Is there a place for mine?

Singed with Latin early, in the library I came upon Cardinal Newman's *Apologia pro Vita Sua,* and proud that I knew what the title meant, read it through. Emerging permanently irritated—at the assumption that the supreme apologias were for cardinals only. Now to find that the writer-vanity can do it up in nines—and without the help of the Lord.

Born at the beginning of the last century, I write this over its cusp and onto the next, in 2003. At this moment the world stumbles, rising painfully as far as its knees. What we call the "space age" seems no more than our planet seeking its excuses. While the churches send up their rockets of piety, single to the end. What may save us for history is the wonderful secular pity, that now and again sends stranger linked to stranger—into the streets.

It's a lovely evening, blessed with family around us, wineglasses in hand. Or else hovering, now grailed in some part of us too undisciplined to name.

Outside there's been a blizzard, bringing the old fairy tale to the park, even to those with no view. At the window is that pattern of safety, the windowpane. Though we kids were warned early that if it got broke, we were the kind of family who would be expected to pay for it.

So we enter the world of obligation. Close the shutters if you have them, good and tight. Yet a childhood, that dawning mix of geography and emotion, can return at any time, whether or not willed.

My father is singing. To all the children who need to be tucked in. He has only two songs, in that ratchety tuneless voice which protects me from all threats. I always felt he should sing "My Old *Kain*tucky Home" last, since it ends with a "good night," but taking me back with him to that other shadow childhood into which I slip noiselessly, as if so born, is he singing what may have tucked in little Joe, in the soft Richmond night? While as the song ends, a voice at the door perhaps says to its servant, "Hurry now, store closes early tonight."

The song I heard was maybe not the Stephen Foster one— I've never checked, nor do I plan to. Never check is my policy— neither the dates nor the songs. Otherwise the true version, mangled to suit, might escape:

> *Who's that I hear, a-co-omin'*
> *Across the fields and slow?*
> *Who's that I hear a-hu-mming? . . .*
> *It's old, uh, bla-ack—Joe.*

While in their bedroom, next to mine, my mother knits for the "1918" war that had lain in wait for her. She nevertheless using the faster in-and-out German stitch, that her American neighbors, knitting with the "over-arm" stitch which energetically and maybe patriotically moves the elbow up and down, up and down, slow and stately, tend to disapprove—even chiding her. Under nightfall, however, in her own dominion, or her half of it, she is making all of us as local as she can.

Emboldened perhaps by a once-strong "Hattie. Hattie!" Until the day when she had had to say to me, "Take your father for a walk."

With which this narrative, straining forward against the undertow of memorabilia, begins. One private vow erupting when I touched the first key:

Tell the unforgettable, I instructed myself. But do it without once mouthing the word that pops from us like a "Watch it!" as we traipse down the steps of history. Save that word for when it will be most deserved.

To survey the landscape of one's family is scarifying, yes:

"To make a number of small incisions in the body, to scratch an outline."

Up there in the balcony of her solitude, my mother breasts her woes. Down below, my father is shouldering the burden of a family second-cousined to a multiple nobody attempts to unravel. He stoops perilously, yet occupies his place. While you as the chronicler merely articulate what you are. Only to find that the truth of events does not lie in the consecutive, but is uncalendared.

My parents lie in anonymous graves, in plots for which the deeds had been purchased from time to time from those cemetery salesmen who devoutly urge one to "prepare." The deeds and their location had long since been in my brother's effects. Pressed, he refused to cede their location—and for once we were agreed, though our reasons were not the same. He did not "believe" in paying sacristans for what he doubted was "eternal care." I felt—only an inkling then—that the untended grave was not always the least visited.

"Do believe in the Resurrection," my two sweet-spirited friends who died last month call out to me, as I sit at the memorial for one of them. Each had left separately, one in London, one in upstate New York; in life they never knew each other. But had exactly the same devotions. What shocked the one in upstate, herself a convert, was that I followed no devotions she could perceive—though she continued to hope.

The one at whose memorial we are all rising (and sitting again) knows better. In her father's house were many mansions, and as at my home place, many of those were books, both the austere and the frivolous. Some of which one might dare to write?

My friend upstate was the reader, not omnivorous but habitual, tolerant but not abject. Of the kind that used to be called the constant one.

So it happened that across seas and state lines, in our not quite joint musings, we all three shared the same joke.

"Oh, I do believe," I would tease either of them, "but not in the resurrection, with that overweening capital 'R.'" Which I consider highly impractical. A fine image, a beautiful one, of course—all those trillions of believers down the ages, lined up, radiant. If a wee smug—as with all those who allot the ruling capital letters to gods, fathers, mothers—and trinities. "But our poor planet, that small ball? Corrugated as it is, it would never in this world provide enough footage for them."

Each looks at me, lovingly but sad, from their so similar vantage point. They know I don't believe in their Heaven either: that infinite expanse of the afterlife, in which those who have inhabited the proper pews beforehand may meet again. To dip the knee, incline the brow, before the Scene all approve.

Even to discover, perhaps at Intermission, as dedicated theatergoers sitting adjacent may, by ticket chance, that they share a mutual friend?

"Oh, her?" the one whom we are at the moment memorializing might say of me. As Oakley & Co. might phrase it, she herself and I had been "in the same line." "Fooled you, did she? The way people of that persuasion often fool themselves. Never attended services in their own creed—or rarely...But believers to the nth actually. In their own...agnostic...atheistic wa-y-ay."

To spit out those last words when just arrived in the heavenly loges—that takes bravery. Then she'll chuckle, if up in that exalted arena one still can. "They inherit the Old Testament, y'know. Quite a burden that is. Safer maybe to feign you're entirely anti-biblical." Then she falls back, worn out.

(The dead are really dead, of course. But I am resurrecting her. Lowercase.)

Up on stage—if one can use that flip directional in a church—a priest sits. According to his inner stance, he is stage right—far right, as a matter of fact. According to my humbler audience view—stage left. Directly in my vision, whatever the term. It is unlikely that I am in his. Singly, that is. As the eulogies go on: measured, stately, humorous, warm, all admirable, I am admiring his gold-embroidered surplice, fastened over the white robe with a clasp, from this distance a round one, and fixed so exactly median that it might serve as a symbol of the Absolute.

Closing my eyes, opening them, I find both of us fixed in that absolving, impersonal stare. In answer, I confess, without grudge:

I believe in the resurrection and the life. By those of us who remain alive. *Credo, credo, credo—credo.* After that first "C," which is merely grammatical, the procession is ever lowercase.

I believe in the secular resurrection—which is memory. Whether by those who have loved or who have fought, who have honored or deceived. What draws my allegiance is that very tide of datelessness, ever fading, ever sweeping on, in the end engorging us all. Exacting from me the pity that for once is not cheap. Squeezing from me the tears that are a boon to the proud.

So then, this account. An attempt to resurrect oneself, well ahead?

In my first decade I too often had "the stomachache." The wrenching ones that came from thinking oneself too noble to be that young? Our benevolent family doctor, using a term then prevalent, diagnosed "autointoxication."

The first-person singular has seemed the trickiest mode in language, ever since. Students embark on its guileless flow as the easiest. Teachers counsel them to, desperate to see the spigots turn. While in self-narration—you swallow the snake.

To find myself in my first try, thrashing away from the seductions of writing for that oh-so-exclusive audience, my own. Nothing more confuses the multiple personae you may think you are. I had an Irish friend who, whether his wife was present under his nose, or in the tub—or in Ireland—unfailingly referred to her in the third person, in a wariness—or admiration?—beyond "she," as Herself. Apologetically, writing of myself I did the same.

But now I am in better luck. I have that envelope. Simple to slip into it, to be included at once in all human sympathy? Breathing in concert, as the hall resounds.

Yet I'm an old army hand at what was fondly called "dissidence," by those who taught us how to "espouse." Understandably, in a world conflict it's at least healing to choose a cause, if from afar. Though now and then, in acts peculiar to American style, somebody more intent on stardom than martyrdom would take a brief whirl at "action." While the groovy backdrop sent bundles, he rallied, funded ads. And poured cream on his porridge—at home.

I don't censure. Having spent much of my middle age in that posture. Translated (as with so many) from private rebellions, in youth unexpressed.

But now I use a different camera, though unsure whether its aperture widens, or is narrowing. Even shamed to focus, if unwillingly (and clicking off, as soon as seen), the ardor of all who swell with red-cheeked empathy. For, say, that woman whose love life got her stoned. Then to publicize: with that shrieking in numbers which is bound to relieve. Then to go home—what else to be done?—to the pleasures of the clit.

Swear to tell "her/my" life story?...Then step, dear, into that leaky barge...Such a comfy, civilian one. Low in the water, below the battleships that swarm. On an untrustworthy planet, that embittered orb always searching for other life in the universe. Where cruelties multiply, with both parties, victim and torturer, wildly chorusing: "Green grow the lilacs, oh—there's nothing wrong."

While the authorities, stealing back onto the scene of action—which is not always a battlefield, but any corner where some are owned—place an e-mail in the mailbox of the injured, or on the very coffin of the unresurrectable.

Saying: "Blessings. We find we have you on film."

Yet on a planet whose forests in their morning innocence are groves where last night the angels picnicked. Whose winding bridges, ending up nowhere, or towers, fallen to wasteland, might someday suggest to an unearthly visitor: "This was the crockery of gods?"

While, even as we are now, in our orphanages there may be some big-eyed stripling or gypsy girl, destined to rule?

That's as it may be. Not to be despised, our good intentions. But History waits. Just as it did on the Ptolemys. To put us down as Profit or Loss.

So, perhaps all the mulling of the autobiographic is not wholly wasted then? For what we might actually yearn for as we flounder in the solipsism of ego is—company. A meeting of minds. Or at least a single vision in the shared telescopes...In an undergraduate course in astronomy once, what was the lesson, as assembled on rooftop, with all academia seething below, we found the single star? Or, rather, a pattern of several ones, then the patterns surrounding it—and a dossier of some suspected of surrounding those.

ONE LAST TIME—my twentieth century kept shrieking, as each century does. We thought it would never get done with, our extraordinary era, ever looming behind our backs, huge and androgynous, not so eager to mess with the "natural" order, as to investigate. Enormously able to switch between virtue and murder. Nudging intellect (that old antiquarian which now and then had plumped for the Good like an eighty-year-old man siring a baby) to role-play with the poisonous, or schooling biology, that slow, enchanting lore of the bloodstream, to market quickie death? While the governors, ever out to thrall the governed, sugar the horizon with battle cries.

So the twenty-first century "dawns"—or stumbles in, already lockstepped and chained. Language fails—or else must learn how to reject its own servitude?

It's afternoon, an old, wise dusk infiltrating my young prodigy of a city. Founded only in the eighteenth century—and by the Dutch, whom the sea taught compromise—New York will not do so, even with the dusk.

In my cigar-band afternoons, clutching cigars for all players, I had traipsed past store windows even on Sundays brewing light. At end of season the group had awarded me a ten-dollar gold piece, enshrined in a satin-lined box no doubt contributed by one of the wives—otherwise alien. That game taught me a lot. It was also election time. My father, bolting that nest of left-over Southern Democrats, was voting Republican against Tammany Hall, and being ribbed for it. "Now maybe you can buy off your dad's vote," one man said. "Oh no," I parroted, chockful of sixth-grade lore. "Universal suffrage. You got to respect it." One of the sleepy-eyed men, scooping in the pot he'd won, drawled: "Hear tell. Some little firebrand you got here, Joe. But we all know how she comes by it. Backroom politics, hmm? Lil ole lady, in the back room."

"Hush, Eleazir," the host, Walter Markens, said. "You go too far. Keep it to poker." He knew my father. Who had turned not red but an ominous white.

"Mind your manners, daughter," he said. "Recollect we don't sass our elders."

Then he got up to go, pulling out his watch. A watch on a chain gives you more gesture, lost to us now. "Time we're wanted home."

Nobody stopped him, though Walter said, "Joe." And to me, catching me eyeing the box, "No take it, hon. It was kindly meant. And earned...And regards to your grandmother." My father put a hand on his shoulder, pressed his hand.

Then we left—never to return. Though without further protest, in the engagingly temperate, social evasiveness that, as a second-generation "native-born," he had absorbed.

As I hold that envelope again in hand, or merely in mind, I know how to interpret now our visitors' always-nervous smile, whether they were related to us or not. A kind of communal smile, spread across all their mouths—not singly. Half admiring its strengths as a bulwark, I learned to tick off any breach. An anecdote, jokey, on "the colored folk," say (implying that down-home Declaration didn't necessarily mean implementation) and as suddenly curtailed. Or a grimace, squirming admission that the very pillow the speaker sat on was "up Nawth."

There's a German word for the possessor of such a smile. Engendered maybe because they, too, were to have so many of such. My mother used the word generally, whether on a hypocritical neighbor, or on me when I denied some infraction impossible to conceal. *Schmeichelkatze!* Smiley-cat. The English lacks the force of the guttural. Also I knew what she was really saying. "Your father's folks"—whose more educated company did flick a response in me that even *Tante*'s sweetness could not—"they're still just as immigrant as mine."

So they were. In the years to come, when grown, I was to meet many a "refugee," fled here to embrace one or the other of our liberties, but conservatively unable to quite embrace all those our Constitution had declared.

Consider my grandfather. Arrived here circa 1827, he might be considered almost a founder, in the widening prospectus of the country as later historicized. But why he had come was never said. Or asked, by me. Certainly that book had detailed a group of German Jews arriving in Richmond around the same time. But there had been no aura of their fleeing religiously, or out of ghetto repression. No "flight" had in fact ever been implied. Rather, I myself had assumed the stimulus as merely the middle-class urge to improve its status moneywise, with perhaps a livelier tinge of that intelligence which seeks the new. (For, ensconced between home and school—Hunter High, to which one was admitted only by exam and a high rating there, then Barnard, which was rumored to have a Jewish quota, I was lamely to admit—when confronted with my caseload, some of whom of whatever race were not merely poor but of that other "minimal" any country must carry, that I had never before met "a dumb Jew.")

So here is my grandfather, observing the custom of the country, whether blithely or resignedly we cannot know. As the steel engraving, married to the lady in the back room, let him rest. And don't blame the Jews—or not specifically. In Sunday school we were taught to think of ourselves biblically—flight out of Egypt and on—as ever oppressed. In history (college level), as ever Inquisitioned.

Finally, under the Holocaust, may we all claim an inch or so of martyrdom's prayer shawl? And Canaan, the promised land, suddenly locates itself with a surety to which no lexicographer can quite attest? But who says that being hunted, driven from pillar to post for what you are, means that once harbored in safety, or at least in asylum, you'll be automatically swamped in sympathy for others so targeted?

The whole 25,000-mile circumference of our earth's patchwork attesting otherwise. But I'm addicted to the single story. Practice not making perfect, as I well know.

That wedding picture of the two "servants"? Long since vanished from our family archive. But still as cardboard clear. They were maybe the two I tried to replace with myself, in that envelope? But couldn't quite evict? "Servants" it says, not indicating how many. But somehow even in a land where such service was "bound," I can't allot my ancestors more than a modest two-in-help. With perhaps a "boy" of indeterminate actual age—maybe even an old retainer?—to chop wood. Plus some turbaned pancake expert, maybe not freed but being worked on, snuck in as kitchen help now and then?

... One day, he of the bow tie and fancy jacket—borrowed for the occasion and long since passed on—can't stop hungering for it. Once of course a white person's, deeded down. (Once, in Rockland County, I lent our "day girl" the family bassinet, in which I myself had been cradled. She never returned it, and knowing what might be progressing, I never asked for it back. I knew it would be assumpted into that group service, and saw that as rightful. Maybe it's still there?)

Anyway, one day that hungerer says to the wife from the bayou, whispers it, "Marster's not a bad one. But I got the belly-growls. Let's railroad ourselves off." She says, "I can maybe pass for Creole? Speaking my French." Neither says the word "underground," ever. Even when only talking ferret dogs. That is not what you do. Did.

"I don't have the belly-growls," the wife says. "*Mais toujours*—what they call here a crick in the neck. Like 'tis not my own?"

Comes from having a price on the head. That's understood. So—they decamp. Maybe their descendants live in Harlem. Or in the broad city, almost anywhere?

When my mother's maid before Frances, Edna, took ill, I went to see her, swinging off the downtown bus to high school at 137th Street—to save pocket money—and walking the rest of the way to 168th, both ways. She was surprised. "Your mother know 'bout this?" No, she didn't. "I came on my own." And kind of proud of it. Which Edna no doubt saw. She was my first dying person, though I wasn't to know that, until she telephoned to quit. I never told anybody I had been there.

But it was she who, long since having spooked out my interest in the Underground Railroad, that day swapped me a piece of it, in thanks. Her folks had come North that way—from "Callina." "And do you know every safe house along the way, that's how those were called—tried to have a player piano in it? Why ever, would you fancy?"

The dying love to riddle. That's what I learned that time. I hope to do the same.

"No'm,"—I said. "Why?"

"To account for the singing," she said. "And for the pedal pumping, to lend the foot strength."

An autobio. I begin to know what it is now. An assemblage of meanings, occurring along the lived path. Not all of mine to be solely black-and-white.

"What's black-and-white and red all over?" That first grade-school riddle. The answer? "A newspaper"—of course.

Each day now the news, printed or wired, hoists the burden of human consciousness over the single head. All woe accessible at the fingertip.

I'm up at the "farmhouse," too early as usual. Kept warmed to fifty degrees by a furnace like an arc light at its core, all its neat, small furnishings stand exactly as left in December, when it was "closed." It doesn't so much greet us as allow us to enter again: a dignity maintained. "Of course, I never really closed."

Up here all the physical lost in the city animates. The snow, deep over the mole huts, has been dragged off as if by helpers we never see, pulling from the earth below, from the sun above, leaving mud not at all primeval, but like the browned smear left by some disgruntled committee come to check damage the county might be liable for, who swore to each other, "All okay for these part-timers. No break-ins"—and left.

I came to see the welkin, that metallic sky which arches here with an abstract depth the city will not allow. The word is no longer even in the *Oxford Universal,* which has waited here, monk-like, as dictionaries will. The welkin is here all right, cobalt-dark. It will allow us to kid ourselves that we had left it, rather than what any local lout knows better—that it has stayed on.

Outside, the "eyebrow" windows held their wisdom, as we walked in. The grate accepts the fire we now put in it. The cold chairs creak under the buttocks that will shortly warm them, once again. The only sound is from a log dislodged as we pull one from the indoor woodpile, left of the mantel, behind the tongs that silently hang. The small grunt the log makes is like a servant saying "yes'm." The servants here serve us well. But as we all know, one wrong jiggle or lack of sense on our part— and they could "declare."

This is no farmhouse anymore. No livestock, not for—how long? The well had to be dug again, as it already had been—before. And before. But this place will tolerate us. Because it must. In reparation we will remind all comers that there are bears up the hill. Nothing unusual of course now, in New York State, where bears are now the tramps at the back doors.

What one is advised to avoid, or to abscond from on the double, is a mother bear if met with her cubs. I'll slog up rea-sonable hills, or staircases, enjoyably; ski lifts seem to me inter-minable. The men go up our hill, guns on shoulder, skinny furless creatures that we are. But not I—and not from fear. Or not precisely. What would I do, if I met her? Out of sheer maternal interest—and the cronydom that comes from it—might I stand there, holding my ground? I have had cubs.

No, this is no longer a farmhouse. We grow nothing, not even flowers, not since the season when even the sunflower, that tall, benign monitor, was eaten—by the deer. Now, too, they encroach. Once they used to appear. Subtly, as in an old children's tale, at the end of the long pasture—now a front yard, where there's a pond. At the doe's flank, the fawn, gamboling. The stag's antlers a filigree, motionless.

At our window we said "Shhh," lyrical. How could they hear us? But they had. Aware always of these aliens at the edge of their cosmos. Gone. Sucked into the trees by woodland parachute.

Nowadays, they idle nearer and nearer that same window. The spring grass, thrilling green, has been mown for them. Eyes downcast, cropping diffidently, they steal ever nearer the front steps, as if about to ask to use the telephone.

"I'm all right, Jack. You all right?" the city construction gangs used to yell from down in the ditches being dug—when there were still open lots on which to construct.

I'm all right. Though this auto-revelation oozing now onto the qwertyuiop keyboard, isn't, we-ell—quite "all." I could hot it up with wild oats, certainly sown, at one time. Or with erotica? On the shelves of our household Eros was already assumpted into literature—as in Boccaccio's miniature shockers, or Shakespeare's easy riff on the "cull"? At university, a spell of erotica can also occur. Any decade, the long Gallic diphthongs can solicit, or those Indian manuals, dug out of the stacks, revolve for the neophyte the three or more profiles facaded on the face of Love. But manuals are so earnest. Like making love in front of a bystander who wishes to name the parts—both of yours—as they exhilarate. And my teenage sessions with the nineteenth-century Gallic crème de la crème—Gautier, Marguerite de Navarre—taught me, those sharp-eyed bedtime chroniclers, agile as good butchers, to merely "french" the roast.

In England I did have a great friend who, among many talents, was also an illustrious porn-master. Though I managed to elude him biblically, I had a great regard for him, as did many not interested in that side of a personality whose energies were multiple. His library is now in the British Museum. Early on, he essayed plying me with items from it, illustrious—and valuable. To my distress, I found them dull. I love secondhand clothes, to the point where I feel guilty if buying from a genuine store. But it seems I can't do with secondhand sex. Or reportage. I tend to laugh.

So, with no hope of extravagant millions derived from episodizing (or sodomizing) a "Story of H" from "O," but in thanks for a valuable insight (the ones from outside authority often the most worthy), I did write a burlesque of sex versus politics, using, as then noted, all the fashionable four-letter terms that if sounded *chez* my parents, would have broken every vase in the house. In gratitude to my friend, I dedicated *Queenie* to him and his wife.

As for porn denigrating women, why bother about that? There being so many worse practices that do.

One thing more I am finding I avoid—as I intoxicate here (for that is the sensation). A writer, especially one who travels, tends to collide now and then with the "famous." From being near enough at a soiree to Tito to worry lest he be bursting his buttons, but never exchanging a word with him—to the "household name" down whose cleavage you can see. To the premier, into whose ear you said, "How shall we two change

the world?"—moving mischievously on before he could respond. Down to the one to whom you would gladly kneel, but
have a cup of tea with instead.

One makes one's own notables really, or I have, listing them
is not consonant with the way I would lead my life. Or have.
While in the biographies they are dry as dust. So, here no names
à la mode.

But now, as I near the finish, that other syllable auto-bursts
into flower. Salving what I never thought could be: The skull at
the bottom of the garden, where we eat while others starve.
The ankle bracelet, gone from the torture cell's iron chain to
embossed silver, lightly linked with the land of the free.

As usual I have begun to mistrust the monologue, here grown
phenomenally, as must happen with all those confined in solitary. Worse is the thesis that sent me here teetering? Am I once
more facing what the thrashers for "equality" dare not admit:
that the "unequal" may cling to and even relish that servitude? I
served my bound years under that shittiest of American eu-
phemisms—homemaker. Yet unlike all the bright girls now out
on the barricades in all the quasi-verbal professions: advertising,
speech writing, pop dialogue cheerfully supplied, I had been
saved from marketing my mind. Or such as it might grow to be.
Meanwhile my kitchen professorship and dawn-to-dusk cleaning—from snotty noses to hair in the sink, and sofa crumbs—
may have supplied me with more plebe metaphor than high art
is comfortable with?

In such a stew I repair to "my" lawyer. Kieran is in fact very
carefully not anybody's. Nor does he plead in court. His pleasure and duty is to supply comfort to the irregular, either private
clients or public, payment from either come-and-go. Kieran's
great-grandparent, clerking at the A&P grocery chain, had

starved his own family in order to buy shares. Selling off before the chain's demise, he had left his heirs "independent"—other than with a slight tendency toward TB, Kieran's hectic cheeks result only from Irish rhetoric. Which I always find as soothing as sailing the sea in a pea-green boat for whose leaks I am not responsible.

For him, the advantage of our friendship is that I'm "literary"—his word rather than mine. But I cherish his explanation. "For me, that's glamour—spelled with an 'ou'... You see—" At that point his eyes mist.

This can't happen often, surely, in a man of the law. Kieran is a short man, rounded rather than flinty, this somehow increasing that lovely accessibility of tongue. Clean-shaven, the chin cupped now in his hands. But no cherub's. Even gloomy, when he croons "Every Irishman worth his salt considers his life a book someone else wrote."

I've no urge to snap "And Irishwomen?" Any insistence that we be right up there in the grammar department has drained from me long ago. You can't earn equality; you assume it. Besides, Kieran is likely more modern there than most of our sex are. Thanks to his wife Bronwen—by her picture on the desk a Welsh beauty whose dimples don't conceal an iron jaw you can trip over—and whose office next door is where one goes either to hammer down a copyright or pursue one. But what's worrying him? Two grown children tease that it was hard lines having a father who's looked like a fifty-year-old boy as long as they've known him. His smirking reply "A lawyer balances his pound of flesh as he can." The "attorney" pomp is beyond him.

But now, with that screw of worry in his forehead, he could be the sixty-five he is.

"You want me to write you up?" I say. "Someday I will, if that's your desire; I promise you. But that's not what I'm here for today." "Thank you," he says with a grin. "There's already quite enough of me, I feel. And Bronwen agrees...No, it's you coming here all of a sudden...We did your two wills for you, years back. We added a clause, for the son's new little girl. And glad to. And we double-checked that lease of yours; co-ops can be tricky these days. But in every other respect—though we charged you the going, as has to be even with clients who are friends—you two were still the kind we could relax over dinner with...I mean—"

Lawyers' faces learn to be featureless, skintight. But on his there's a glow. "That North Italian place last month? Good enough. But the bottom-line treat was not being quizzed on how we could do better, or on some new dodge that's occurred to you—on Yours against Whozit?...Like: Give us the dope, Kieran. Have we really got a case?" He falls back, exhausted.

"But, Kieran, you know we don't sue. That is—we haven't. That's not why I—I mean I'm only here to—?" What am I here for? "On...on something I've inherited."

Hunched over conspiratorially, he could be that dwarf who everybody in the thriller thinks did it. Who did.

The voice creeps like syrup. "Who you suing?"

Gone, I think. Work fatigue? No, aping his West Coast clients, Kieran always knows when to take off. Skiing in the Alpes Maritimes was only the beginning. He knows lie-down islands where you go to laze off from your massage spa. In court, where I'd heard him plead a couple of times because he was my only access to a milieu I ought to see, he was never languid, but never sauced the judge. As one of those toughie blond Hibernian angel-faces who can look like the head boxer on Saint Peter's team, and never go bald, he still was able—by slumping and wearing cheap in-stock clothing—to tone down his aureole. Indeed, when I heard him, he defending a settlement house against which a team of workmen had filed allegations of injury obviously faked, it was said he had rinsed his golden hair and beard to a safer brown.

"Suing?" I said. "Kieran Kilroe, who would I sue?"

I never call him that—a name he himself says is the kind chosen by parents of modest origin—his father had been a trolley-car conductor who hoped their kids would advance to monogrammed towels. But he has angered me. By idly misconceiving me. Which old friends are not supposed to do.

"*You* tell *me.*" He blows a smoke ring at me. I blow one back. In those days we smoked. Floating those rings from school lounges to barrooms, to signal that we shared the same love dreams, and passions on how to save the world. Which in spite of militarist weddings—or because of them—seemed a heavy-breathing but gloriously heightened place. Where even on the badlands one walked among oracles that promised pinnacles.

In law school Kieran had sworn never to sell anybody cheap, including himself. This now enables him to serve clients both rich and poor—the bills going to the former, and all his "bias" toward the latter. "Bias," as he says, "being all the heart any sensible advocate should boast."

"All you nice sentimentalists," he says. "Singing out against the world's ills. And then sitting on your hams."

"You're so right," I say. "I used to lilt like that. Why does social protest always alliterate? Terrible. Like part-singing with the sopranos off-key. So I went back to the page. But it still happens there. Know what? Humans are supposed to be the only animals who've developed consciousness. Been yakking our glory ever since. But maybe—just now and then—we merely bark and hiss?"

His swivel chair has allowed him to lean back far enough to put his feet on the desk—a vanity posture more often of the tall. I'm careful not to laugh—until I see he's laughing at me.

"How you divagate, honey. You should be in court."

"Oh—my dance training," I smirk. *"Plié"*—I cross my ankles—*"Grand jeté"*—I fling out an arm. *"Attitude."* Freeze.

He smirks back, that last fling before the ironic grow serious. Sighs. "We're swamped with litigants. All suing the government, ours or others, over injustices that have existed next door to their kind three thousand years. And no doubt B.C."

"Before that," I say dreamily. "Let's not limit."

"Agreed. And highly profitable for us in the law. In publicity alone. If we didn't have to deflect. Like the client who wants to sue—what's the country once was Burma?—for incarcerating that lovely insurgent of theirs—he saw her picture. He wants damages for each hour of her house arrest. According to some scale of compensation he's figured out. And he would prove formidable. Only glitch is he's a slum landlord of national scope... And here's—"

"Don't tell me," I interrupt.

But he overrides. "And here's one, Wang McGoldrick Jonathan III, solid Chinese citizens, three generations Frisco, all American named. But they run those backward, in honor the homeland. Pays us an honorarium for listing us on their stationery—and to oversee contractual agreements. All so far, word of mouth. They're so honest that just being with them an hour or so is like breathing at high altitude. But now their senior potentate, head of the Breath of Beijing restaurant-supply outlets, has just returned from a long-courted reception there—furious. He found out that having more than one child there is discriminated against. Or worse. He dumped it all on us. Don't they know that their secret of empire is to populate?" Kieran grins—more normally. "And put one descendant at every outlet... So?" He ruffles hair too short to "let down," to him a gesture of intimacy. "Are people getting to admit the world's a damn cruel place—the way they used to? Or papering it over?"

"In case the aliens we find turn out to be on such a higher plane—all good works and goodwill? So that we'll want to hide our dirty planet? On which there's so much misery?"

"Oh, you," he says. "I'm sure there'll be enough in my lot they'd be jealous of. And maybe in yours."

Kieran doesn't really believe in the existence of anybody else that much—except for a few willing to be his interlocutors—like me. As for me, I'm on the fence. I don't mind going along with those physicists who assert there must be other life in the universe (and did once posit and have fun with an elliptical one). But I can't afford to give Whatever-Whom that much more of my time. *Ad astra,* or universe-wise, we're now into our new century—and peanuts though that may be to the black-hole crowd, I've already overstayed.

…In fact Kieran, like many of my contemporaries within a certain range, has begun to fade. Particularly those who have had reputations to keep up. A delusive exercise at best. Maybe worse for those who were once almost enthroned. The man in the street being the ultimate authority…I once knew a university president, hobnobber of leaders in every capital, who prophesied correctly, "I'll lose my box at the races, minute I step down."

Kieran, noting I've fallen into a brown study, has done the same, though owing to his complexion the effect is more auburn, and less likely to last. I've always had the luck to have friends so matching me they almost might have been custom-made to fit—by me? If so, watch it, K.K., in his three-piece pin-stripe, and with that profession stuck like a bone in his throat may be a warning. My women friends do far better, having had to work harder to be seen as individuals. Or even to get off first base—which for them has to be located between waist and knee.

"Don't fade on me," Kieran says suddenly. "These days, I have trouble dividing which of my friends is dead or alive. What with seeing a lot of us on old television. As well as on live."

He stands up, begins to pace, like when we were students spelling each other, or boning up for exams. He hearing me sour-faced on what would likely be tested for the English comprehensive, me crouched over, following with a finger his recital from a "trot" smuggled from old bar exams. "In fact, that's what's wrong with those poor buggers who're swarming in here: 'Don't trust anything digital,' one said to me. 'It can't show dirt. Or any agony. It's just too damn clean.'"...And then he says, "Okay, lead in the pipes could kill us. But what else can we use?"

"Stop walking round and round me."

He stops. "You're doing the same. Inside. I can tell. So who're you suing?"

It's like water torture, but of course he's right. "My grandfather. Only he's outside the statute of limitations."

He's quiet enough of a sudden. Like some doctor you've just told that your headache comes from elves picking at your hairline. Finally he says, "Not directly, we couldn't. But—if there is an estate?"

"There jolly well is...Yes." Now and then I go British, for emphasis, thanks to living there now and then—and they do it so well. Nor do the friends over there so often fade, dead or alive. That's an American custom. Giving ground less doggedly, because we have so much of it?

"Not settled yet?" He looks eager.

"Never will be."

"Hah."

I'm being a tease, with no excuse except the eternal one: That was then. This is now...Speak, Clio.

"When'd he die?"

"Dunno. Nor when he was born. Came here 1827? Married 1852—for sure."

He whistles through his teeth. A boy's bleat. Not good enough for an alley, too shrill from behind an office door.

"You do want something of me." His eyes screw.

I'm ashamed that this is true. There's another side of humanity where one gives without taking, but I'm not paranormally able to be there for long.

For Kieran—one puts away such childish things. All that Belfast can mean to him now is a revolutionary gloss on a social process that he thoroughly disavows. If with a thrill, each time he enunciates the word, of having been just near enough the juggernaut to qualify as an Eire-ishman.

And I'm just as much the fraud. Wanting to be told why I'm so emotional about my discovery, I've sought out the person least likely to understand why. Frauds seek out frauds, eh? Many critics may find the "analyst's" fees unconscionably high for a technique that must cling to exemplary fellow feeling. Yet the fee doubles when the analyst is oneself. And the clues?

For as I hand Kieran the envelope safely enclosed in a braw white modern one, and like its enclosure a century and a half ago, left unsealed, what am I thinking?

Set a thief to catch a thief—that's what. Aren't I trying to steal a sense of honor for myself. Of obligation long gone and never mine. Out of moral indignation merely...(That of course being what moral indignation is.)

"Servants?" he says, at first blankly. Then, "Arr-r, you one of those can't employ without guilt? Always paying their cook and bottle washers more than the going rate—and doing half the work themselves?"

"Well, I have scrubbed floors. But I've got over that empathy." I haven't. I not only thieve, I lie.

Kieran's third wife is a Spanish grandee who until her family had fled, post-Franco, had never combed her own hair. When they met she was a call girl. Corrupted beauty fascinates him. That of course being what moral obligation is. Like many in the law, he feels he must be near corruption but not of it. But those above the law fill him with rage, all the stronger because it's envious. When I explained what "servants" meant and he examines the evidence, he says nothing at first except "Marvelous paper stock. Feel it."

But the dates interest him, 1856...1865. "Your grandfather was within his legal rights. So rest easy."

"That's the trouble."

"Ah." Then, "Want me to hunt those servants up, do you. So you can apologize to their heirs? Or maybe even compensate?"

"Don't be absurd."

"Good thing. In case your grandparents had too many."

"It's just that: I never thought. I didn't appreciate. Or maybe I half did...like—all those sweet-talking lady cousins of ours. Bending their pretty mouths to protest something—maybe nothing more than a needle prick. Saying, 'Oh, shoot.' Always did wonder about that etymology. Their conversation was peppered with it. Prolly still is."

We laugh. The way you do.

"Guess I do maybe want to apologize," I say. "To history."

He sits up then. Like any professional who's been giving of his valuable time to a friend for free. But maybe smells payback for himself? "I go South now and then," he says. "I'm the partner who travels. To keep the firm personalized. I could scout around. Any facts might still be there. Insurance leaves a long trail."

"I don't even know their names. The servants I mean. So-called."

"We have your grandfather's."

"So we do. So...we...do." How can I dislike a man I never knew? "Don't even know whether he came North. Or died before. My father was near fifty when I was born. His father—when he was, maybe even older." I get tired of repeating this. "Used to happen—maybe more. Or in countries where older men still marry young girls." Though my mother hadn't quite qualified.

"You Ivy Leaguers," Kieran says. "I had friends at Columbia, Yale. The law can equalize a student early. And all of them taught to believe the one-world-to-come. But on a tight little island—where maybe you sneak a quarter mile off and their god is different—you know the score. We used to tease my grandmother she came over here with potatoes in her pocket. Just in case."

"I always thought you Irish believed in the one flag—more than we wanderers could." Though we try. Every time.

"Oh, we do"—flashes that smile. "Temporarily."

The same white-toothed American smile I have. The Depression never affected it. Nor gave us the rickets and bow legs. Hospitals saw pots of those later on, but we weren't that sort.

Instead, for me—the caseload. Then—the parental deaths, like a slowly turning key. Finally the stories, pouring like atonement from the congested heart.

He gives me back my peculiar treasure. "But so long ago," he marvels. "Why bother now?"

"I felt it back then, when my father died. I must have. It just didn't hit. And I was busy with the family."

As we all are. He follows my glance to the pictures on his desk. The Spanish wife and the daughters in their timeless bodices, the several grooms, led by him, the small children—of which generation? If asked, he would enumerate. Once in a while—I do...Rather a display. But he has the desk for it. And the forty-first-floor view.

We both stand up. "Well, we're no detective agency," he says, "but I can poke. But promise me—"

"Not to—expiate?...How could I?"

"We keep natural here," he says. "We have to. No matter what we see. It's built in. But your crowd—" He's not insensitive. "I mean—you writers..."

"Oh, Kie-eran." I have always felt it easiest to confess to the Irish. All of whom, even my one aunt by marriage, have been Catholics. To whom confession, in or out of church, is more happily routine. Once, in a foreign church, seeing the box the priest must put his ear to, I went in, though no one was about— and leaned there. Breathing nothing, having nothing to say, except—"I exist." That queerishness, when it comes over you that you do.

"When I started—," I say. "When I became one, so to speak." Because you really are one only intermittently. As what you do appears. "I thought it would bring me—into the fold. Just normally. I could now say what I was. Like other people: lawyer, doctor, preacher, manager, all the etceteras. To which people nod. But it doesn't bring us in the fold. You keep us out. You think there's something cockamamy about it; don't you. And about us...Oh, we get to sport our cockades—in some downbeat hall. Or maybe London's Guildhall, places like that— when we gather big. But we're not to be trusted, really. Especially not with our own lives."

I see by his look that I'm proving that. He pats my shoulder, then my cheek. "Don't do anything I would do. In case."

We both have to laugh. But I have the last word. As all too often?

"A partner—," I say, sweeping the establishment with a glance maybe not jealous enough. That, too, is my trouble. "And you have other partners. What luck."

Funny thing: in all this interchange, though he's seen the envelope and its markings, and tallied my explanation with that tempered, nodding silence all lawyers award your tale—neither of us has once said the word: Slave.

So here I am, back at the monologue. That being only the furthest, yet not-quite-out-of-bounds sign that I must work alone. This time, I interlace my fingers tight, the palms forming a hollow between. Sincerity is the invisible egg held there, that I must not crack. I'm permitted to create deception—as the dancer swooshes out a veil that, as it settles toward her, she at the last moment eludes. But I must not ever wholly deceive. To err is so human. But not human enough?

It is possible—nay, probable—that we will not see Kieran Kilroe again. Nor will I hear from him, unless I set it up. Perhaps I imagined him? I needed an interlocutor. On whom to test, try, repercuss, and finally offer (like larks shot on the wing and served by the distraught cook when roasted but not unfeathered) the propositions toward which this narrative tends:

Proposition I. Resolved: "That this earth-ball we live on, snowy with Everests, chartered with omni-green, as if chlorophyll is hope, and weighed by cities whose glitter makes Babylon a peddler's cart—and pushed about by homunculi ever nose-in-the-wind toward the slightest drizzle of enlightenment—that this earth, so poised between its Gulf Streams and melting Arctic wastes, so that it may end in an apoplexy of atmosphere, is yet worthy to be its universe's star."…Capable even of imagining other universes—surely the height of cosmic good-sportsmanship?

Proposition II. Resolved: "That any corner of this planet not under the looking glass (and of most right there) is so snot-clotted with misery as to be graphless in that realm. While in the crevices not quite beyond the mildly audacious flashlights of the rights-watchers—the cell-torturers operate." Yet be proud, Awnt Nell. It is reported that almost the whole of a—is it a nation? call it Gambia—is illiterate.

I had a cup of tea just now; ASSAM, the tin says. Smooth and encouraging as a flower-burst of Indian air. Trouble is: I believe in both those propositions.

While around the rim of my work spot, this bowl of reflection which I have sought, people hang by their fingernails, waiting to be characterized. The nail analogy is unfortunate. On the TV screen, which I pop now and then for news—a bomb factory. Each bomb curved like a harpy's ever-growing fingernail.

But I've been through this before. Before. Hard as it is to believe in the worst of us, easy as it is to credit the best of us (or reverse the "hard" and the "easy") that is what we alternately do. On into that night where both the unbearable and the delight of being will be borne away.

Ah—that was a swoop of language, last night's entry. Forgive me—such of you parishioners as are left to me—I minister as I can. Never entered a church that I didn't want to dance in. Never open a book wherein I don't want to pray. If such is religion, then I am a proper catechumen. Ready to convert:

I believe in the resurrection, in which a wine is poured by the living. Into the cups of the dead. In the open-all-night restaurant. At dawn we close. By pulling up all the window shades.

When I came in—it was 1924. I was twelve, going on thirteen. Where we are now—if you be still with me, you very well know.

So now are we going to hear from everybody? Why not?

In apology.

In the sitting room, the steel engraving looks down. "I was a storekeeper. Dry goods. Lots of heavy liftables, to be shifted about. I had to shift with them. Some of us have to be slave keeper as well. I came from Europe, Eyerup—and Stirrup! Where my son Joe never got to go. Brought with me the big Doré Bible...Famed for such steel engravings as will ever out-shine me. Yet my little wife of the wardrobe trunks—that is what we called them—walked ever handmaiden, at my side. Joe's daughter owns that Bible now. For any explanation of our lives let her pore over its text...That is my bequest."

My grandmother and my mother? Each has spoken her piece—as handmaidens will. Using the lore of the house, and the rite of giving birth. Each of those garnered, so to speak, from whatever and whomever was at hand.

While my father has sung. And still sings.

Only one has not been heard from. Who might that be?

"They gave me my letters. She did. That's what they call it. When they give the eyes—a child's mostly—the power to pick up what the letters say. All she said was 'Nell, my eyes are going. Cain't read the labels enny moah.'...When she spoke to us, even to me—she kind of spoke lak we do...Lot of them do. Sometimes, it's speaking down at us. But sometimes, it's reaching out. Never held it against her. Even if, all those hours she stewed me in those schoolbooks of Joe's, I had to read out egg-zact like she. 'You stewin' me white,' I say. 'Gwine be sorry for it.' And she hisses back, 'Go-ing. Not gwine.' Which was right—we-ell. Ruther not say. Cause when she got forceful, you could hear the German tickle in it. So I can't truly quote, but she did say 'I mought pour out the molasses. 'Stead of the milk. So you got to help me out.'"

Because everything liquid seemed to come in the same size bottle—my father said. "After the war. Had to do with the bottle factory. Which was up North. Anyway, it was like they were sending us insults, of a sort. Narrow, squared-off bottles you couldn't mistake. Bury them long enough—for we had no other disposal—and they would take on a pearly blue-green, almost what you would see in a museum, in an amphora."

I was old enough by then for him not to have to explain what that was. "Nowadays," he'd said, with a hint of scorn, "nowadays, people collect."

"Nell was always very careful not to put in her two-cents' worth," my father said, the one time I pushed him to expatiate on this tender matter. "Now that her own outside family, not to say our neighbors, knew she'd been 'overeducated'—as both sides would have said."

In general he preferred not to speak of her. An aging man speak of his "mammy"—and up here in the quick-bottling North? But I see another reason now. Watching her, still a boy in his first teenage jobs, he had been alerted to the word power that could noose a compromise between eye and tongue. "She did say," he admitted, "that she had got herself a private procla-mation." His eye had lingered on one or other of the Josies my mother had substituted for *die Schwarzen*. He made one of those odd sounds—between chuckle and cough—which suggest what one wants to say, but won't. Not in black-and-white.

So, hail and farewell, all my hearties. *Ave, atque vale.* There's no way of translating Virgil's *atque*: that *and* which makes the two sides of a salute absolutely equal. My Virginians would feel the same. Nor would we be merely showing off our small Latin. That double sound is the choral echo which apologia leaves in one's own ear. As if—after improvising through all the sharps and flats, minor and major—one finds oneself resolving, not too loud and with one forefinger, on middle C. Into which any occasional and accidental notes melt away.

When you tell a story, it's kind of a scramble for partners. All the more so, when you are telling your own. The trick (or the desperate gesture?) is to involve everybody you can think of—whom you may have touched. Or have touched you. Even if they didn't know.

Can't hope to omit the "I" entirely. But discount that descending tri-syllable: *Re-mem-ber,* which drips through such accounts, and through maybe all history? Like that bugle an obedient soldier must listen for. Sometimes it sounds reveille (pronounced to rhyme with Beverly), as if to goose the dreamer out of some once lived-in bed. Sometimes sounding taps—like a shoulder being batted and counseled: "The graves are over there."

I intend to save that word for my finish. When it will make that particular call, defined as "that one which by successive blows of bugle or drum in the evening, signals the soldier to return to his quarters in garrison, or to the tents in camp."

It is evening now. Perhaps my father, as mnemonic a man as ever I knew, will join me there? In the early days in the States, salesmen were called "drummers." Later, as the category grew and became formalized, what these man did, barnstorming from town to town, sending in their cards to a large backslapping acquaintance, and at the trade's apex patronizing the hotels especially known for accommodating such, the term changed. Acquiring that overblown dignity it perhaps needed. For many of these men, like my father, were no tobacco-chawing itinerants ready for an evening out with the gals, but family men, who night after night, week after week, might have to assume the accoutrements of jollity, but yearned to be home. While some, like him, represented businesses they owned.

In his effects is a small oblong brass tray, about the size of an ashtray, and perhaps chosen so, as an amulet of membership, one that could also be used in the culture of the cigar—before that of the cigarette. The maker, stamped tiny on its reverse, dates it: METAL ARTS, ROCHESTER, N.Y.—originator of the celebrated Rochester brass oil lamps, porcelain shaded, which later, when electrified, would flood antique shops. On the little tray, an elaborate design centers on a double-wreathed circle. The outer one inscribed U.C.T., the inner one explaining: UNITED COMMERCIAL TRAVELERS.

But it is the line drawing in the center that can still cause a pang. I'd always dismissed it as mere design. Until my sharper-eyed husband showed me it under the magnifying glass: a traveling bag. In fact, a valise made up of those soft sections, flappable backward, into which numberless dry goods might be stuffed. The straps of any valise I had ever seen had been leather. But under the glass the two attached here are clearly chains. This tray's owner, as said, dangled no emblems on his watch chain, nor sported any decorations in his buttonhole. Men of his era could put a posy there, when escorting a woman, or she might so adorn him. I seemed to have seen that once or twice when very young, but not since. In his drawer, along with the cuff links, dress-shirt studs, and tie pins, had been a pair of large, flat silver links, embossed JHC, through which suspenders could be threaded. Though only black silk, or white in summer, would have been threaded through them.

I sent those to my son, who had never known his grandfather. As a West Coast wearer of jeans, and at times red suspenders, he appreciates eras—perhaps it is hereditary. The traveler's tray is to me a symbol of his grandfather Joe's envelope—that continuity. And there is still his great-grandfather's to come.

What shall we do with these continuities which overflow all lives? No matter how bleak a life, there is always something that may be carried on. Even for that classic infant left on a doorstep, wrapped in a shawl. Even to the fetus left in a garbage can, that the most fact-worn city, recoiling, will try to keep hushed.

I have a sneaky fondness for the marriage page. Where each couple erects the frail architecture it plans to inhabit—and maybe populate? While publishing the plans for all to see. The world knows writers who hate their past. Or shamed by it, club it down ceaselessly. Or those who, with good reason, cannot escape history's bloody hand. There are those who must ennoble—often from countries like Britain or France, where the snobbery of primogeniture is indeed prime. In one friend's account, it would seem that the very genes come ennobled: the male ones properly titled, with perhaps just a spot of ermine contracted illegitimately; the female genes at least bordered with hereditary lace...Or there are, more thankfully, those comics who entertain us with family eccentricity, ridiculed. All, all in response to the power of generation? This narrative, then, is mine?

Or so it has taught me, as the self, when revisited, cannot help but do. Observing, as if under thrall, the thrust of the generations by which it has been conceived. A dire engagement, in which that cool talent—the so-called brain—collaborates with that hot jigsaw puzzle—the so-called heart. The psychoanalysts, those sidewalk observers, call this enthrallment "projecting." A petty thievery at which one can smile. Both the process and its name, stolen from all the poets, dramaturgists, and dancers, of history. From all the arts, doomed as these are to the virtue of the repeat.

And so to bed?

As it happens, far too appropriately. For this family bed on which I repose, harking back, this arrant challenge to its heirs, a bed far too huge and darkly awesome for modernity, is that same bed in which I saw my grandmother die.

It was still there, you see, in its time migrated from household to storage, and back again—and at my marriage could not be ignored. Humbly it submitted to the restorer who lengthened its sideboards for its taller occupant-to-be, we protesting weakly meanwhile "It's not really an antique." The mattress of course renewed, to a quality and expense we would not have felt obliged merely for ourselves. Guests, to whom we now cede it, proclaim that they last night embarked on a wider-than-usual space. But that's illusion, concocted by a footboard broad enough for children to sit on, as they immemorially have. Plus a central panel, which when stared into while its name is murmured, "Circassian walnut," seems to initiate them into all the mysteries of wood. Actually, it's only a double bed, no wider than those from any department store. That's the marvel. That the measurement for mortals should so precisely remain.

If I am here only because "the pater"—as my dad's English cousins might have said it—was conceived here, as seventh of eight, so be it. As we two sleep, that pair does not seem to impose. Not my grandmother—once seen here in a young person's pellucid gaze. Nor my grandfather, who so lacks anecdote that any vision of him, now and then inserted here, can be banished for lack of detail.

The headboard, arrogant as always, continues to measure us.

As for that envelope: when first encountered it measured him, founder of our brief dynasty. Then it measured me. Now, all considered, it has the humble radiance of a document, however small, that yet covers a multitude. My panicky impulse to crawl into its confines was not aberration. Nor even atonement. Merely that impossible craving which overcomes the enlightened—to switch the company one was born to travel with. If only for a breather—to join the rock-bottom crowd. Now and then the "investigator" who was I had almost persuaded herself it could be done.

Standing on a staircase, say, watching a coffin go bump-a-dump down the stairs, inside it the girl whom no cashmere sweater (secondhand from the "relief" stock) could save. Or sitting down to drink a cup of cambric tea, gently offered by the widowed Scotswoman, relic of an American citizen but the certificate lost, whose dole had been kept pending—while she starved. Until that day, when bringing her at last her allowance, I dared to set beside it my lunch thermos—of milk.

Once (upon a time), and "up in the country" as tactless city dwellers say of any region outside it, we found a cot-bed contraption of wooden slats attached to a fold-up metal frame. Asked its period, or rather, "When'd they use these things?" the dealer shrugged. "Used to see them, not anymore. Horse-and-wagon, maybe. Horse alone couldn't carry. Or about when the first Fords." He gave me a sharp look. "You like collapsibles, huh—anything that does." How could he tell?

Junkmen. Diagnosticians of a sort. In their lower orders, they can be like garden griffins gone buggy, stone-fleshed against any ripple of talk. But when smart, even nice, like this one, sterling characters, or at least Rogers silverplate, they can slip a hint as to why you—and they—have to collect.

Once we'd bought—for ninety bucks, which seemed steep but he wouldn't bargain—he expanded some, for free. "Have a fella, he'll buy any accordion I can find. Have a lady—she'll go for any handbag has those compartments, enough of them. Tried to sell her one of those hanging shoe bags? Nothing doing. 'Unh-unh, Jason,' she says—everybody calls me that—'has to be something at first it don't show what it can do.' Found her an article—just a four-inch square, thick paper, with one of those dime-a-piece brass locks. Hung out, opened onto a marriage license a yard long. She nearly went out of her mind."

The cot, unwrapped, eased into the back hatch of the Volvo, new and shiny then, and crouched there like a dog will, out of its habitat, only comforted when the window is opened for its muzzle to protrude.

"Have a museum lady, stops here," the junkman says. "Told me the covered wagons had similar. Spot me one of those, and she and I, we could both take off junking—on the dot." He smoothes the car's rump. "What you pay for this job?"

At our answer his head retracts under the jacket hood a man who sits all day against the wind will naturally wear. "You bought it new? New?" He turns his back, on the clods we are.

Set the cot up in the "guest room," also my studio, it yawns a bit, then settles down, next to the drop-leaf table that can take a computer or be a nightstand, or a dressing table. The folding footrest, also a seat, migrates between. But when we dust and scrub the cot free of the junkyard, there, hung on a white cotton twist, is the maker's tag. On it, in the curly black print that wasn't born yesterday: "Salesman's Bed."

I'm not fond of the symbol-hunting one meets in the classroom. Where Prince Myshkin, say, in Dostoyevsky's The Idiot, that image of a Russiandom already charismatic enough under a master's skill, has to be Jesus as well. I prefer truth plain. Truth is what's scoured down, undistorted, like in the bathhouse at the beach, that cubbyhole where there's nothing between you and your underwear. Then to the water, where all the poetry can play, from "Full fathom five thy father lies" to "the multitudinous seas incarnadine." If you're lucky you haven't had to wear a suit.

The new bed can stay. A country message.

City or country, chosen or inherited, one's furnishment instructs, proscribing the boundaries, even commanding the only kind of house or flat it will fit into; that's a Southern habit too.

A loft? My grandmother's three-piece love seat and two side chairs, all mahogany meringue with air in between, and seats that only the one-buttocked may find perch on? Sell?...If it's "by Belter," that Old South wood twirler, as some say it is, you can damn well buy the loft—and recline on your built-ins like a movie star.

"That's what they do now—," the Bible intones deep, from within its wrappings. (The black-leather cover with its gold JHC is frayed, needing the bookbinder, if an antebellum expert can be found.) "Sell their birthright for a mess of pottage." The love seat knows better. Pleading as I had once been teased to plead for an aunt's birthday gift, "Oh, please?" And humbly, when that doesn't do it: "Pretty please."

Keep me.

And forgive me? For I know what I do. I have spent my life in the habit of images. In the business of empathy. Nothing arcane about that. We are born to be enchanted by the cosmos the minute we open our eyes. And to puzzle forever over the teeming inanimate that houses us—how did it come to be? *Atque*— we, the animate. This landscape with figures, which is us. Which we cherish with overweening tenderness, praying that we be allowed to stay. For the lifetime. For those who come after us. How long will we all be allowed—to stay...Pretty please?

Some of us turning to remark to one another, "What a fool question to pose to a cosmogony?" Or not turning. Or not asking.

Then: Lucky he, or she, who has the apology to offer.

At a proper distance, it is not only mine, but shines like a hoard anybody would wish to glimpse at waking, as well as end of day. It is what as children we thought we saw—before. When all the adults, rising like monuments, are still mystical.

Then the wars will arrive. To advise us on which among us are to be the Blue, which the Gray. The frightening? Or the beloved?

Who's to tell us: *Never separate?*

So, I have my bequest. From my grandfather—who else? While the little lady of the trunks walks handmaiden at his side. While those who served them rose every morning to the howls of the day.

According to my mother, poking her head out of her parenthesis, those old trunks were lost in storage, as all the objects we live with eventually are. This is what she came to *Amerika* already knowing. Giving her an aura she will never lose.

My father shakes his head: nay, nay, nay—too short a word to be awarded voice. I feel a tingle in both palms, as when he used to tuck between them "see what I brought you...back." All his presents coming from that area. Traveling to me, from where nothing is lost. Is it a praline, from Atlantic City? Sugary and breakable as a smile? Or one of those Little Blue Books, scarcely larger than a stamp, guarding no more than a tiny paragraph. Wee booklets that swayed the continent of his boyhood with the will to educate?

It's his blessing. The kind that the grave gives best. That needs no pointed forefinger, smile or voice, but is compounded of all the autobiographical past:

"She'll find us, and with all our paraphernalia," it says of me. "She is our museum—that collects."

L'ENVOI

Many of the old real books we had, some family, some his, had that just ahead of the end, sticking up on the page like a sail. As if the book owned itself. Well, let it, I always thought, half resentfully. I have it now.

Which at last allows me the use of that three-syllable word—Remember—held back until now as one holds a lifelong breath, at last expelled. A word ever too casually used, that drips both blood and lace.

With it, permit me that other word, a stingy one-syllable. The burden of a hated song. Under which those who walk to its beat are dateless, no color or any color, lipless. Or the palate cleft, its speech a dribble, as all the freighted caravansary passes. Say it: slave—and the head of such a person, dislocating slightly at the neck, will at once have a price on it. Not at all impeding the body's toil.

A marvel, really. See how they dance, laugh, writhe in the hot slime of love. (And forever have done, under the historical moon.) Breed them, in all the dirty crevices of the planet. If lost (or wandered off, more likely), the premium can always be cashed.

Homebound, some are, as the saying goes—always with us. On the same pavement, side by side. Raise the ante, and hear us all chortling together our weekend lunacies?

Guests of the planet, are we? And who's to pay? Always on the light adventure, which will end in dark. But the story is always visible. Whether or not it gets told. And we get it for free.

So, did I find my vocation there? In the warm-chill, chest-bosom of family? Or in that borderland where those others walked, in somber travesty?

Let me say...ah, yes, that's of extreme importance. You—let *me* say.

Then (and how good of you)—I can serve out my obligation, as vowed...While—would you care to try out your envelope? You'll have one. Not a family who don't.

Ah, I see. You've had no luck with it. Neither did I.

Then stand up, for Christ's sake. As in oratorio. Now repeat after me (there's always virtue in the repeat):

Remember. Remember. Remember.

Remember the...the...did you hear that? They must be somewhere out there, listening. Dateless. In their apartheid of the soul.

Ah, here it comes. I knew it would. They too have their garrison. Are they practicing?

No—it's a full bugling...And below that, the drums. It's the tattoo. And three times over:

Remember the slave.

Remember the slave.

Remember the slave.

Nobody is dateless for nothing. It's only that you last forever—if you are.

Down home anywhere—you listening, from your envelope? Holler back.